L S W R
LOCOMOTIVES

'T9' class No. 729 with a 4,000 gallon double bogie tender and decorated for the visit of the German Kaiser to Windsor.

AN ILLUSTRATED HISTORY OF

L S W R
LOCOMOTIVES

THE
DRUMMOND CLASSES

BY

D. L. BRADLEY

WILD SWAN PUBLICATIONS LTD.

ISBN 0 906867 42 8

Designed by Paul Karau
Typesetting by Berkshire Publishing Services
Printed and bound by Butler & Tanner Ltd., Frome

Published by
WILD SWAN PUBLICATIONS LTD.
1-3 Hagbourne Road, Didcot, Oxon OX11 8DP

CONTENTS

J. E. Kite Collection

A pre-1910 view of Eastleigh Works yard.

GENERAL STORE. COPPER SMITHS.*

PAINT SHOP. SMITHY. AXLE SHOP* & POWER HOUSE.*

FORGE. IRON STORE. BRICK MAKERS. BRASS FOUNDRY. PATTERN SHOP.

* MEANS:- LYING AT BACK OF FIRST NAMED SHOP.

IRON FOUNDRY.

CORE MAKERS OVENS.

The locomotive works were moved from cramped quarters at Nine Elms to a spacious new site at Eastleigh in 1909. This view shows the new facilities circa 1911.

J. E. Kite Collection

INTRODUCTION

London & South Western locomotives have a special appeal to railway historians for most were designed and built by well-known and highly respected mechanical engineers, since Joseph Beattie, William Adams, Dugald Drummond and Robert Urie all completed distinguished careers in charge of the company's locomotive department. With some 1,500 engines involved, the history cannot be contained by a single volume, therefore this part of the survey only covers the Drummond classes.

In pursuit of knowledge the engine, boiler and tender registers, drawings, diagram books, coal returns and the rough notes of the Locomotive Committee meetings made available by the staff at Eastleigh Works in 1965-6 proved invaluable. Reference was also made to the minute, account and other registers held by the Public Record Office at Kew and to the Nine Elms and Eastleigh drawing office registers, drawings and photographs in care of the National Railway Museum at York. In all instances the dates of ordering, construction, entry to service, modification, rebuilding, reboilering, withdrawal, breaking up and sale have been taken from the engine and boiler registers, which detail all the engines owned by the South Western from 1841 to 1922, details of which are confirmed and amplified by the Nine Elms and Eastleigh Works repair journals of 1892-1932. For the later period, use has been made of the Southern Railway and British Railways

engine, tender, boiler and frame cards, the Waterloo mileage registers, the weekly works return sheets and notices of withdrawal, breaking up and sale. Assistance was also sought from the Sharps Stewart, Dübs, Neilson, Robert Stephenson and Beyer Peacock order books and drawings preserved by the Science Museum, South Kensington, the Greater Manchester Museum of Science & Industry and the Mitchell Library, Glasgow.

The dimensions were obtained from the South Western and Southern Railway diagram books, general arrangement drawings and the order books of private manufacturers. Unfortunately, these sources often fail to agree, while it was not unknown for Nine Elms and Eastleigh to issue contradictory figures. The company's weights in working order were computed for engines in light steam with 5 cwt of coal in the firebox, 2½ in. of water showing in the glass, full tender, saddle or side tanks and 5 cwt of coal in the tender or bunker. As a result, these weights, particularly the tenders, were considerably less than those appearing in the manufacturers' order books, Board of Trade accident reports, weigh house records and Southern Railway diagram books. Dimensions and weights, like final mileages, are not an exact science.

Engine allocations before Grouping have often caused historians difficulty, but fortunately many of the lists issued each year in March by Nine Elms Works recording

1

View showing the rail entrance to Eastleigh Works, with the station in the background. The Southampton and Bournemouth main line is to the left of the view and the Fareham and Portsmouth line is to the right. The 'M7' is standing on one of the engine roads leading to the running shed.

J. E. Kite Collection

the current position of the engine stock, including those away for repair, have been preserved. After this establishment closed, responsibility for these lists was transferred to Waterloo, where those for 1878-1922 were available in 1965. Human nature being what it is, all railways are beset by accidents, although by good fortune and able management, the South Western only suffered one major disaster, at Salisbury in June 1906. All accidents, trivial or serious, have to be reported and the subsequent Board of Trade or Ministry of Transport accounts of the events leading to the incidents provide useful sources of train formations and speed, company practice, dimensions, weights, mechanical details and repair mileages.

Nine Elms ex-works dates almost invariably indicated the date when construction or repair was completed, with a further two or three weeks elapsing for painting and trial running before revenue earning service was entered. At Eastleigh Works, the date of transfer from yard to the nearby running shed was recorded as the entry or return to traffic, despite most engines requiring further attention by fitters sent across from the works. After Nationalisation the entry to traffic dates recorded by the engine cards were entirely fictitious for their main purpose was to ensure on paper that the specified quotas of general, intermediate and casual repairs were being completed. Often the entry to traffic was a month or more after the official date.

This book could not have been written without the help of many people too numerous to name individually. However, special thanks are due to Peter Swift, chairman of the South Western Circle, Ted Fry, photographer supreme of Salisbury, Sid Nash, John Edgington and the late George Woodward, who recorded all the Eastleigh Works arrivals and departures from mid-1926 to the end of steam.

DUGALD DRUMMOND

MECHANICAL ENGINEER 1895-1912

THIS celebrated Scottish railway engineer was born at Ardrossan, Ayrshire, on 1st January 1840 and grew up in the mixed atmosphere of railways and Clyde navigation, for his father was the permanent way inspector of the Bowling Railway. Destined from birth for an engineering career, Drummond served his apprenticeship with Forest & Barr of Glasgow before gaining further experience on the Dumbartonshire and Caledonian Railways. Later, time was spent in charge of the boiler shop at Thomas Brassey's Canada Works, Birkenhead, before moving to the Cowlairs Works of the North British Railway in mid-1864. There, under the skilled tuition of S. W. Johnson, some eighteen months were served as a wheel shop chargehand before ambition drove him to Inverness and the Highland Railway, where he became foreman erector under W. Stroudley at Lochgorm Works.

Thereafter, his rise in railway service was meteoric for he was appointed works manager in 1867 and, following Stroudley's departure to Brighton in February 1870, had charge of the Highland's locomotive department until the appointment of David Smith. Later the same year, Stroudley found him a position at Brighton Works, where Drummond remained until appointed locomotive superintendent of the North British Railway in February 1875. After seven years he was again on the move, on this occasion to the neighbouring St. Rollox Works of the Caledonian Railway. By now approaching middle age, it might be assumed that his wanderings, if not over, would be more restrictive, but this was not to be, for in April 1890 he suddenly tendered his resignation to form a consortium with business acquaintances to establish the Australasian Locomotive Engine Works at Sydney, New South Wales.

Unhappily, the hitherto good fortune deserted him for within months the scheme had foundered and he was back in Scotland with sorely depleted funds and no immediate prospects of resuming high railway office. In desperation he turned to the private sector and with borrowed capital founded the Glasgow Railway Engineering Company, and sought orders for the design, erection and supply of industrial engines, rolling stock and plant. Some success was achieved, but this type of activity, particularly the canvassing of orders, had no lasting appeal to a man of his talents and disposition, so after five years he gratefully accepted the locomotive superintendency of the London & South Western Railway, despite the remuneration of £1,500 per annum being considerably less than enjoyed at St. Rollox.

At last his good fortune returned, for William Adams had left the South Western's locomotive affairs in such excellent order that he was able to carefully assess the future motive power requirements before designing his 'T9' express passenger, '700' goods and 'M7' suburban classes. All gave the same high standard of reliability and performance as engines built earlier for the North British and Caledonian Railways. Indeed, following superheating by his successor, Robert Urie, the 'T9s' became acknowledged as one of the most useful passenger classes to work in this country, not only on the South Western, but also after Grouping on all three sections of the Southern Railway. In 1903-5 these well-liked 4—4—0s were followed by classes 'L12' and 'S11',

in which all the well-proven standard Drummond features were fully exploited without restricting the front-end or the coupled wheel-bearing surfaces.

As a result, the South Western in 1905, with a hundred modern express 4—4—0s in service, was well supplied with passenger motive power and Drummond had reached the peak of his railway career. Having attained this, most loco-

motive engineers would have been satisfied, but not Drummond for he appreciated that the next decade would demand higher speeds and the provision of heavier and more luxurious rolling stock. Of necessity, engines would have to work harder and, capable as the current 4—4—0s might be, he rightly concluded that six-coupled wheels and larger boilers would be necessary. Consequently his allegiance was transferred to massively constructed multi-cylinder 4—6—0s. Sadly, the early classes failed to meet expectation, although those built later performed adequately, if seldom excelling his 4—4—0s.

By now a septuagenarian, Drummond could have allowed his department to drift quietly along until time offered honourable and well-earned retirement, but the determination to succeed lingered on and in 1911 he designed the 'D15s'. Ten well-proportioned piston valve 4—4—0s for the Bournemouth expresses, which possessed all the sparkle lacked by the 4—6—0s. Unfortunately, little time was granted to savour the success for death came on 8th November 1912.

In recent years most South Western historians have mentioned Drummond's irascibility and fiery rhetoric, traits which undoubtedly were present, but these same writers failed to remark that they were reserved for those who failed to apply the company's safety code or display the high standard of diligence Drummond demanded of himself and employees of all grades. Those performing their duty had little to fear and much to gain. Drummond may not have been as well liked as William Adams, but he was equally respected.

Today Drummond is probably most readily recalled by the preserved 'T9' working on the Mid-Hants Railway, although his greatest achievement can be found at Eastleigh, where the locomotive works stand in lasting memory of a truly great railway engineer.

'L12' class 4—4—0 No. 421 in Drummond livery, with balanced crank axle, firebox water tubes, Duplex fuel pumps and a double bogie tender, at Nine Elms in October 1904.

V. Chambers

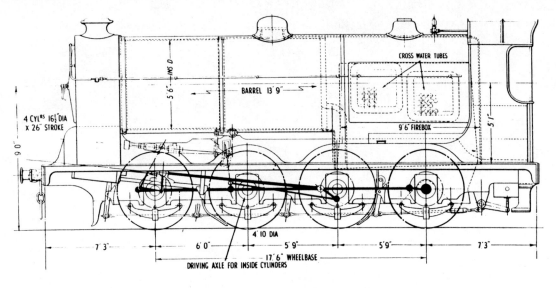

Dugald Drummond's LSWR proposal for a heavy goods engine.

LOCOMOTIVE LIVERIES

DUGALD DRUMMOND

Passenger Classes

At first the Adams pea green livery without splasher monograms was used, but commencing with 'T6' class No. 677 in September 1895, express engines had the company's coat-of-arms applied to the leading splashers. The next change occurred with 'X6' class No. 657 in early December 1895, when royal green replaced the pea green on the cab, boiler, dome cover, splashers, valances, main frames below the platform, wheel bosses, spokes and rims, footsteps and the tender panels, backplate and frame exteriors. The lining followed Adams style, but with 'X6' class No. 661 at the end of the year, Drummond introduced his own lining. This was bold and striking for the dark brown bordering was edged by fine white, black and white lines, while the black boiler bands were white edged and had 3 inch wide tan stripes on the cladding.

Heat resistant Olympia black appeared on the smokebox and chimney, while standard glossy black was used for the tops of the main frames, platform, splashers and sandboxes, the exterior of the cab roof, footstep treads, guard irons, lamp brackets, axles, axle ends, tool boxes, coal rails, tender and bunker interior, tender base, coping edges, hornplates, springs, buckles, hangers, axleboxes and brake gear.

The motionplate and interior of the main frames were tan, the cab interior grained to resemble pine and the buffer beams vermilion with gilt numerals; the 'No' being to the left and the numbers to the right of the draw hook. The '700' class 0-6-0s and 'M7s' Nos. 242-56 were lettered 'SWR' and 'T7' class No. 720 and 'M7s' Nos. 667-76 'LSW', but thereafter 'LSWR' in widely spaced 8½ inch black shaded letters without stops was standardised. Early built engines carried numberplates on the cab or bunker sides, but from mid-1903 these were superseded by transfer numerals. Express and mixed traffic classes, except the 4-6-0s, had the company's coat-of-arms on the leading splashers.

Despite Drummond referring to his livery as royal or tartan green, in reality the colour was only marginally darker than the Adams pea green for the formulae were very similar. Details are:-

Royal Green	Pea Green
4 lb cypress green	4 lb Buckingham green
2 lb zinc white in oil	2 lb zinc white in oil
1 lb lemon chrome in oil	1 lb yellow ochre in oil
¼ lb black	Touch of black
Dark Brown	
6 lb purple brown	
¼ lb burnt sienna in oil	
¼ lb burnt umber in oil	

In March 1909 the cost of painting the Drummond classes was:-

	Labour £	Materials £	Total £
4-6-0	30 10 1	10 6 0	40 16 1
4-4-0 express	22 15 2	9 0 7	31 15 9
4-4-0 mixed traffic	18 11 10	7 12 8	26 4 6
0-4-4 tank	12 8 2	5 11 5	17 19 7
0-6-0 goods	16 8 3	6 10 11	22 19 2
0-4-0 tank	9 5 2	4 8 5	13 13 7

At this period passenger engines averaged 26 months and goods engines 34 months between repaints.

Experimental Passenger Livery

This livery was only applied to one engine, 'T7' class double-single No. 720 when built in August 1897. In effect it was Adams style with LB & SCR Stroudley improved engine green (yellow) replacing the apple green, dark brown instead of black bordering and square cornered lining. The tender was lettered 'LSW' in widely spaced block capitals. In May 1899 this flamboyant and quite unsuitable livery gave way to royal green.

Goods Classes

The boiler, dome cover, exterior of main frames below the platform, cab, tender, tank and bunker panelling, valances, footsteps, splasher and sandbox sides, frame exteriors of six-wheeled tenders and all the wheel bosses, cranks, spokes and rims were holly green, a colour which darkened rapidly and long before repainting was necessary had become black.

The cab front, sides and rear, splasher, sandbox and tank sides, valances, footsteps and the tender and bunker sides and ends were black-bordered and edged with a fine bright green line. The boiler bands were black with green edging, although when new the '700' class had tan stripes on the cladding like the passenger classes.

The smokebox and chimney were painted heat-resisting Olympia black, while standard black was applied to the tops of the frames, splashers, sandboxes, platform and tanks, exterior of the cab roof, tank ends, footstep treads, guard irons, brake gear, axles, axle ends, tyres, tender frame interiors, base and interior of the tender and bunker, coal rails, coping edge, toolboxes, hornplates, springs, buckles, hangers, axleboxes and lamp irons. The motion plate and interior of the main frames were tan, the cab interior grained to resemble pine and the buffer beams vermilion with numerals in gilt. The '700' goods were lettered 'SWR' when new, but thereafter, following a brief period of 'LSW', 'LSWR' was standardised.

Numberplates

Drummond introduced his pattern numberplates on 'X6' class 4-4-0 No. 657 in December 1895 and fitted them to all new construction until 'L11' class No. 154 in May 1903, when they were superseded on the cab or bunker sides by 6 inch transfer numerals. The smooth oval numberplates measured 17½ in. by 11 in. and were lettered 'South Western Railway'.

Tender and Tank Lettering

After commencing with 'SWR', and briefly employing 'LSW', 'LSWR' became standard. Details for the Drummond classes are:-

S.W.R (wide spacing)   'M7' No. 242 February 1897.

SWR	(wide spacing)	'M7s' Nos. 243-56, '700s' Nos. 687-716 March-August 1897.
LSW	(wide spacing)	'M7s' Nos. 667-76, 'T7' No. 720 August-December 1897.
LSWR	(wide spacing)	'M7' No. 31 March 1898 and all later construction and repaints.

Duplication

Only three Drummond engines, 'C14' class Nos. 741/4/5, were duplicated before Grouping. This should have been denoted by a line below the side tank numerals, but photographs dated 1920-2 show Nos. 744/5 still carrying capital stock numbers, while No. 741 had the duplicate line when photographed at Strawberry Hill in October 1921, but not when recorded at Southampton in April 1922. After Grouping these three engines became Nos. E0741/4/5 and in June 1925 were joined in the duplicate list by 'P14' class 4—6—0 No. E0449. When the E-prefix was discarded in mid-1931, Nos. E0741/4 became 3741/4. No. E0745 had been transferred some years earlier to Service Stock, becoming E77S and finally 77S.

ROBERT URIE

Passenger Classes

After taking office Urie retained the Drummond livery, without the splasher coat-of-arms and with some lining variation on the 'H15' class, until December 1914 when the royal green was replaced by olive green. Urie referred to the colour as sage green, but this it certainly was not for it was marginally softer and darker than the Drummond green and akin to a ripe green olive.

The dark brown bordering and intricate lining remained until October 1917, when wartime economy caused a change to a 3 inch black border separated from the olive green by a fine white line. The boiler bands were black with white edging and the outside cylinders olive green with a black band edged by white at the extremities. Drummond style numerals and lettering remained in use.

After some months weathering and cleaning the olive green became more yellow, which probably accounts for the confusing references to the hue in contemporary railway journals.

Goods Classes

Holly green with black edging and white lining was used until late 1917, when the lining was often omitted to save labour and materials until after the Armistice.

R. E. L. MAUNSELL

Passenger Classes

All the early Eastleigh Grouping repaints were in Urie livery, but from November 1923 the white line separating the black border from the olive green was changed to yellow and 'Southern' inscribed in 6½ inch extended primrose yellow lettering across the tender or tank sides above similarly coloured 18 inch numerals. Until mid-1931 a 3 inch letter 'E', also in primrose yellow, appeared between the lettering and numerals on Western Section engines to

distinguish them from those of the Eastern (A) and Central (B) Sections. After the first eleven Southern repaints, small oval brass numberplates were attached to the cab sides and tender backplates of tender engines and to the bunker backplates of tank engines. At first the background was black, but from mid-1928 this became buffer beam red. On the front buffer beam the E-prefix appeared on the left of the draw hook and the numerals in 5 inch characters to the right.

In February 1925 the Urie olive green was superseded by a deeper and more attractive green, known as Maunsell green, while the line edging the black bordering reverted to white. When the E-prefix was removed 'No' appeared to the left of the front draw hook, the numerals remaining to the right. At the same time the tender and bunker backplate numberplates were removed and replaced by transfer numerals below the coping.

Goods Classes

The Urie holly green livery remained in use until November 1923, when it was replaced by black with dark green lining. The style followed that of the passenger classes and the same changes occurred.

'S15' Class

The original livery was goods black, but because of their regular use on passenger trains this was changed to Maunsell green from February 1928.

Goods Livery Lining

To save expense this was omitted after mid-1935, the first Drummond engine to enter traffic plain black being '700' class No. 691 in August 1935.

Side Tank Numerals

Commencing with Nos. 46 and 246 in August 1931, the 'M7s', 'C14s' and 'K14s' were given 15 inch instead of 18 inch side tank numerals.

O. V. BULLEID

'King Arthur', 'N15' and 'H15' Classes

The first indication of a livery change came in May 1938 when 'N15' class No. 749 was painted brilliant unlined light green by Eastleigh Works. Block numerals replaced the small cabside numberplates, while one side of the tender was conventionally lettered 'Southern' and the other 'SR' in very large block capitals. It would appear that the colour was considered too bright, for the following month No. 749 was painted a less startling green (later known as malachite) with black and white lining and 'Southern' applied to the tender in lined block lettering. On one side the numerals were painted on the cab sides and on the other the smoke deflectors. No. 749 was returned to traffic in Maunsell livery, but the second experimental style with cab side numerals formed the basis of the new Bulleid liveries. These came in three shades of green, Maunsell, olive and malachite, with black/white, black/yellow, or green/yellow lining. Full details will be found with the respective classes. Because of the Second World War plain black became standard in March 1942. After the cessation of hostilities, the 'King Arthurs' and 'N15s' were painted malachite green, but the 'H15s' remained black.

Secondary Passenger Classes

The Maunsell green livery with minor lining variation remained in use until September 1939, when repaints were either unlined Maunsell or malachite green with cab or bunker numerals and Bulleid lettering. The use of green ceased because of wartime shortages in March 1941, when plain black became standard. After the war the royal 'T9', No. 119, and a handful of 'M7s' were painted malachite green, but otherwise plain black remained in use until after Nationalisation.

Goods Classes

These remained plain black with Maunsell lettering and tender or tank numerals until September 1939, when cab or bunker numerals and Bulleid lettering became standard.

BRITISH RAILWAYS

The 'King Arthurs' and 'N15s' continued to be painted malachite green until August 1949, when Brunswick green with orange and black lining was substituted. Secondary passenger classes, including the 'H15s', were painted black with red, cream and grey lining and goods classes plain black. Numerals appeared on the cab or bunker sides and numberplates were attached to the smokebox doors. Full details of these liveries and the temporary S-prefix are contained in the text.

LIVERY REFERENCE DATES

British Railways lettered tender and tank sides	January 1948
Smokebox numberplates	June 1948
Unlettered tender and tank sides	December 1948
1st British Railways totem	August 1949
2nd British Railways totem	March 1957

URIE POWER CLASSIFICATION

In March 1916 Urie introduced a lettered power classification for all the main line engines, with A denoting the most powerful. At first the letters were inscribed inside the cab, but from September 1916 they were transferred to the platform valance immediately to the rear of the front buffer beam. Details for the Drummond classes are:-

'T9' class No. 703 and 'L12' class No. 417 at Waterloo displaying post-1911 headcodes.   *J. E. Kite Collection*

A   F13 (superheated No. 333)
B   F13 (Nos. 330-2/4), G14, P14, T14. (Nos. 330-2/4 were
                                originally classified A)
C   700
D   D15, L12
E   S11
F   K10, L11
H   T9
I   C8, E10, T7
K   M7

Unclassified K14, C14, Terrier No. 735 and Drummond's Car. After Grouping the Southern Railway retained this classification for Western Section engines while for a time it was perpetuated by British Railways.

BRITISH RAILWAYS POWER AND LOAD CLASSIFICATIONS

Power	Load	Classes
4P	—	T14
3P	3P	D15
2P	3P	L12, S11, T9
2P	2P	M7
1MT	—	K10, L11
4F	3F	700
0F	1F	K14
0F (later 0P)	0F	C14

ENGINE DISC AND LAMP BRACKETS

When Drummond assumed responsibility for LSWR locomotive matters disc and lamp headcodes were displayed on five brackets, at the top and on either side of the smokebox, one on the smokebox door above the locking handles, and one on the running plate at the centre of the buffer beam. The position on the smokebox door was only for discs and lamps indicating special trains and was not greatly used. Being liable to confuse signalmen at night, or in poor visibility, it was abolished in 1897 when a new system of route codes was introduced. Employing six brackets, at the top and on either side of the smokebox and three on the platform above the bufferbeam, this layout (apart from the transfer of the two smokebox side brackets to the door in the 1930s) remained standard until the end of steam, although the arrangement of headcodes changed at intervals over the years.

ENGINE HEADCODES 1905

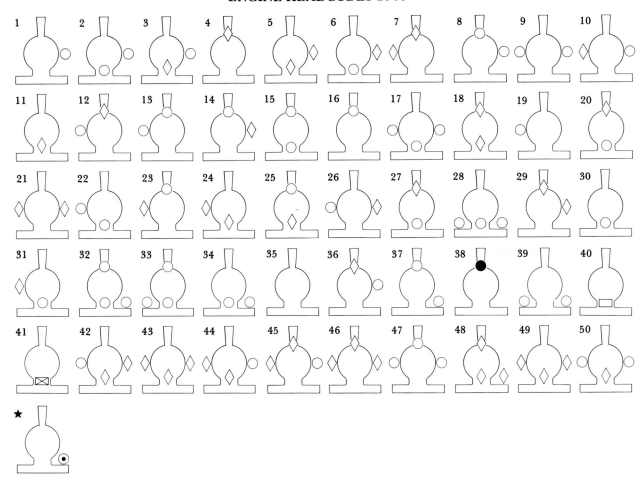

ENGINE HEADCODES 1911

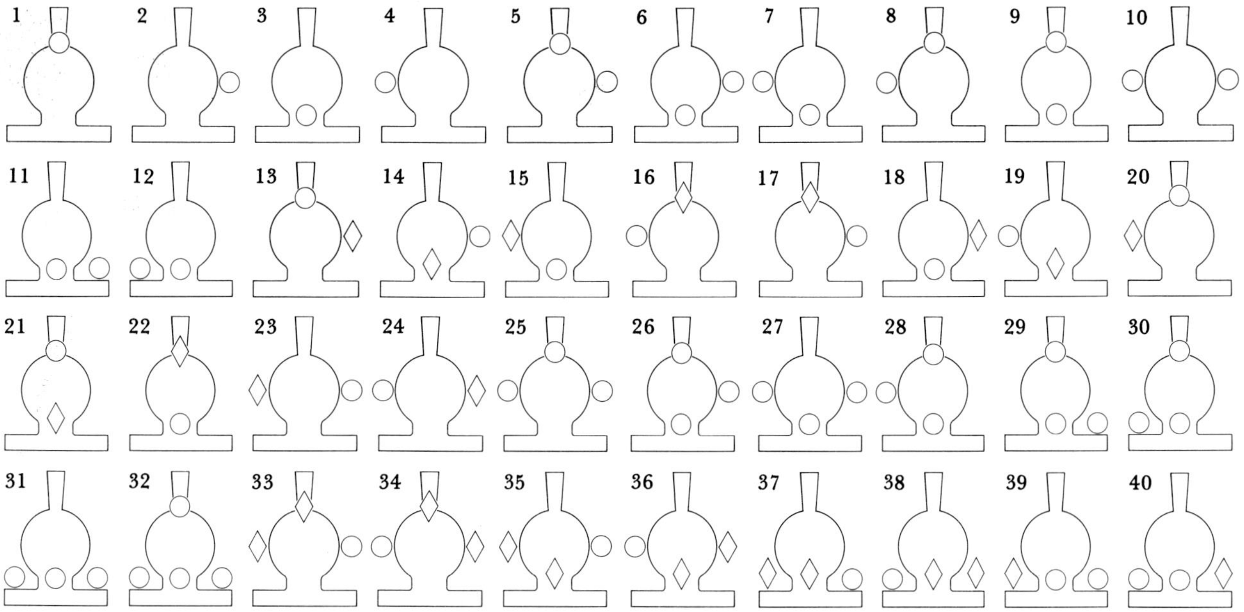

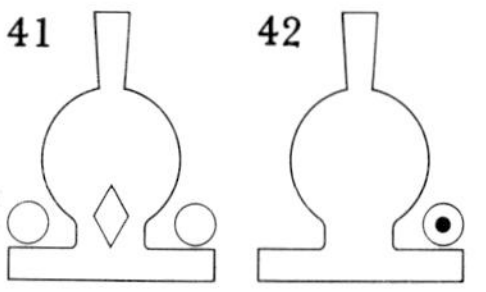

ENGINE HEADCODES 1911

1. Kensington & Woking via Richmond. Guildford & Farnham. Waterloo & Wimbledon Pk. Sidings, via East Putney (Empty Trains). Eastleigh & Bulford via Chandlersford & Andover. Southampton Docks & Brockenhurst & Dorchester via Wimborne.* Weymouth & Portland & Easton (Passenger Trains). Plymouth & St. Budeaux.
2. Waterloo or Nine Elms & Southampton Docks via Main Line. Willesden & Brentford via Gunnersbury.
3. Waterloo & Kingston via Kensington. Staines & Weybridge. Brockwood & Bisley Camp. Alton & Fareham. Bentley & Bordon. Fort Brockhurst & Lee-on-the-Solent. Hamworthy Jn. & Hamworthy. Salisbury & Bulford. Axminster & Lyme Regis. Tipton St. John & Exmouth. Plymouth & Cattewater. Winchester (Cheesehill) & Southampton Docks. ** Barnstaple (GWR) & Barnstaple Jn. & Ilfracombe.** Bodmin (GWR) & Wadebridge.** (Great Western Co's Trains, see Notes)
4. Waterloo or Nine Elms & Reading, via Loop Line. Willesden & Brentford via Kew East Jn. Weybridge & Virginia Water. Guildford & Aldershot. Exeter & Sidmouth.
5. Waterloo or Nine Elms & Guildford, via Leatherhead. Waterloo & Wimbledon via Main Line. Waterloo or Nine Elms & Southampton Docks via Brentford, Chertsey & Woking. Salisbury & Dorchester via Wimborne.*
6. Waterloo & Kingston & Shepperton, via East Putney. Ludgate Hill & Richmond New, via Kensington. Brentford & Neasden via Kew East Jn. Woking & Windsor, via Byfleet Curve. Southampton Docks & Andover. Basingstoke & Alton.
7. Waterloo to Waterloo via Twickenham, Whitton Jn., & Hounslow. Brentford & Brent via Kew East Jn. Wimbledon Station or Durnsford Rd. Sidings & Waterloo, via the Main Line (Empty Trains).
8. Waterloo or Nine Elms & Hampton Court. Waterloo & Twickenham via Barnes. Waterloo & Shepperton via Twickenham. Brentford & Brent via Chiswick Jn.
9. Waterloo or Nine Elms & Plymouth. Clapham Jn & Twickenham via Kensington & Chiswick Jn. Battersea & Brent, via New Kew Jn. Southampton Docks & Portsmouth via Netley. Windsor & Ascot via Staines High Street.
10. Waterloo or Nine Elms & Guildford via Cobham. Waterloo or Nine Elms & Reading via Twickenham. Clapham Jn. & Kensington. Ascot & Farnham. Guildford & Godalming Goods. Eastleigh & Portsmouth. Salisbury & Bournemouth West via Wimborne.
11. Waterloo or Nine Elms & Woking via Richmond & Chertsey.
12. Waterloo & Nine Elms Goods Yard.
13. Waterloo or Nine Elms & Windsor via Twickenham. Woking & Chertsey & Reading, via Virginia Water Curve.
14. Waterloo & Wimbledon Pk. Sidings via East Putney (Passenger Trains). Southampton Docks & Nine Elms, via Main Line (Market Goods, Fruit, or Potato Trains).
15. Southampton Docks & Nine Elms via Chertsey & Brentford (Market Goods, Fruit, & Potato Trains).
16. Waterloo or Nine Elms & Southampton Dks. via Alton. Waterloo or Nine Elms & Windsor, via Loop Line. Waterloo & Barnes & Feltham via Loop Line.
17. All stations to Nine Elms Loco Depot. Nine Elms Loco Depot & Nine Elms Goods Yard, via Engine Line or Queens Road. Portsmouth to Fratton Loco Depot. Exeter & Exmouth Jn.
18. Exeter & Nine Elms (Market Goods & Fish Trains). Southampton Docks & Bournemouth West via Sway.
19. Waterloo & Virginia Water via Main Line. Gunnersbury & Twickenham. Salisbury & Southampton West & Portsmouth via Netley. Bournemouth Central & Dorchester.*
20. Nine Elms & Neasden via New Kew Jn. All Stations to Eastleigh Loco Depot.
21. Waterloo & Clapham Jn. (Empty Trains). Nine Elms Loco Yard to Clapham Jn. Ludgate Hill & Wimbledon, via Merton Abbey. Brentford & Southampton Docks via Ascot & Farnborough Curve. Ringwood & Bournemouth West, via Christchurch. Wareham & Swanage. Exeter & Torrington.*
22. Waterloo & Waterloo Roundabout Service via Kingston. Ascot & Woking via Frimley. Southampton Docks & Salisbury via Redbridge. Exeter & Padstow.*
23. Waterloo or Nine Elms & Portsmouth, via Woking & Guildford. Waterloo & Wimbledon, via East Putney. Southampton Docks & Salisbury via Eastleigh. Fareham & Gosport. Bodmin & Wadebridge.
24. Waterloo or Nine Elms & Southampton Docks via East Putney. Petersfield & Midhurst. Havant & Cosham. Fratton & East Southsea. Botley & Bishops Waltham. Fareham & Stokes Bay. Brockenhurst & Lymington Pier. Bournemouth West & Dorchester.* Whitchurch & Fullerton. Yeovil Jn. & Yeovil Town. Chard Jn. & Chard Town.* Seaton Jn. & Seaton. Exeter & Exmouth. Barnstaple Jn. & Ilfracombe. Halwill Jn. & Bude. Plymouth Friary & Turnchapel.
25. Waterloo or Nine Elms & Brockenhurst & Bournemouth West, via Sway.
26. Kensington & Wimbledon via East Putney.
27. Waterloo & Waterloo, via Hounslow & Twickenham. Clapham Jn. & Richmond New via Kensington. Ludgate Hill & Wimbledon, via Haydons Road.
28. Waterloo & Richmond New via Kensington.
29. Nine Elms & Brent, via New Kew Jn. Weymouth & Portland & Easton (Goods Trains).
30. Nine Elms & Willesden, via New Kew Jn.
31. Shepperton & Twickenham & Willesden via Gunnersbury. Nine Elms to Nine Elms, via Chertsey & Brentford, or vice versa. Cattewater Jn. & Plymstock.**
32. Royal Trains.
33. Members & 1st Class Race Trains, via Earlsfield.
34. Members & 1st Class Race Trains, via East Putney or via Twickenham.
35. Fast Race Trains (1st, 2nd & 3rd Classes) via Earlsfield.
36. Fast Race Trains (1st, 2nd & 3rd Classes) via East Putney, or via Twickenham.
37. Stopping Race Trains (1st, 2nd & 3rd Classes) via Earlsfield.
38. Stopping Race Trains (1st, 2nd & 3rd Classes) via East Putney or via Twickenham.
39. Waterloo & Hampton Court, via East Putney (Excursion Trains).
40. Waterloo & Leatherhead & Guildford via East Putney (Excursion Trains).
41. Waterloo & Oxshott & Guildford, via East Putney (Excursion Trains).
42. Special Train:- By Day: White Disc with Black Centre. By Night: Purple Light.

NOTE

* Trains running over the GWR will carry the GW Co's Code.

** GW Co's Engines will carry unlighted lamps instead of disc shaped boards by day.

ENGINE HEADCODES 1905

1. Waterloo or Nine Elms & Southampton via Main Line. Waterloo & Basingstoke. Willesden & Brentford via Gunnersbury.
2. Nine Elms & Southampton Docks, via Main Line.
3. Southampton Docks & Nine Elms (Market Goods, Fruit or Potato Trains), via Main Line. Waterloo & Twickenham via Kensington & Hounslow.
4. Waterloo or Nine Elms & Bournemouth West, via Direct Line. Ludgate Hill & Wimbledon, via Haydons Road. Waterloo & Richmond New, via Kensington. Brent & Brentford, via Gunnersbury & Chiswick Jn.
5. Brentford & Wimbledon via Chertsey. Basingstoke & Alton.
6. Exeter & Nine Elms (Market Goods & Fish Trains). Clapham Jn. & Richmond via Kensington.
7. Waterloo or Nine Elms & Dorchester, via Ringwood. Gunnersbury & Twickenham. Brentford & Neasden. Waterloo to Clapham Jn. (Kensington Arrival Platform) on Down Windsor Local Line from Queens Road.
8. Waterloo or Nine Elms & Guildford via Leatherhead (trains to carry No. 10 code between Guildford & Portsmouth). Waterloo & Wimbledon via Main Line. Salisbury & Dorchester via Wimborne. Waterloo or Nine Elms & Southampton via Brentford, Chertsey & Woking.
9. Waterloo or Nine Elms & Guildford, via Cobham. Guildford & Godalming Goods. Ascot & Farnham. Clapham Jn. & Kensington. Waterloo or Nine Elms & Reading, via Twickenham. Eastleigh & Portsmouth. Salisbury, Wimborne & Bournemouth West.
10. Waterloo or Nine Elms & Portsmouth via Woking & Guildford. Southampton, Eastleigh & Salisbury. Waterloo & Wimbledon via East Putney. Fareham & Gosport. Bodmin & Wadebridge.
11. Waterloo & Kingston via East Putney. Portsmouth & Hendon (MR) via Eastleigh, Chertsey, Richmond & Gunnersbury. Amesbury Branch.
12. Waterloo or Nine Elms & Aldershot, Farnham & Southampton via Alton. Waterloo or Nine Elms & Windsor, via Loop Line. Waterloo, Hounslow, & Feltham (including Trains terminating at Barnes).
13. Waterloo or Nine Elms & Hampton Court. Waterloo & Twickenham, via Barnes. Waterloo & Thames Valley Line via Twickenham. Kensington & Woking via Chiswick Jn.
14. Waterloo or Nine Elms & Windsor via Twickenham. Woking & Reading via Virginia Water Curve.
15. Waterloo or Nine Elms & Salisbury & Exeter. Southampton & Portsmouth via Netley. Clapham Jn. & Twickenham via Kensington & Chiswick Jn. Battersea & Brent, via New Kew Jn.
16. Kensington & Woking via Richmond. Guildford & Farnham. Waterloo & Wimbledon Park Sidings, via East Putney. Dorchester & Southampton via Wimborne. Weymouth, Portland & Easton. Passenger Trains.
17. Waterloo to Waterloo via Hounslow & Twickenham.
18. Waterloo & Kingston via Barnes. Waterloo to Waterloo Roundabout Service via Kingston. Special Race Trains, Reading & Surbiton via Virginia Water. Brentford & Brent, via Old Kew Jn. Southampton & Bournemouth via Sway. Exeter & Plymouth.
19. Guildford & Aldershot. Sidmouth Branch (Exeter & Sidmouth). Waterloo or Nine Elms & Reading, via Loop Line. Virginia Water & Weybridge.
20. Ascot & Woking. Southampton & Salisbury via Redbridge. Exeter & Padstow.
21. Southampton & Andover. Wimbledon, Kingston, Richmond & Brent via Gunnersbury. Woking & Windsor via Byfleet Curve.
22. Winchester (GW) & Southampton. Empty trains, Wimbledon Station or Sidings & Waterloo via the Main Line. Waterloo to Waterloo via Twickenham, Whitton Jn. & Hounslow.
23. Nine Elms & Neasden via New Kew Jn. All stations to Eastleigh Loco Depot.
24. Salisbury, Southampton West & Portsmouth via Netley. Dorchester & Bournemouth Central. Waterloo & Virginia Water, via Main Line.
25. Empty trains, Waterloo & Clapham Jn. Nine Elms Loco Yard to Clapham Jn. Ludgate Hill & Richmond. Ringwood & Bournemouth West via Christchurch. Brentford & Southampton via Ascot & Farnborough Curve. Swanage Branch. Exeter & Torrington.
26. Waterloo or Nine Elms & Southampton via East Putney. Midhurst Branch. Lymington Branch. Southsea Branch. Fareham & Stokes Bay. Yeovil Branch. Seaton Branch. Ilfracombe Branch. Turnchapel Branch. Bishops Waltham Branch. Cosham & Havant. Whitchurch & Fullerton. Dorchester & Bournemouth West. Chard Branch. Exmouth Branch. Bude Branch. Kensington to Wimbledon via Clapham Jn. & East Putney.
27. Ludgate Hill & Wimbledon via Merton Abbey. (Diamond Top of Smokebox between Ludgate Hill & Tulse Hill & additional White Round Centre Buffer Beam, Tulse Hill to Wimbledon)
28. Shepperton, Richmond & Willesden via Gunnersbury.
29. Nine Elms & Brent via New Kew Jn.
30. Staines & Weybridge. Plymouth & Cattewater Branch. Waterloo & Kingston via Kensington. Clapham Jn. & Bournemouth via East Putney. Alton & Fareham. Tipton St. Johns & Exmouth. Axminster & Lyme Regis.
31. Southampton Docks & Nine Elms (Market, Fruit & Potato Trains) via Chertsey & Brentford.
32. Willesden & Brentford via Kew East Jn. Willesden & Kew East Sidings (L & NW Co's Goods Trains). Weymouth, Portland & Easton Goods Trains.
33. Willesden & Nine Elms via Kew Curve.
34. Waterloo or Nine Elms & Woking, via Richmond & Chertsey.
35. Engines, Nine Elms Loco Yard to Waterloo. (To carry the Headcode of the Train it has to work from Waterloo. When Two or more Engines are coupled together, each must carry its distinct headcode, but only the last engine to carry a Tail Lamp)
36. All Stations to Nine Elms Loco Depot. Exeter & Exmouth Jn.
37. Bollo Lane Jn. & Richmond New (North London Co's Ordinary Trains) (Also White Oval, side of Chimney).
38. Bollo Lane Jn. & Richmond New. (North London Co's Special Trains).
39. Hammersmith & Richmond New. (Metropolitan & GW Co's Trains.)
40. Bollo Lane Jn. & Kensington High St. (Midland Co's Goods Trains). Square with diagonal cross, centre of buffer beam.

CODES FOR SPECIAL RACE TRAINS IN THE LONDON SUBURBAN DISTRICT

42. Fast Trains with 1st, 2nd & 3rd Class Passengers.
46. Stopping Trains with 1st, 2nd & 3rd Class Passengers.
44. Members & First Class Trains, via East Putney or Twickenham.
45. Members & First Class Trains via Earlsfield or Earlsfield & Kingston.
46. Thames Valley Line Special Trains. Waterloo & Ascot via Hounslow.
47. 1st, 2nd & 3rd Class Trains via East Putney & Kingston.

SPECIAL EXCURSION TRAINS

48. Waterloo & Hampton Court via East Putney.
49. Waterloo & Leatherhead via East Putney.
50. Waterloo & Oxshott via East Putney.

*Special Trains (except Nos. 42-50 above) will carry a White Round Disc with Black Centre (Purple Light at Night) over Near Side Buffer.

*The Heavy Lifters Train going to an accident will carry the Special Disc or Lamp over each buffer.

*Trains passing onto the GWR will carry the GW code from the Last Stopping Station on the LSW, & vv.

'T7' class No. 720 in service at Waterloo before 1900 with narrow width cab and splashers and speed recorder mounted on front platform.

THE DOUBLE-SINGLES

For more than a decade after the introduction of steam locomotion, railways in this country successfully operated their main line passenger services with singles, but, as train loads and speeds increased, they proved wanting and were replaced first by 2—4—0s and later 4—4—0s. However, in the 1890s singles made a come-back, notably on the Midland, Great Eastern, North Eastern and Manchester, Sheffield & Lincolnshire Railways, where daily they had charge of the best expresses, a resurgence made possible by the combination of steam sanding and greater driving axle weights overcoming the earlier load restrictions.

Singles were considerably cheaper to build, maintain and operate than similarly powered 4—4—0s, factors which obviously influenced directors and major shareholders in their favour. As a result, many locomotive superintendents, including Adams, came under intense and often uninformed managerial pressure for their reintroduction. Indeed, Nine Elms completed drawings of an 8 ft outside cylinder 4—2—2 in 1893, although no further action had been taken before Adams' retirement, leaving Drummond to satisfy the Locomotive Committee's aspirations, yet at the same time providing engines capable of meeting current operating requirements. It would appear that the density of traffic over the double track east of Basingstoke and the steep gradients between Salisbury and Exeter created design problems not present on those railways successfully operating modern singles, so Drummond developed a more powerful double-single in which four cylinders drove two independent pairs of driving wheels. The intention was to retain the freedom and economy of the single, yet overcome its disadvantage when starting heavy trains and when climbing banks, an ingenious and intriguing concept, which unfortunately failed to meet expectation; consequently double-singles never seriously rivalled 4—4—0s.

'T7' Class

Throughout his long railway career, Drummond was never renowned for caution, but when introducing double-singles he displayed commendable restraint by ordering only one engine from Nine Elms Works at a cost of £3,160 in March 1897. Numbered 720 and classified 'T7', it was completed on 16th August 1897 and had the following dimensions:

Cylinders (4)	15″ x 26″
Bogie	3′ 7″
Driving wheels	6′ 7″
Wheelbase	6′ 6″ + 8′ 5″ + 11′ 0″ = 25′ 11″
Boiler diameter	4′ 5″

'T7' class double single No. 720, as built with narrow cab and splashers, organ pipe whistle, single slide bars, separate smokebox, front hand-railing and painted Stroudley yellow, at Nine Elms on 16th August 1897. *J. B. Ashford*

Boiler length	12′ 0″ (Tubeplates 12′ 4″)
Firebox length	8′ 4″
Heating surfaces:	
Tubes (271 x 1½″)	1,307 sq. ft.
Firebox	142 sq. ft.
Cross water tubes	215 sq. ft.
Total	1,664 sq. ft.
Working pressure	175 lb
Grate area	27.4 sq. ft.
Weights in working order:	
Bogie	16T 17C
Leading driving wheels	18T 18C
Trailing driving wheels	18T 16C
Engine total	54T 11C
Tender	48T 18C
Engine & Tender	103T 9C

The inside cylinders with the valves between were positioned conventionally below the smokebox and operated by Stephenson link motion, while the outside cylinders had the valves below and were located to the rear of the bogie and employed Joy's valve gear. Of necessity the drive was divided, with the inside cylinders powering the leading driving wheels and the outside cylinders the trailing pair.

The boiler was pitched at 7 ft. 9 in., while the 11 ft. spacing of the driving wheels permitted the use of a much longer firebox than was possible with contemporary 4—4—0s. The firebox contained eighty-three 2¾ in. diameter cross water tubes in pods of 50 and 33, but unlike later engines, there was no provision for inspection or repair without stripping the cladding.

Other interesting details included separate driving wheel and connecting rod splashers, steam reversing, single slide bars for the outside cylinders and an organ pipe whistle. The double bogie tender carried 4,500 gallons of water and 5 tons of coal, and was equipped with exhaust steam heating tubes.

It was quite a surprising engine, although perhaps even more startling was the livery, for No. 720 was painted Stroudley yellow and the tender lettered 'LSW'.

It has been suggested that when new, 16½ in. cylinders were fitted and that these were lined up to 15 in. in October 1897, but this is not confirmed by the cylinder register or drawing E7567 of August 1897, both of which record the smaller diameter. A possible reason for the error is to be found in the cylinders themselves for they were unusually thick-sided, suggesting that the casting was for machining to 16½ in., but restricted to 15 in. Confusion is also possible from the cylinder register's reference to a new left-hand outside cylinder being fitted in October 1897, the diameter being shown as 16½ in., later corrected in purple ink to 15 in.

During Adams' superintendency the engine register frequently contained observations against new construction, but after Drummond took office these asides closed, except for this engine, which is noted as being the replacement of Beattie 6 ft 6 in 2—4—0 No. 017 *Queen*, the latter to be broken up and the scrap value deducted from the cost of No. 720.

As soon as run-in, reputedly on the Waterloo-Salisbury semi-fasts, No. 720 was used for a lengthy series of fuel and haulage trials between Clapham Junction and Eastleigh. Apparently the weight distribution did not prove entirely

satisfactory for the engine register records the weight carried by the bogie being decreased by 14 cwt to 16 tons 17 cwt. The release to general service came in November 1897, when Nine Elms employed it on the Bournemouth expresses, but with only moderate success for the coal consumption was excessive and the performance little better than the final Adams 4—4—0s. There were also hot box failures, while at mileage 15,944 flats on the leading driving wheels and loose outside cylinders caused a return to Nine Elms Works on 30th November 1898, when advantage was taken of its presence to reduce the blast pipe diameter by ½ inch, replace the organ pipe with a standard whistle, provide grab rails over the front footsteps, replace the ash pan and fit an experimental chimney with a heavier top and greater taper. Several test runs with indicator gear on the reversing shaft were made in April 1899, but the chimney did not assist steaming, so when traffic was re-entered, painted royal green on 31st May 1899, the original pattern had been refitted, together with a Boyer speed recorder at the leading end of the right platform. Unfortunately, there was little improvement in performance or

The experimental chimney fitted to 'T7' class No. 720 in April 1899; it later reappeared on Adams '445' class 4—4—0 No. 448.
Author's collection

Another pre-1900 view of No. 720 in service.

J. E. Kite Collection

'T7' class No. 720 at Bournemouth West on 22nd August 1901 with full width cab and splashers, standard whistle, continuous boiler hand-railing, 4,500 gallon double bogie tender and painted green.

C. H. Eden

'T7' class No. 720 at Nine Elms on 4th April 1905 with the 5 ft boiler, water tube inspection covers, shortened chimney and dome, double slide bars, resited steam reversing and 4,500 gallon tender.   *F. Burtt*

'T7' class No. 720 at Nine Elms on 5th July 1905, fitted with indicator gear and a smokebox shelter.   *F. Burtt*

The chance of 'E14' No. 335 and 'T7' No. 720 meeting at Eastleigh Works must have been infinitesimal, nevertheless it did occur in October 1910.

Author's collection

availability and almost as much time was spent stopped on Nine Elms shed or in the works as in service. Details are:-

18/1-20/1/1900	Speed recorder removed, hot box, tender calibrated.
30/4-6/7/1900	Heavy repairs, wide cab and splasher fitted.
30/7-3/8/1900	Tyres reprofiled.
12/9-15/9/1900	Blast pipe renewed.
26/11-14/12/1900	Attention to firebox and valve gear.
18/4-20/4/1901	Attention to cross water tubes, Bessemer steel driving tyres.
23/4-27/7/1901	Adjustment to blast pipe.
7/4-2/8/1902	Inside cylinders lined to 14 in., new 14 in. outside cylinders, double slide bars.
11/11/1903-31/3/1905	Laid aside awaiting a larger boiler (mileage 73,651).

Details of this boiler are:-

Diameter		5' 0"
Length		12' 0" (Tubeplates 12' 3½")
Firebox length		8' 4"
Heating surfaces:		
Tubes (247 x 1¾")		1,392 sq. ft.
Firebox		173 sq. ft.
Cross water tubes (72 x 2¾")		195 sq. ft.
Total		1,760 sq. ft.
Working pressure	175 lb	
Grate area	27.4 sq. ft.	

Weights in working order:

Bogie	18T 18C
Leading driving wheels	20T 13C
Trailing driving wheels	20T 10C
Total	60T 1C

The boiler was based on the 'S11'/'L12' pattern with the barrel and firebox lengthened to accommodate the larger wheelbase. The larger diameter and higher pitching necessitated the use of shorter mountings, which not only improved the appearance but also gave a passing resemblance to the 'L12s'. Other changes included the provision of large cross water tube maintenance covers, resiting the steam reverser between the frames, enlarging the sand containers, providing Duplex feed pumps and fitting Krupps steel driving wheel tyres.

On returning to traffic, No. 720 was employed almost exclusively on the Waterloo-Bournemouth expresses, including the well-patronised 12.30 p.m. luncheon car train due at the Central station in 160 minutes at 3.10 p.m. In early July 1905 indicator gear and a smokebox personnel shelter were fitted and a series of trials run with 'T9s' Nos. 282 and 728 on the 2.00 p.m. Waterloo-Bournemouth and the 6.55 p.m. return. All trains were loaded to seven corridors and a Pullman or dining car. Details are:-

Brockenhurst in mid-1912 with 'T7' No. 720 heading the 12.30 p.m. Waterloo-Weymouth, 'O2' class No. 204 the 2.45 p.m. Brockenhurst-Lymington, and 'X2' class No. 593 the 3.02 p.m. Brockenhurst-Wimborne-Weymouth.

Collection Ian Harrison

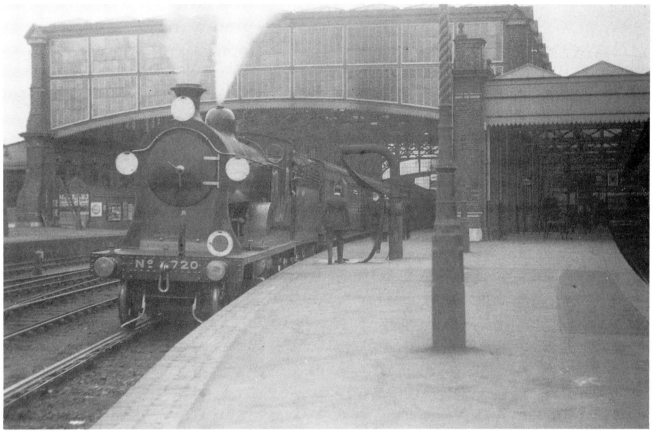

A pre-1914 view of 'T7' class No. 720 at Bournemouth Central on a special train to Waterloo.   *J. E. Kite Collection*

No.	Class	Mileage	Coal burnt per mile Allowed	Actual	Oil & Tallow per 100 miles	
720	T7	2,483	31 lb	41.4 lb	4¼ lb	10.2 lb
282	T9	2,798	31 lb	33.1 lb	4¼ lb	6.1 lb
728	T9	3,147	31 lb	32.4 lb	4¼ lb	6.0 lb

The coal and oil allowances were probably deliberately optimistic to encourage economy for most locomotive superintendents would have gladly accepted the 'T9' consumption. No. 720's indicator cards recorded an unequal power output of the outside and inside cylinders; at 45 mph the inner pair generated 59 per cent of the total, which probably accounted for the frequent overheating of the inside driving bearings and the slipping at speed experienced with the leading driving wheels. The 166 lb average boiler pressure of the 'T9s' was entirely satisfactory, but the 132 lb recorded by No. 720 suggested that the new and large boiler was incapable of supplying four 14 inch cylinders. No time was debited the 'T9s', but No. 720 lost a total of 17 minutes by poor recovery from station and signal stops.

No. 720 remained at Nine Elms and in the summer months was usually employed on the slower and lighter Bournemouth and Salisbury services, while most winters were spent in store or carriage heating at Clapham Junction.

The now unnecessary 4,500 gallon tender was exchanged for the 4,000 gallon pattern of 'E14' class 4–6–0 No. 335 in January 1908, while at the September-December 1912 general repair (total mileage 222,824) the Stroudley two-arm regulator was replaced by a more sensitive single-arm balanced pattern and larger sand containers provided. In 1914 drawings were authorised for rebuilding as an inside cylinder 4–4–0 but, because of the war, no further action occurred.

In the summer months of 1911-4 the 12.30 p.m. Waterloo-Weymouth was regularly worked, an easily timed train stopping at Southampton West (5 mins), Brockenhurst (5 mins), Boscombe (2 mins), Bournemouth Central (5 mins), Parkstone (2 mins), Poole (3 mins) and Dorchester (3 mins), with Bournemouth Central being reached in 155 minutes at 3.05 p.m. and Weymouth at 4.10 p.m. The return was with the 7.35 p.m. slow, reaching Waterloo at 12.04 a.m., a poorly patronised train with stops at most stations *en route* to collect GPO parcels.

From early 1916 an 11.50 p.m. army mail train ran from Waterloo to Southampton docks, where the mail bags were transferred to a ferry for Cherbourg, a train which included a first class carriage for staff officers conveying despatches to Army Headquarters on the Western Front and was intended to relieve the congestion at Folkestone Harbour following the destruction of the Folkestone-Dover line by a landslip. This duty was regularly covered by No. 720 which returned in the early morning with a leave train to Waterloo or empty carriage stock to Clapham Junction.

The mileage only increased by 21,632 in 1919-21, so use was probably restricted to the summer months, when it

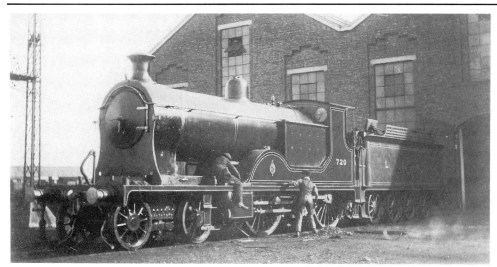

No. 720 receives attention from
cleaners in Eastleigh Works yard.
J. E. Kite Collection

could usually be found working the 7.00 a.m. Waterloo-Eastleigh horseboxes and the 1.15 p.m. return.

Southern Railway stock was entered at Grouping, but being in store and retaining the 1905 firebox, it was not expected to receive Maunsell livery. However, when taken into Eastleigh Works on 15th September 1924, it not only received general repairs and a repaint, but also a new firebox without cross water tubes. Traffic was re-entered on 30th May 1925, with the remainder of the summer being spent working the 7.20 a.m. Waterloo-Salisbury and the 3.33 p.m. return to Woking, from where vans were taken to Waterloo. These duties ceased with the winter timetable, when the only regular working became the weekly 11.10

a.m. Fyffes Waterloo-Southampton docks boat express, which was routed via Alton and usually loaded to three corridors and a bogie van. No. 720 was last noted in charge of this special on 27th December 1926 and being withdrawn on 8th April 1927, this was probably its final main line appearance.

ENGINE SUMMARY

No.	Date	Order No.	Reboilered	Southern Livery	Mileage	Withdrawn
720	8/1897	T7	3/1905	5/1925	357,207	4/1927

Built at Nine Elms Works, and broken up at Eastleigh Works. The 1905 boiler was converted for carriage heating at Clapham Junction.

'T7' class No. 720 in Urie livery, with boiler barrel clack boxes and No. 335's 4,000 gallon double bogie tender, at Nine Elms on 16th September 1922.
W. Beckerlegge

'E10' class double single No. 370 with smokebox sand containers, firebox water tubes and numberplates, at Nine Elms on 21st August 1902.

J. B. Ashford

'E 10' Class

Despite No. 720's trials and tribulations, Drummond persevered with the double-single concept and in May 1899 ordered five more of an improved design from Nine Elms Works at a cost of £2,950 each. As Nos. 369-73 and classified 'E10', they entered traffic in mid-1901 and had the following dimensions:-

Cylinders	14″ x 26″
Bogie wheels	3′ 7″
Driving wheels	6′ 7″
Wheelbase	6′ 6″ + 8′ 5″ + 11′ 0″ = 25′ 11″
Boiler diameter	4′ 5″
Boiler length	12′ 0″ (tubeplates 12′ 3½″)
Firebox length	8′ 4″

Heating surfaces:

Tubes (280 x 1½″)	1,344 sq. ft.
Firebox	156 sq. ft.
Cross water tubes	190 sq. ft.
Total	1,690 sq. ft.
Working pressure	175 lb
Grate area	27.4 sq. ft.

Weights in working order:

Bogie	17T 18C
Leading driving wheels	19T 10C
Trailing driving wheels	20T 7C
Engine total	57T 15C
Tender	49T 0C
Engine & Tender	106T 15C

The boiler was based on that originally carried by 'T7' class No. 720, although the firebox was marginally larger and the cross water tubes were provided with external access openings having large rectangular covers. The motion was also similar, but the Joy's valve gear was more robust and had double slide bars, while the cab and splashers extended to the full width of the platform. Reversing was by steam, and boiler feed by hot water injectors via clack-boxes at the base of the front tubeplate. Sanding was by steam from containers sited within the smokebox and delivering ahead of the rear bogie wheels where the possibility of any useful purpose being served was remote. Equally impractical were the small brass covered replenishing openings high up the smokebox and only accessible by ladder. In 1905-6 gravity sanding was substituted from containers sited inside the frames with delivery ahead of the leading driving wheels.

When new all were stationed at Nine Elms and shared the Bournemouth and Salisbury expresses with the 'T9s' and the later Adams 4—4—0s, but by mid-1904 they had been transferred to the ocean liner specials, troop trains, seaside excursions and other secondary main line passenger duties. The last mentioned included the Waterloo-Alton-Southampton Town services, trains, which being easily timed and seldom loading to more than a four bogie set and

'E10' class No. 373 passing Woodmill Lane bridge, Swaythling, with a Waterloo-Southampton Terminus semi-fast on 26th July 1902.

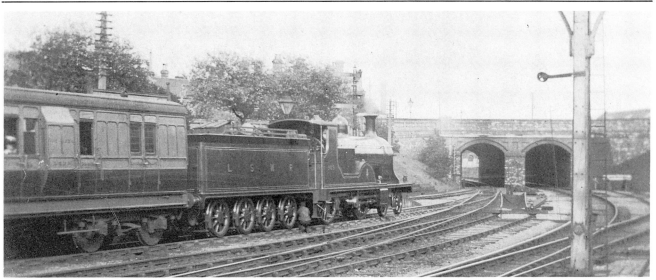

'E10' class No. 373 awaiting departure from Bournemouth Central.

J. E. Kite Collection

a six-wheeled van, were well suited to double-single operation. During the winter, five or six months were spent in store which gave rise to the nickname of 'Butterflies'.

The August 1911 London District coal returns give the following details of the coal consumption and mileage:-

No.	Mileage Worked	Coal Burnt per Mile Allowed lb	Coal Burnt per Mile Actual lb	Oil per 100 miles Allowed lb	Oil per 100 miles Actual lb	Duties
369	2,174	32	40.3	5½	9.1	
372	2,953	32	41.1	5½	8.8	Waterloo-Alton-Southampton Town.
373	3,048	32	39.5	5½	8.6	
370	2,417	34	42.2	6	9.4	Ocean liner and other specials.

No. 371 was in Eastleigh Works for general repairs.

After taking office, Urie considered rebuilding the class as 4—4—0s and in April 1914 estimated the costs as:-

£925 each   Four-cylinder 4—4—0s with original frames, conventional fireboxes, part new motion, clack boxes on barrel, cold feed and Detroit lubricators.

£1320 each   Two-cylinder 4—4—0s, part new frames, 10 ft coupled wheelbase, 7 ft 4 in. firebox, 19 in. cylinders and Stephensons valve gear.

Possibly because of the war, no action was taken and modifications were restricted to conventional fireboxes,

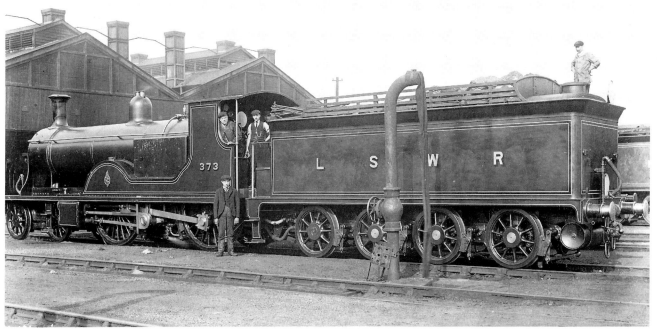

'E10' class No. 373 with conventional gravity sanding and transfer numerals at Eastleigh on 10th March 1910.

J. B. Ashford

A broadside view of 'E10' class No. 373 in post-World War 1 livery.   *J. E. Kite Collection*

'E10' class No. 373 in post-World War 1 livery, with boiler barrel clackboxes, Urie smokebox door and platform valance power classification, at Nine Elms in March 1920.
                                                                                        W. Beckerlegge

'E10' class No. E372 in Southern Railway livery (no cabside numberplates) with additional sanding for the trailing driving wheels, at Eastleigh Works on 18th May 1927.   *H. C. Casserley*

boiler barrel clack-boxes, Urie pattern smokebox doors and in the case of Nos. 369/70/2/3 additional sandboxes feeding the trailing driving wheels.

The entry of 'H15s' Nos. 482-91 to traffic and the heavy December 1913 withdrawals, led to numerous shed and duty changes, including the transfer of Nos. 369-71 to Eastleigh for the light Salisbury-Portsmouth and Southampton-Bournemouth services. By March 1917 all five were again stationed at Nine Elms and were usually employed piloting heavy expresses or main line goods. Occasionally light specials were worked to Southampton docks, often via the Watercress line.

All entered Southern Railway stock at Grouping, although by this date No. 371 was lying unserviceable at Eastleigh and was never steamed again. Only two, Nos. 372 (May 1925) and 373 (February 1925), received the E-prefix and Maunsell livery. During the 1923/4 summers Nos. 369/70 appeared regularly on the Waterloo-Basingstoke-Salisbury semi-fasts, but before their 1925 general repairs Nos. 372/3 were seldom seen in steam. However, on their return to traffic, they took over the Salisbury duties from Nos. 369/70 as well as occasionally working four or six carriage ocean liner specials via both the main line and Alton routes. Nos. 369-71 were withdrawn in September 1926, but Nos. 372/3 lasted until April 1927, with No. 372 making the final double-single main line appearance on 24th March 1927 with a six carriage ocean liner special.

ENGINE SUMMARY

No.	Date	Order No.	Final Mileage	Withdrawn
369	4/1901	E10	373,169	9/1926
370	6/1901	E10	417,869	9/1926
371	6/1901	E10	323,743	9/1926 (Laid aside 10/1922)
372	6/1901	E10	419,611	4/1927
373	7/1901	E10	407,548	4/1927

All built by Nine Elms Works and broken up at Eastleigh Works. The boilers from Nos. 369-72 were modified for stationary duty at Eastleigh Locomotive Works, Lancing Carriage Works, Longhedge Carriage Sidings and Battersea Repair Shop. The boiler from No. 373 was sold to Blackpool Council for heating greenhouses.

'E10s' Nos. 369/71 awaiting breaking up at Eastleigh on 7th July 1926.   *H. C. Casserley*

'C8' class 4—4—0 No. 290, as built with cabside numberplates, splasher coat-of-arms, single link front coupling, splasher sandboxes and a six-wheeled tender, at Nine Elms on 14th June 1898. *J. B. Ashford*

The boiler for 'C8' class No. 290 standing in the Nine Elms boiler shop on 12th May 1898. *Author's collection*

'C8' class No. 297 passing Swaythling with the 9.30 a.m. Waterloo-Bournemouth Pullman Car Express on 6th March 1900. Note the burnt smokebox door, a feature of many 'C8' photographs taken at this period.
Dr. Sellon

THE EARLY EXPRESS 4-4-0s

The first four-coupled express engines built by Drummond for the South Western, 'C8' class Nos. 290-9 of 1898, were undoubtedly a misconception of the company's main line passenger requirements for not only were they smaller and less powerful than the final Adams 4—4—0s, but also incapable of maintaining time with the best Bournemouth and Salisbury services. This was a possibility which probably occurred to Drummond for in the interval between ordering the material and entry to traffic, he lengthened the wheelbase to accommodate a larger firebox before ordering more 4—4—0s from Dübs and Nine Elms Works. These later engines were the renowned 'T9s', 4—4—0s which formed the basis of South Western passenger motive power and, after superheating, gave excellent service on all three sections of the Southern Railway.

'C8' Class

On taking office, Drummond found orders existing for thirty Adams 4—4—0s, 'X6' class Nos. 657-76 and 'T6' class No. 677-86. As assembly of the latter had commenced and much of the material for the first ten 'X6s' was on order; their construction could not be cancelled without financial loss, but this was possible for 'X6s' Nos. 667-76, so Drummond took the opportunity of substituting a like number of 6 ft. 7 in. 4—4—0s of his own design. The drawings were presented to the Locomotive Committee in July 1896, but because Nine Elms was fully committed with double-single

No. 720 and 'M7s' Nos. 242-56, 667-76, assembly was delayed until April 1898 and only then became possible by obtaining the frames, cylinders, boilers and tender plating from Beyer Peacock & Co.

As Nos. 290-9 and classified 'C8', they entered traffic between June and November 1898 at a cost of £1,930 each. In appearance, design and power they were reminiscent of engines provided some years earlier by Drummond for the North British and Caledonian Railways. The dimensions were as follows:-

Cylinders	18½" x 26"
Bogie wheels	3' 7"
Coupled wheels	6' 7"
Wheelbase	6' 6" + 6' 9" + 9' 0" = 22' 3"
Boiler diameter	4' 5"
Boiler length	10' 6" (Tubeplates 10' 9 3/8")
Firebox length	6' 4"
Heating surfaces:	
Tubes (216 x 1¾")	1,067 sq. ft.
Firebox	124 sq. ft.
Total	1,191 sq. ft.
Working pressure	175 lb
Grate area	20.4 sq. ft.
Weights in working order:	
Bogie	15T 2C
Leading coupled wheels	16T 4C
Trailing coupled wheels	15T 10C
Engine total	46T 16C
Tender	40T 14C
Engine & Tender	87T 10C

'C8' class No. 297 at Waterloo on a main line train.

J. E. Kite Collection

The boiler was also carried by classes 'M7' and '700', but was pitched 7 ft. 9 in. above rail level as against their 7 ft. 6 in. and 7 ft. 3 in. The six-wheel tender carried 4 tons of coal and 3,500 gallons of water, the same as the '700' class, but the wheelbase was increased by 1 ft. to 14 ft. Unlike the '700' class and the early 'M7s', reversing was by steam.

All were stationed at Nine Elms and rostered for the best Salisbury, Bournemouth and Portsmouth services, but, being smaller and less powerful than the final Adams 4—4—0s, they regularly lost time, so when the 'T9s' entered traffic they were relegated to the semi-fasts, excursions and ocean liner specials. Even so, it is noticeable in an era when engines were meticulously maintained how many photographs taken in 1900-5 record badly burnt smokebox doors. In secondary service the coal consumption was higher than the Adams 'X2s', while the tender capacity proved too small for the Bournemouth trains.

In preparation for the return of the Grand Duke and Duchess of Serge to Russia, No. 294 worked a six carriage special from Windsor to Dover (LC & DR) on 20th November 1899. No major problems arose apart from one of the carriages failing with a hot box, so three days later the same engine and the South Western royal train repeated the journey with the Grand Duke's party. On the London, Chatham & Dover, the train was piloted by rebuilt Martley 2—4—0 No. 49 *Zephyr*, with the return journey being made via Redhill and Guildford. The deficient water capacity was overcome in 1902-7 by transferring the 3,500 gallon six-wheeled tenders to the 'K10' and 'L11' mixed traffic 4—4—0s and replacing them by the 4,000 gallon double bogie patterns. Details are:-

290	10/1906	295	3/1907
291	2/1903	296	6/1903
292	5/1903	297	9/1904
293	5/1907	298	10/1904
294	9/1902	299	12/1903

With these 44 ton 17 cwt tenders, the total weight in working order was increased to 91 tons 13 cwt. At first there was no interchange of boilers either within the class or with the '700' goods and 'M7' bogie tanks, but with the provision of five spare boilers in 1905-7 regular exchanges commenced between these three classes and also with the 'K10s' after Urie removed the latter's firebox water tubes.

In 1903 Nos. 290/1/3/6 were transferred to Eastleigh and with those remaining at Nine Elms superseded the Adams 'X2s' and 'T3s' on the Waterloo-Alton-Southampton Town services, not, however, with unqualified success, for in October 1903 the Eastleigh and Nine Elms shed foremen were instructed not to employ those members of the class retaining 3,500 gallon tenders to avoid time being lost taking water at Alton, where the mains pressure was poor.

As a result Nine Elms commenced rostering the 'E10' double-singles for these services, and when their performance proved superior, only the Eastleigh 'C8s' appeared regularly on these trains. Obviously, with such a reputation, the class was always overshadowed by the 'T9s' and references in the contemporary railway press are few, therefore the August 1911 coal returns are especially important. Details are:-

No.	Mileage Worked Passenger	Goods	Coal Burnt per mile (lb)	Duties
290	2,150	176	46.6	Portsmouth, Netley and Eastleigh.
296	3,927	75	37.2	Portsmouth-Waterloo semi-fasts.
299	4,003	—	36.0	
291	4,087	240	33.9	Ocean liner and other specials.
293	3,164	183	33.2	
294	2,863	239	35.4	Waterloo-Woking-Basingstoke-Salisbury semi-fasts.
297	3,008	146	36.1	
292	2,816	196	39.2	Reading passenger and vans.
298	2,543	283	38.8	

No. 295 was under repair at Eastleigh Works and No. 290 had worked 86,437 miles since its last general overhaul.

After 1913 the clack-boxes were repositioned on the sides of the boiler barrel, while all replacement smokebox doors were of Urie pattern with four clips round the lower sector where warping often occurred. Otherwise there were few alterations for the class was not considered worth superheating.

During the First World War, Nos. 295/7/8 were employed by Eastleigh piloting ambulance and leave specials over the difficult Alton line, while Nos. 290/2/9 were stationed at Guildford in 1915 for working troop and van specials from Aldershot to Southampton docks. Later in the war, probably from mid-1917, Nos. 291/2/4 appeared on troop specials to Tilbury docks and Nos. 297/9 were working from Plymouth on the Exeter services.

After the Armistice Nos. 296-9 were transferred to Fratton for the Eastleigh, Southampton and Salisbury services, while Exmouth Junction gained Nos. 291-5 for the Plymouth and North Devon trains. However, the latter's stay in the West Country was only temporary for as soon as superheated 'T9s' became available, they were sent away to Salisbury.

All entered Southern Railway stock at Grouping to be painted Maunsell green and receive the E-prefix, details being:-

290	1/1924	295	12/1925
291	10/1925	296	6/1925
292	2/1925	297	12/1925
293	3/1924	298	9/1925
294	9/1925	299	11/1923

When first released to traffic, No. 299 was without the small cabside numberplates.

Other post-Grouping changes included the removal of the splasher mounted sandboxes and the provision of containers inside the frames on all, except No. 291, in

'C8' class No. 293 in post-World War 1 livery, with Urie smokebox door, valance power classification, boiler barrel clackboxes and a double bogie tender at Strawberry Hill on 9th October 1920.
G. E. Mitchell

'C8' class No. E291, in Maunsell green livery, but retaining splasher sandboxes, at Eastleigh on 7th September 1930.   *H. C. Casserley*

1926-8. This engine was noted repainted in Eastleigh Works on 30th November 1930 still retaining the original layout, but it is not known whether it was later modified. A minor livery modification, but nevertheless one which greatly improved the appearance of tender engines was the use of buffer beam red, instead of black for the background of the small cabside numberplates. The first Eastleigh repaint was No. 295 in June 1928. A further livery change in 1931-2 saw the removal of the E-prefix, details being:-

292	6/1931	298	9/1931
293	4/1932	299	12/1931
297	10/1931		

Nos. 290/1/4-6 were withdrawn before this occurred.

For several years after Grouping, Nos. 290-4 were stationed at Basingstoke for the Waterloo semi-fasts, but following complaints of late running and delays to other services, they were replaced in early 1926 by Adams 'T3s' and transferred to Yeovil. However, their stay was brief and by June 1926 the allocation was: Eastleigh Nos. 290/1/3/6; Fratton No. 294; Nine Elms No. 295; Salisbury Nos. 292/7-9. At Nine Elms No. 295 worked the Reading vans during the week and excursions from Western Section suburban stations to the Central Section seaside resorts on summer Sundays and bank holidays, while those at Salisbury worked slows to Eastleigh, Portsmouth, Yeovil and Bournemouth, the type of mundane passenger duties expected of the class at this period. Because of the loss of 'T9s' and 'L12s' to the Eastern Section, the repertoire of Eastleigh's Nos. 290/1/3/6 was considerably more enterprising for they had two return duties to Waterloo via Alton, one from Southampton Terminus to Reading and return, several Eastleigh-Southampton and Eastleigh-Salisbury locals and goods turns to Southampton docks and Basingstoke. The last mentioned were coal wagons, which in the winter months regularly loaded to 32 wagons and must have proved a heavy task on the climb up through Winchester for such large wheeled engines. Additionally, in the summer months there were soft fruit trains from Fareham to Salisbury or Basingstoke and weekly Fareham line cattle trains. In May 1932 Nos. 298/9 were transferred to Feltham for the Sunday Wimbledon-Brighton excursions via Raynes Park and Dorking on which weight restrictions forbade the use of 'T9s'. During the week they substituted as required for 'K10s' or 'L11s' on London area goods duties. Later the same year No. 295 was sent to Yeovil for an early morning Exeter slow, returning on vans.

Withdrawal commenced with Nos. 290/4 in 1933 and was followed by Nos. 291-3/5-7 in 1935-6. For a year or so prior to withdrawal, No. 295 had lain derelict at Yeovil, while at Salisbury Nos. 292/6/7 had only been steamed spasmodically for station piloting, the Templecombe goods or to release 'T9s' at busy periods for main line duty. At Feltham Nos. 298/9 lasted somewhat longer, working London area goods, vans and empty carriage stock, with the last, No. 298, not being discarded until January 1938, which left the Beattie well tank it had replaced in November 1898 to work on for a further quarter of a century. After withdrawal the tenders of Nos. 290-6 were transferred to Urie 'S15s' Nos. 509, 506, 504/7/8/10, 510, so that their 5,000 gallon pattern could be released to the 'N15X' rebuilds.

ENGINE SUMMARY

No.	Date	Order No.	Withdrawn
290	6/1898	C8	10/1933
291	6/1898	C8	1/1935
292	6/1898	C8	1/1936
293	7/1898	C8	2/1935
294	8/1898	C8	2/1933
295	10/1898	C8	8/1935
296	11/1898	C8	11/1935
297	11/1898	C8	6/1936
298	11/1898	C8	1/1938
299	11/1898	C8	8/1937

All were built by Nine Elms Works and broken up at Eastleigh Works. Final mileages: Nos. 290 — 805,247; 292 — 800,694; 294 — 796,411; 296 — 739,899; 299 — 813,117.

'C8' class No. 298, with the sandboxes resited between the frames, at Feltham in July 1937. Although only employed on Sunday excursion, empty carriage stock and local goods duties, it is reasonably well groomed and apparently in good mechanical order.

P. Ransome Wallis, courtesy National Railway Museum

'T9' class No. 702 passing Brockenhurst with the 2.15 p.m. Waterloo-Bournemouth Pullman Car express (non-stop to Christchurch) on 8th May 1899, of the 1899 Dübs series with narrow cabs and splashers, firebox water tubes and six-wheeled tenders. On the left 'O2' class No. 194 has charge of the Lymington branch train.

Dr. Sellon

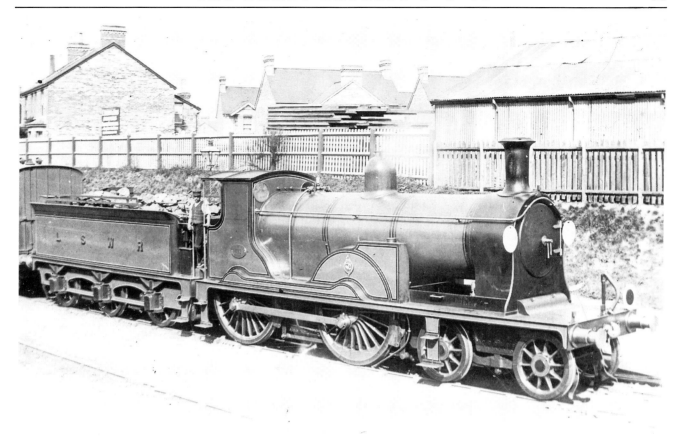

'T9' class 4—4—0 No. 113 standing at Branksome with a Weymouth-Bournemouth train in August 1900, of the 1899 Nine Elms series with narrow cabs and splashers, fireboxes without water tanks and 3,500 gallon six-wheeled tenders.   *C. H. Eden*

'T9' Class

The express classes built by most mechanical engineers gave adequate if unpretentious service, although in each decade a few exceeded expectation and gained the acclaim of both professional and amateur railwaymen. During the final years of British main line steam, the Gresley 'A4s', Stanier 'Black 5s' and Riddles '9Fs' immediately come to mind, while at the turn of the century there were the McIntosh 'Dunalastairs', Ivatt 'Atlantics' and Holden 'Claud Hamiltons'. To the latter must be added the Drummond 'T9s', 4—4—0s which formed the basis of South Western passenger service from 1899 until Grouping, when, revitalised by superheating, they played an important role on all the sections of the Southern Railway.

Tenders for the supply of the first thirty, Nos. 702-19/ 21-32, were sought on 2nd February 1898, with those received being considered by the Locomotive Committee at the following month's meeting, when the offer of £2,945 each by Dübs & Co. was accepted. Details of the other tenders are: Neilson & Co. £3,117; Sharp Stewart & Co. £3,150; Vulcan Foundry £3,190; Beyer Peacock & Co. £3,220; Kitson & Co. £3,360; Robert Stephenson & Co. £3,800. The very competitive Dübs tender suggests that the order was so urgently required to retain the work force intact that management was prepared to accept the bare

costs or even a small loss. Under the circumstances the temptation to save expense by 'cutting corners' must have been intense, but to Dübs' credit this was resisted.

The February 1898 drawings incorporated a conventional firebox, but these were recalled on 30th March 1898 and a modified series substituted in which the firebox and grate were marginally larger, the ashpan deeper, the clackboxes repositioned at the base of the front tubeplate and cross water tubes added. These modifications increased the cost by £255 per engine, bringing the total to £3,200 each.

Delivery was scheduled for 30th November 1899, but a boiler shop dispute delayed completion of Nos. 728-32 until the end of the year. In appearance there was a marked resemblance to Drummond's Caledonian 4—4—0s and the recently completed 'C8' class, although the coupled wheelbase was noticeably longer to accommodate the larger firebox. The dimensions were as follows:

Cylinders	18½″ x 26″
Bogie wheels	3′ 7″
Coupled wheels	6′ 7″
Wheelbase	6′ 6″ + 6′ 9″ + 10′ 0″ = 23′ 3″
Boiler diameter	4′ 5″
Boiler length	10′ 6″ (Tubeplates 10′ 9 3/8″)
Firebox length	7′ 4″

'T9' class No. 311 at Nine Elms on 1st March 1901, of the 1900-1 Nine Elms series with full width cabs and splashers, steam sanding from smokebox containers, firebox water tubes and 4,000 gallon double bogie tenders.
J. B. Ashford

The stark simplicity of the 'T9' cab, No. 702 at Nine Elms shortly after delivery by Dübs.
Author's collection

'T9' class No. 712 passing over Kent Road bridge, Swaythling, with the 9.30 a.m. Waterloo-Bournemouth Pullman Car express on 23rd May 1901.
Dr. Sellon

Heating surfaces:

Tubes	1,187 sq. ft.	
Firebox	143 sq. ft.	
Cross water tubes	138 sq. ft.	
Total	1,468 sq. ft.	
Working pressure	175 lb	
Grate area	24 sq. ft.	

Weights in working order:

	Nos. 702-14	Nos. 715-9/21-32
Bogie	15T 6C	15T 1C
Leading coupled wheels	18T 7C	18T 1C
Trailing coupled wheels	17T 9C	16T 9C
Engine total	51T 2C	49T 11C
Tender	39T 4C	39T 4C
Engine & tender	90T 6C	88T 15C

On delivery the weight of Nos. 702-14 was found to exceed specification by 2 tons, so Dübs were instructed to lighten the drag boxes of Nos. 715-9/21-32 and fabricate the splashers, sandboxes and cab sidesheets from thinner steel. Those already delivered had the drag boxes modified at Dübs' expense during the first visit to Nine Elms Works for heavy repairs.

The mild steel boiler was constructed in two telescopic rings and except for the larger firebox, was similar to that carried by classes '700', 'C8', 'K10' and 'M7'. The dome was positioned on the rear ring and was capped by two brass encased lock-up safety valves pressed to 175 lb per

sq. in. The firebox cross water tubes were mounted in two pods, one containing 36 and the other 25 tubes, with a diameter of 2¼ in. and a length of 3 ft 7 in. Large rectangular external inspection covers were provided for cleaning and repair. The tender was not equipped with exhaust steam heating, the contents being fed to the boiler by means of two injectors and clackboxes at the base of the front tubeplate. The chimney was of the well-proportioned tall lipped pattern used with minor differences on all the Drummond 4—4—0s, except the large boilered 'D15s', 'L12s' and 'S11s'.

The direct Stephenson link motion was neatly but robustly constructed, with the motionplate positioned midway along the slide bars, where the maximum stress could be absorbed. Further advantage was gained by using long eccentric rods and providing generous bearing surfaces for the valve spindle bushes, which were housed in the motionplate. To avoid heat being conducted from the cylinders to the slipper blocks, the leading ends of the slide bars did not make contact, while equally practical was their trough pattern which partially enclosed the crossheads and protected the working surfaces from abrasion by grit, ash and sand, a failing of the Adams single bar layout. The pistons were conical and the connecting rods of rectangular section with marine-type big-ends, while the 10 ft coupling rods were unusually lengthy and exceeded those of the Crewe Black Prince compounds by 4 inches.

'T9' class No. 773, the Glasgow exhibition locomotive, resplendent in its special livery as received from Dübs in 1901.

J. E. Kite Collection

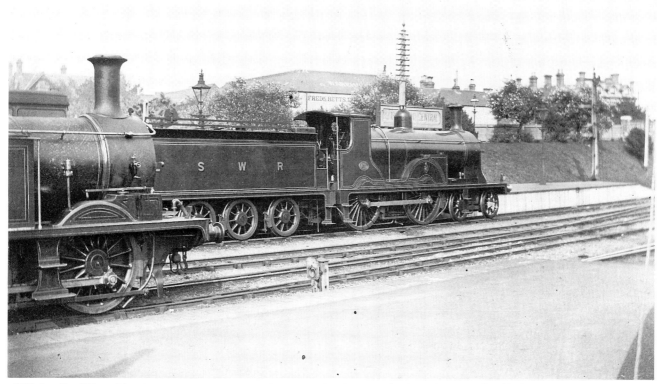

'T9' class No. 281 awaiting departure from Bournemouth Central with the double bogie tender received in 1904.   *J. E. Kite Collection*

The 18½ in. by 26 in. cylinders followed normal Drummond practice by having 1 in. thick barrels and 2 ft. 3 in. centres. The steam chests were between, but nevertheless were relatively spacious with the exhaust ports divided into separate halves, one above and the other below the centre line. The exhaust steam passages from the lower set reached the blast pipe by passing round the cylinders, expanding fan-like until at the sides, where the main frames formed the retaining walls, they practically encompassed the cylinder barrel and had no difficulty accepting half the steam of each cylinder. No doubt Drummond's intention was to insulate the cylinders from the cooling effect of the atmosphere, although in all probability greater advantage ensued from the reduced heat lost and thereby avoiding that most pernicious cause of back pressure, a wet and rapidly condensing exhaust. In theory, the use of the main frames as cylinder retaining walls was disadvantageous, but practice proved this a fallacy for the standard Drummond front-end gave the best performance of cylinders having back to back valves between them. The generous 8 in. by 7½ in. coupled axle journals ensured freedom from hot boxes.

The cab and splashers did not extend to the edge of the platform, which necessitated the provision of separate casings for the coupling rods. Sanding was by gravity to the leading coupled wheels from containers combined with the front splashers. The drive was left hand, the regulator being of Stroudley pattern, while reversing was by steam.

The six-wheel 3,500 gallon tender was basically similar to the '700' class goods, but had the wheelbase lengthened by 1 ft. to 14 ft. Dübs recorded the fully laden weight as 39 tons 4 cwt, but the LSWR diagram books give 39 tons 12 cwt, the same as the tenders of the Nine Elms-built Nos. 113-22, 280-9.

On 28th February 1900 Dübs sought permission to build an additional engine at a cost of £3,525 for exhibition at the Glasgow Trade Fair, with delivery promised for 30th November 1901. The Locomotive Committee agreed providing the price was reduced to £3,200, including delivery to Nine Elms. Dübs accepted these terms on 28th March 1900, when it was allotted No. 773. It was similar to the 1899 series, but was magnificently finished with extra lining, and the buffer faces, wheel centres, coupling rods, tyres, piping, safety valves, window surrounds and footplate controls highly burnished. Indeed, such was the standard of craftsmanship and paintwork that it was October 1905 before general repairs and repainting became necessary, the mileage being 136,067.

Ten more, Nos. 113-22 (originally intended to be Nos. 733-42), were ordered from Nine Elms Works at a cost of £2,275 each in December 1898 and delivered in June-September 1899. They were similar to the Dübs series apart from having fireboxes without cross water tubes, being 3 tons lighter and having marginally heavier 3,500 gallon tenders. They were followed by Nos. 280-9 at a cost of £2,345 each between October 1899 and February 1900. The changed dimensions were:-

Heating surfaces:
Tubes (280 x 1½")	1,187 sq. ft.
Firebox	148 sq. ft.
Total	1,335 sq. ft.

'T9' class No. 773 being lifted for repair at Nine Elms shed on 18th May 1902.

C. H. Eden

Dual-braked 'T9' class No. 338 photographed circa 1915, with Westinghouse air pump positioned on side of smokebox.

J. E. Kite Collection

Weights in working order:

Bogie	14T 0C
Leading coupled wheels	17T 0C
Trailing coupled wheels	15T 4C
Engine total	46T 4C
Tender	39T 12C
Engine & Tender	85T 16C

A final fifteen of an improved design, Nos. 300-5/7/ 10-4/36-8 were ordered from Nine Elms Works at a cost of £2,685 each in May 1900 and delivered between December 1900 and October 1901. All were fitted with wide cabs and splashers, firebox cross water tubes, steam sanding and 4,000 gallon double bogie tenders. The sand containers were sited inside the smokebox, with small hinged brass filler caps below the handrailing, and delivery pipes passing through the platform to deposit sand to the rear bogie wheels where little useful purpose was served. As with other Drummond engines having these sanding arrangements, the containers were later resited inside the main frames with gravity feed to the leading coupled wheels. The changed dimensions were:-

Heating surfaces:

Tubes (280 x 1½")	1,187 sq. ft.
Firebox	148 sq. ft.
Cross water tubes	165 sq. ft.
Total	1,500 sq. ft.

Weights in working order:

Bogie	15T 8C
Leading coupled wheels	17T 15C
Trailing coupled wheels	15T 14C
Engine total	48T 17C
Tender	44T 17C
Engine & Tender	93T 14C

Nos. 337/8 were dual-braked, the Westinghouse air pump being carried below the footplate where access for maintenance or repair proved so inconvenient that in 1909-10 it was repositioned low down on the left hand side of the smokebox. The air brake was removed from No. 337 in February 1935 and No. 338 in November 1934.

In express service all three series proved smooth-riding, free-steaming and reliable, while, for the period, the coal and water consumption was moderate. Nevertheless, the performance on the Bournemouth, Salisbury and Portsmouth expresses was not outstanding, but over the undulating West of England line the class really excelled for it was there that the free-running and speed gained them the nickname of 'Greyhounds'.

In July 1906 Drummond reported that engines with firebox water tubes gave a yearly fuel saving of £31 12s 8d, but cost an additional £17 16s 5d in labour and maintenance. Since the fuel used by different crews on similar duties varied by 15%, the actual savings were probably minimal and did not warrant the added complication and reduced availability.

On the Caledonian Drummond strongly advocated the use of fully opened regulators and short cut-offs, but despite obtaining excellent results in a series of trials, he was unable to gain its adoption. On coming south, the scheme received a further airing and, although the Adams classes could not be driven in this manner, his own could and he insisted that they were. North of the Border crews were not impressed by Scottish wrath and fiery rhetoric, but to South Western men the new chief was beyond their ken and therefore feared. As a result wide open regulators and short cut-offs received a fair trial and in time became the accepted way of driving the Drummond classes. After Grouping this was particularly noticeable when the new 4—6—0s were introduced on all sections of the Southern Railway for Western Section men automatically drove them by the reversing wheel, whereas most Eastern and Central Section drivers adjusted their progress by means of the regulator. In practice and despite current thinking, either method in skilled hands gave very similar results. This was confirmed by a series of trials held by Drummond with 'T9s' Nos. 712/23 on the fast Bournemouth expresses in mid-1901, details being:-

No.	Driving Method	No. of Journeys	Average Load	Coal Burnt per train mile	Oil Consumed per 100 miles	Average time lost
712	Cut-off	7	257 tons	32.6 lb	5.9 lb	1 min.
723	Regulator	8	264 tons	33.2 lb	6.1 lb	1½ min.

The weather varied from warm and sunny to cool with blustery showers.

The mid-1902 allocation was: Nine Elms Nos. 114/5/20/1, 283/5, 303/7/10/37, 705/13/8/23/5/8/30/73; Salisbury Nos. 122, 280, 314, 712/29; Eastleigh Nos. 116/7, 311/2, 717; Fratton Nos. 338, 732; Bournemouth Nos. 113/8, 282, 301, 702/8/14; Dorchester Nos. 289, 726/7; Yeovil Nos. 286, 703; Exmouth Junction Nos. 304/5/13, 707/15/22; Plymouth Nos. 288, 719/21; Nine Elms Works (for repair) Nos. 119, 281/4/7, 300/2/36, 704/6/9/10/1/6/24/31.

In the summer months the six-wheel tenders of the Dübs and 1st Nine Elms series proved adequate for the non-stop Bournemouth expresses, but in the winter months most drivers insisted in stopping *en route* to take water. Although time was seldom lost, the Running Department found the practice objectionable, so in November 1901 Drummond agreed to transfer thirty of these tenders to the 'K10' class mixed traffic 4—4—0s under construction at Nine Elms Works and supply twenty-eight 'T9s' and two 'C8s' with new 4,000 gallon double bogie tenders. Details are:-

No.	Date	Small Tender to	No.	Date	Small Tender to
114	9/1902	137	710	12/1902	146
117	12/1902	149	711	12/1902	152
118	7/1902	391	712	12/1902	145
121	8/1902	392	713	10/1902	141
122	4/1902	384	714	4/1902	381
282	6/1902	388	717	10/1902	139
286	6/1902	386	719	12/1902	144
287	12/1902	151	725	5/1902	385
288	6/1902	389	726	4/1902	380
289	6/1902	390	727	4/1902	383
702	12/1902	150	728	8/1902	135
705	11/1902	152	729	4/1902	382
706	10/1902	140	731	5/1902	387
708	9/1902	138	732	11/1902	143

In 1903-7 the remaining twenty-three 6-wheel tender 'T9s' and eight 'C8s' similarly received new double bogie tender, these having been constructed with the 'L11' class mixed traffic 4—4—0s. Details are:-

No.	Date	Small Tender to	No.	Date	Small Tender to
113	8/1906	414	707	12/1906	437
115	8/1904	170	709	6/1904	168
116	11/1906	436	715	6/1903	158
119	10/1904	173	716	11/1903	165
120	6/1907	442	718	5/1904	134
280	10/1903	163	721	5/1904	167
281	5/1904	166	722	4/1907	440
283	9/1903	159	723	5/1903	154
284	3/1907	439	724	10/1904	172
285	5/1904	148	730	6/1903	156
703	10/1906	435	773	10/1906	406
704	9/1903	161			

The 4,000 gallon double bogie tenders were usually referred to as Drummond water carts because of their habitual spraying of the permanent way with water as the rivets attaching the bogie centres to the base of the tank worked loose. At this period, of course, it was common practice in the summer months for councils to dampen down the dust of the untarred roads with large horse-drawn water carts, with which South Western crews noted an affinity.

During 1900 competition with the Great Western Railway for the lucrative and prestigious West of England passenger traffic became more severe. Consequently, in July orders were placed with Eastleigh Carriage Works for the supply of three new trains of corridor bogie carriages and restaurant cars to encourage regular travellers to patronise the Waterloo-Exeter route. Details are:-

8 first class (27 tons) at £1,100 each
4 second class (27½ tons) at £1,190 each
4 first class (28 tons) at £1,200 each
4 composites (25½ tons) at £1,050 each
3 dining cars (32½ tons) at £1,750 each
4 guards vans (19½ tons) at £480 each

The intention was to have all three trains in service before the end of the year, but the decision to fit steam heating and the late delivery of the dining car cookers and food-warming cabinets delayed completion until April 1901. For working these trains eleven 'T9s', Nos. 114/9/20/1 of Nine Elms, Nos. 280/3, 314, 729 of Salisbury and Nos. 707/9/15 of Exmouth Junction, were fitted with the necessary equipment and hose connections at the rear of the tender. At this period it was not considered necessary to provide connections at the front of tender engines.

On test between Salisbury and Exeter, it was found that carriage heating increased the coal consumption by 6 ozs per vehicle mile, which, when all the carriage stock had been equipped, would increase the annual coal consumption by 6,000 tons at a cost of £4,700, a price which several directors found too high for passenger comfort and questioned the need for such luxurious travel, especially for third class passengers. As a result, in January 1902, Drummond was instructed to investigate the means of lowering the cost. Over a four week period the engines working the 11.00 a.m. down and 12.00 p.m. up West of England expresses had their coal consumption measured while the carriage heating equipment was in use, and the findings compared with those obtained with the same trains in June 1902, when the weather was warmer and no heating was provided. To the surprise of Drummond and the recorders, the difference between the two sets of figures was considerably less than anticipated, as the original assessment had failed to account for the human element, in particular the ingenuity of engine crews to make life on the footplate as comfortable as circumstances and experience permitted. With this intention, it had become standard practice to heat trains as thoroughly as possible while standing awaiting departure at Waterloo and Exeter, since the steam then being generated was serving no other practical purpose and, what is more, was liable to be lost via the safety valves. At the 'right-away' the carriage heating was reduced to minimal to conserve steam and only returned to full power when steam was in surplus, such as running down banks, at stops *en route* or when time was in hand. As a result, the additional coal cost was re-assessed as £1,260, a figure acceptable to the directors, although not, of course, giving passengers full carriage comfort.

At this period the best West of England expresses were booked 210 minutes to Exeter (171¾ miles) and 319 minutes to Plymouth (234 miles). Details are:-

DOWN

Waterloo dep.	Exeter arr.	Time mins.	
10.50 a.m.	2.20 p.m.	210	Plymouth express (arr. 4.09 p.m., 319 mins.)
11.00 a.m.	2.55 p.m.	235	North Devon express (arr. Ilfracombe 5.08 p.m.)
11.10 a.m.	3.13 p.m.	243	North Cornwall express (arr. Padstow 6.40 p.m.)
1.00 p.m.	5.11 p.m.	251	Plymouth express (arr. 7.15 p.m., 375 mins.)
3.00 p.m.	6.45 p.m.	225	Plymouth express (arr. 8.46 p.m., 346 mins.)
5.50 p.m.	10.05 p.m.	255	

UP

Exeter dep.	Waterloo arr.	Time mins.	
10.20 a.m.	2.35 p.m.	255	
12.00 p.m.	3.30 p.m.	210	Plymouth express (dep. 10.08 a.m., 322 mins.)
12.15 p.m.	4.00 p.m.	225	North Devon express (dep. Torrington 10.20 a.m.)
12.50 p.m.	5.18 p.m.	268	North Cornwall express (dep. Padstow 8.35 a.m.)
1.05 p.m.	6.53 p.m.	348	
4.15 p.m.	8.00 p.m.	225	Plymouth express (dep. 2.15 p.m., 345 mins.)

All trains changed engines and crews at Salisbury and Exeter, with the fastest services in either direction being booked non-stop Waterloo-Salisbury and Salisbury-Exeter in 210 minutes.

In 1901 the Great Western was still running its Plymouth services via Swindon and Bristol, but little advantage was taken of the easier route for the timings were only marginally better than the South Western. Details are:-

10.50 a.m. Paddington-Plymouth (318 mins.)
10.30 a.m. Plymouth-Paddington (313 mins.)

There was no direct competition for the lucrative Bournemouth traffic, but nevertheless in October 1900, concurrently with 'T9s' replacing the Adams 4—4—0s on the best services, there was a long overdue improvement of schedules with the well-patronised 9.00 a.m. up and 4.10 p.m. down being booked non-stop over the 108 miles in 130 and 126 minutes respectively. The engine of the 4.10 p.m. worked through to Weymouth and, with a 7.28 p.m. arrival, gave a journey time of 198 minutes. The crew and engine spent the night at Dorchester and next morning

worked the 7.50 a.m. Weymouth-Waterloo, which departed Bournemouth Central at 9.00 a.m. and ran non-stop to London. On Sundays there were no through Weymouth workings; consequently on Mondays a Dorchester 'T9', usually No. 289, worked this train as far as Bournemouth Central, where the Nine Elms engine off the newspaper train took over. At first the non-stop expresses were restricted to eight bogies, but when the 'T9s' with 4,000 gallon tenders were found capable of improving on schedule the standard formation at busy periods became ten bogies.

Apart from the Monday working of the 7.50 a.m. up, the three Dorchester 'T9s', Nos. 289, 726/7, worked the 8.30 a.m. Waterloo via Wimborne, returning with the 2.15 p.m. down over the same route, together with a number of Weymouth-Bournemouth Central duties. For some years they had the reputation of being the best groomed and maintained members of the class.

These fast Bournemouth services proved very popular and for the 1901 summer the 12.20 p.m. Waterloo-Bournemouth Central and the 1.50 p.m. Bournemouth Central-Waterloo also became non-stop, while the 2.15 p.m. down only called at Christchurch. The last mentioned was particularly well-patronised and regularly loaded to ten bogies and two vans, but nevertheless gained an excellent reputation for punctuality.

Pullman cars had been available on this route since 1890, but after the turn of the century, possibly to make the facilities available to passengers not travelling throughout, the four cars, *Duchess of Albany, Duchess of Fife, Duchess of Connaught* and *Princess Margaret*, were restricted to those services having stops *en route*. Details for May 1902 are:-

DOWN

9.30 a.m.	Waterloo-Bournemouth Central			(194 mins.)
12.30 p.m.	,,	,,	,,	(160 mins.)
2.15 p.m.	,,	,,	,,	(143 mins.)
4.53 p.m.	,,	,,	,,	(171 mins.)

UP

8.01 a.m.	Bournemouth Central-Waterloo			(158 mins.)
9.26 a.m.	,,	,,	,,	(180 mins.)
11.10 a.m.	,,	,,	,,	(175 mins.)
2.10 p.m.	,,	,,	,,	(155 mins.)

This policy, unfortunately for the Pullman Car Company, led to many first class passengers transferring their patronage to the non-stop services, especially after the introduction of breakfast, luncheon and dining cars in 1904. As a result, the Pullman cars commenced running at a loss, with two being withdrawn from the Bournemouth services in December 1905 and the remainder in November 1911. After a period of use on the ocean liner specials, Sunday excursions to Bournemouth and Weymouth, private trains and race specials, all were transferred to the LB & SCR for the Brighton and Eastbourne expresses.

Although superseded on the best services by the 'T9s', the later Adams 4—4—0s were still rostered by Bournemouth for the Basingstoke and Woking semi-fasts, the slow Waterloo services, many of the Weymouth trains and holiday reliefs, consequently the coal returns of May 1903 offer an interesting comparison between the two engineers' 4–4–0s. Details are:-

Class	No.	Mileage	Coal burnt per mile	Oil & tallow per 100 miles
T9	113	5,592	31.2 lb	5.4 lb
T9	118	5,398	32.1 lb	5.6 lb
T9	285	4,764	32.0 lb	5.7 lb
T9	301	4,447	31.4 lb	5.3 lb
C8	291	4,087	33.1 lb	6.4 lb
X2	580	3,094	38.1 lb	7.1 lb
X2	590	2,016	37.8 lb	7.4 lb
T3	563	4,897	36.2 lb	6.9 lb
T6	685	3,198	36.4 lb	7.0 lb
T6	686	3,569	35.7 lb	7.3 lb

No engine attained the allowance of 31 lb of coal and 5 lb of oil/tallow for these duties, although the 'T9s' only proved marginally more extravagant, suggesting that the well-designed front-end and larger firebox made lengthy periods of hard driving unnecessary, whereas the Adams classes, particularly the smaller 'X2s', frequently had to be fully extended. Like most outside cylinder engines, the latter's oil and tallow consumption was considerably higher.

An interesting comparison is also possible with the double-single No. 720, details being:-

Number of Days in Works 1900-13

Year	No. 720	No. 728
1900	97	–
1901	6	–
1902	117	43
1903	50	–
1904	365	47
1905	151	32
1906	68	31
1907	56	23
1908	18	71
1909	91	18
1910	95	–
1911	86	87
1912	89	–
1913	–	65
TOTAL	1,289 days	417 days
Yearly average	92.1 days	29.8 days

General Repair Mileages 1899-1913

No. 720		No. 728	
30/4/00-6/7/00	35,986	18/7/02-30/8/02	86,306
11/11/03-31/3/05	37,665	17/10/04-3/12/04	77,612
30/10/07-21/12/07	36,798	22/4/08-4/7/08	98,923
19/2/09-8/5/09	53,943	17/1/11-3/6/11	89,169
23/9/12-21/12/12	61,432	7/4/13-21/6/13	74,864
Total Mileage	222,824		426,874
Yearly average	17,371		32,836

Like most railways at the turn of the century, South Western engines almost invariably retained their own boilers when undergoing heavy repairs at Nine Elms Works, but in 1905-7 Drummond decided to reduce the inevitable delays awaiting the return of boilers by establishing an exchange system and to this end provided a number of spares for his

own and most of the Adams classes. Two boilers at a cost of £688 were provided for the 'T9' class and fitted to Nos. 303 (August 1907) and 718 (May 1908). Unfortunately, a complication still remained because of the two types of firebox, Nos. 113-22, 280-9 being of conventional pattern, whereas Nos. 300-5/7/10-4/36-8, 702-19/21-32/73 and all the 'L11' class mixed traffic 4–4–0s were fitted with cross water tubes. This was not an insurmountable problem if Drummond agreed to the transfer of boilers having the feature to engines without it, but he refused to permit this, so delays still occurred until Urie removed the cross water tubes and supplied six more spare boilers with conventional fireboxes. These were fitted to: 303 (7/1913); 713 (1/1913); 714 (5/1913); 721/32 (3/1913); and 728 (6/1913).

These boilers followed Drummond practice by having dome top safety valves, but were fitted with Urie pattern smokebox doors and barrel clackboxes. Existing boilers had their clackboxes similarly repositioned, while all replacement smokebox doors were of Urie pattern, but because of wartime shortages the removal of the firebox cross water tubes was prolonged and Nos. 702-4/9/15/24/30 still retained theirs at Grouping. They finally disappeared from No. 715 in December 1923.

The class was little affected by the early 4–6–0s, but when 'T14s' Nos. 443-7/58-62 and 'D15s' Nos. 463-72 entered traffic in 1911-2, they took over all the hardest Bournemouth and Salisbury expresses, thereby permitting the transfer of Nos. 113/5, 702/4 to Plymouth, Nos. 119, 706/23/8/30 to Exmouth Junction and Nos. 116/7, 300 to Yeovil. These transfers caused the down-grading of the later Adams 4–4–0s and the laying aside of classes '0135' and '0380'. Fortunately, numerous secondary main line duties, ocean liner specials, cross-country services, excursions and summer reliefs remained for the 'T9s', while should replacements be required for the larger engines, they proved worthy substitutes.

At the outbreak of the First World War, most of the Urie 'H15s' and later Drummond 4–6–0s were removed from their normal passenger duties and concentrated on the many troop, ambulance, van, explosives and heavy goods specials bound for Southampton dock. Their place on the public express services was filled by classes 'T9', 'L12' and 'D15'. Later in the war there were daily workings by 'C8s', 'L11s' and 'T9s' from Aldershot and Salisbury to Tilbury docks via Kew, Cricklewood, Kentish Town and the Tottenham-Hampstead line, while, after the establishment of a tank warfare range at Wool, 'T9s' frequently worked trains of flat wagons conveying armoured vehicles to Southampton docks. One of these specials, headed by No. 717, overran signals approaching Bournemouth Central on the early morning of 6th October 1916 and crashed into a set of empty carriages standing on the up through road. Damage to stock was not extensive and no one was seriously injured, but the station was closed until the following day and No. 717 was not returned to traffic until March 1917. At the subsequent enquiry it was disclosed that the engine's brake hose had not been connected to the four carriages at the front of the train and the guard had not tested the brakes before the journey commenced. In the following year a similar train, headed by No. 702, on 23rd November 1917 came to grief approaching Brockenhurst, when a

'T9' class No. 304, with conventional gravity sanding and transfer numerals, at Nine Elms on 20th September 1907. *J. B. Ashford*

'male' tank (with projecting guns) broke loose from its fastening and played havoc with the lineside furniture before the train could be stopped.

After hostilities ceased, the return of 'H15s' to passenger service, the construction of 'N15s' Nos. 736-45 and the superheating of classes 'L12' and 'D15' left the South Western adequately provided with express motive power, but lacking in modern engines for working the many summer reliefs and excursions over routes forbidden the 'D15s' and 4—6—0s, a need which Urie fulfilled in May 1921 by ordering the superheating of twenty-five 'T9s' at an estimated cost of £495 each. The drawings were completed in July 1921 with intention of having the lead engine in traffic by the end of the year, but delays in obtaining the necessary material and lack of workshop capacity prevented this and it was April 1922 before No. 314 left Eastleigh Works for trials.

In addition to the Eastleigh superheater, No. 314 was provided with an extended smokebox supported by a saddle, 19 inch cylinders, a Urie smokebox door and a tall stovepipe chimney with a capuchon. The Drummond boiler had been stripped to the shell and fitted with new tubes, tubeplates and firebox, while the expense of fitting piston valves was avoided by using a four-feed Detroit lubricator. To compensate for the weight of the superheater, a large drag box was provided below the footplate, this also being necessary on classes '700', 'S11', 'L12' and 'D15' when superheated.

The changed dimensions were:-

Cylinders	19" x 26"
Heating surfaces:	
Small tubes (124 x 1¾")	610 sq. ft.
Large tubes (21 x 5¼")	311 sq. ft.
Firebox	142 sq. ft.
Total evaporative	1,063 sq. ft.
Superheater	195 sq. ft.
Total	1,258 sq. ft.

Weights in working order:

	Dübs	*G9, K0, O2*	*T9, X9, G10*
Bogie	16T 4C	17T 2C	17T 1C
Leading coupled wheels	18T 10C	18T 7C	17T 12C
Trailing coupled wheels	17T 2C	16T 9C	16T 14C
Engine total	51T 16C	51T 18C	51T 7C
Tender	44T 17C	44T 17C	44T 17C
Engine & Tender	96T 13C	96T 15C	96T 4C

Unlike the other superheated Drummond classes, the boiler pitch was not raised, but this did not mar the appearance and the rebuilds remained extremely attractive looking 4—4—0s.

Before Grouping Nos. 300/4/5/11/3 were similarly modernised, leaving Nos. 119, 282/4/7, 301-3/10/36/8, 702/4/9/14/21/2/4/9/73 to be dealt with by the Southern

Superheated 'T9' No. 702 outside Eastleigh Works in May 1923 with an extended smokebox, conventional firebox, boiler barrel clackboxes, Urie smokebox door, fluted coupling rods, capuchon-topped stove-pipe chimney and double bogie tender.   *F. Burtt*

Railway in 1923-4. Hitherto the performance had been good, but now it was completely transformed with only the heaviest and fastest express services being beyond the class. Despite their larger boilers, the superheated 'L12s' and 'D15s' never gained the same popularity or acclaim.

Therefore at Grouping, 6 superheated and 60 saturated 'T9s' entered Southern Railway stock, when after the initial superheating order had been completed, it was decided to extend modernisation to the entire class. At first with Eastleigh superheaters, but commencing with No. 707 in October 1924, the Maunsell pattern with a heating surface of 213 sq. ft. was substituted. It could, of course, be readily distinguished by the smokebox top snifting valves. As the earlier rebuilds required heavy superheater repairs, this pattern was also fitted.

All were painted Maunsell green and given the E-prefix. Dates when this occurred, the E-prefix was removed and the fitting of superheaters are as follows:-

One of the last saturated 'T9' class, No. 718, at the west end of Reading GWR station in early Southern Railway green livery.   *J. E. Kite*

No.	Southern Livery	E-prefix Discarded	Eastleigh Superheater	Maunsell Superheater
113	11/1923 (a)	4/1932	–	11/1925
114	6/1925 (a)	9/1933	–	11/1927
115	3/1925 (a)	5/1933	–	8/1927
116	8/1925	7/1931	–	8/1925
117	4/1925 (a)	10/1931	–	11/1927
118	7/1925 (a)	12/1931	–	6/1928
119	10/1925	7/1931	9/1923	10/1925
120	6/1925 (a)	9/1932	–	5/1927
121	2/1924	9/1933	2/1924	2/1927
122	4/1926	5/1933	–	4/1926
280	8/1924 (a)	7/1932	–	7/1927
281	5/1924 (a)	11/1933	–	6/1928
282	4/1924	4/1932	12/1923	4/1925
283	10/1925	5/1933	–	10/1925
284	3/1926	11/1932	7/1923	3/1926
285	2/1924 (a)	5/1932	–	1/1926
286	12/1923 (a)	11/1931	–	6/1926
287	12/1923	8/1931	12/1923	7/1925
288	3/1924 (a)	1/1932	–	2/1926
289	3/1925 (a)	10/1931	–	12/1927
300	2/1924	5/1932	10/1922	6/1925
301	3/1925	8/1932	1/1923	7/1925
302	11/1925	5/1932	6/1923	11/1925
303	1/1926	5/1933	4/1923	1/1926
304	2/1925	4/1932	6/1922	2/1925
305	2/1924	2/1933	7/1922	8/1925
307	8/1924	9/1932	8/1924	7/1925
310	1/1925	10/1933	2/1923	1/1925
311	5/1925	7/1933	12/1922	5/1925
312	2/1925	3/1933	–	2/1925
313	11/1924	6/1934	7/1922	8/1925
314	1/1925	10/1931	4/1922	1/1925
336	7/1925	10/1931	3/1923	7/1925
337	5/1925	4/1933	–	5/1925
338	11/1924	11/1932	1/1923	9/1925
702	5/1925	9/1931	5/1923	5/1925
703	6/1924 (a)	10/1933	–	9/1926
704	5/1925	2/1932	6/1923	5/1925
705	5/1924	7/1932	5/1924	10/1925
706	1/1924 (a)	9/1931	–	9/1925
707	10/1924	9/1931	–	10/1924
708	9/1924 (a)	12/1932	–	5/1927
709	10/1925	2/1932	5/1923	10/1925
710	5/1925 (a)	6/1931	–	7/1929
711	11/1924 (a)	10/1932	–	8/1927
712	7/1925 (a)	9/1931	–	3/1928
713	7/1925	4/1932	–	7/1925
714	2/1924	7/1932	2/1924	9/1925
715	12/1923	7/1932	12/1923	7/1925
716	6/1924 (a)	4/1932	–	7/1927
717	3/1925 (a)	11/1931	–	9/1927
718	11/1925 (a)	8/1933	–	9/1928
719	4/1925 (a)	11/1932	–	8/1926
721	12/1925	1/1932	8/1923	12/1925
722	4/1926	10/1932	10/1923	5/1928
723	3/1925 (a)	2/1932	–	2/1928
724	3/1924	8/1932	5/1923	3/1926
725	2/1926	4/1933	–	2/1926
726	2/1924	9/1933	2/1924	3/1926
727	5/1925	12/1931	–	5/1925
728	1/1926	6/1931	–	1/1926
729	1/1926	4/1932	8/1923	8/1927
730	2/1925 (a)	3/1932	–	12/1927
731	5/1924 (a)	6/1932	–	1/1927
732	4/1924 (a)	7/1933	–	3/1927
773/733 (b)	3/1926	12/1932	6/1923	3/1925

(a) Southern livery before superheated.
(b) Maunsell superheater before receiving Southern livery.

Most received renovated boilers, but those provided for Nos. 119/21, 287 were new, while two spare superheated boilers were built in July 1927 and fitted to Nos. 312/38. Nos. 113-22, 280-9 and 702-19/21-33 were built with combined leading coupled wheel splashers and sandboxes, a layout retained on those superheated in 1923-6, but thereafter the sandboxes were resited inside the frames, while those superheated earlier were similarly modified, usually when the Maunsell superheater replaced the Eastleigh pattern.

Only one Western Section engine ran in LSWR livery with a Maunsell superheater, this being No. 773 (renumbered 733 in December 1924), which received an Eastleigh superheater in June 1923, but owing to continual trouble with the elements it spent much of the next 18 months under repair at Nine Elms shed or Eastleigh Works until a Maunsell superheater was substituted in March 1925. As the paintwork remained in good order, it was returned to traffic without being repainted, leaving the Southern livery to be applied at the next heavy repair in March 1926.

At this period the class was widely employed throughout the Western Section on main line and secondary passenger duties, particularly between Waterloo and Portsmouth, Southampton (via Alton), Bournemouth and Weymouth (via Wimborne), while on summer Saturdays regular appearances were made on holiday reliefs to Lymington, Bournemouth, Swanage and Weymouth. Numerous excursions were also worked on summer Sundays, while in 1924-5 regular appearances in partnership with 'L12s' and 'S11s' were made on the Waterloo-Portsmouth services via Horsham. For some reason the latter failed to gain public approval and were abandoned, whereupon Nine Elms transferred these classes to excursions from Clapham Junction, Wimbledon, Surbiton and other Western Section suburban stations to Bognor Regis and Littlehampton via Horsham, duties which continued until electrification.

Another interesting and demanding early Grouping duty was the two day Bournemouth West-Birmingham (Snow Hill), which at first was monopolised by Bournemouth 'D15s', but when that class was transferred to Fratton in 1925, the duty passed to superheated 'T9s' Nos. 282/8, 707/14. After the 1927 summer the service was restricted to Fridays and Saturdays, although at busy periods still loading to ten bogies. The service was abandoned in September 1930.

In 1924, with large numbers of express and mixed traffic 4–6–0s, 'L1' class 4–4–0s and 'N' class 2–6–0s about to enter traffic, it was evident that a large surplus of elderly, medium-powered passenger tender engines would arise on all three sections. Many of these could with advantage be laid aside and broken up, but it was imperative to discover which could best be retained for further secondary service. Consequently, in April and May 1924, a series of fuel consumption and costing trials were conducted with classes 'B1', 'B2X' (ex-LB & SCR), 'F1' (ex-SE & CR) and 'T9' between Brighton, Hastings and Ashford. Each engine was prepared by its home shed, driven by crews familiar with the class and fired with the type and quality of coal normally employed on their section's secondary passenger services. At the time no details of the trials were made

'T9' No. 773 on an up train at Exeter in May 1925, the only Western Section engine fitted with a Maunsell superheater and smokebox
snifting valves before receiving Southern Railway livery.   *Lens of Sutton*

public, but a summary was found at Ashford Works in 1960
when the drawing office was being reorganised for dieselisation. Details are:-

No.	Class	Average time Lost/Gained mins.	Coal burnt per train mile lb.	Maintenance costs units	Remarks
B172	B1	−4	35.9	133	Primed badly, 1 faulty injector.
B206	B2X	−8	39.9	137	Top feed, steamed badly, excessive smoke.
B208	B2X	−7	42.1	124	Side feed, steaming erratic, much fire throwing.
E314	T9	+2	28.8	100	Superheated, much steam lost by safety valves.
A204	F1	+3	31.4	92	Very poor quality coal, free steaming.

All trains were formed of two three-carriage ex-SE & CR
non-corridor bogie sets and a bogie van, of which only the
leading set was available for public use. For the purpose of
the trials the three ex-LB & SCR engines were provided
with vacuum ejectors, while the annual maintenance costs
were standardised at 100 units for the 'T9', the only class
for which accurate figures were readily available. The other
four were graded accordingly. During the period of trials
the weather was mainly dry with light winds and did not
materially affect the findings. The 'T9' was always working
well within itself and probably lost as much steam via the
safety valves as was gainfully employed until the crew
gauged the moderate demands of the lightly loaded and
easily timed trains. The performance and reliability of the
Stirling 'F1' class 4—4—0 came as a pleasant surprise, while

the two 'B2Xs' gobbled up alarming quantities of coal to
little visible account, except dense clouds of smoke.

As a result of these trials, it was decided to withdraw
all the 'Gladstones' and the 'B2Xs', and replace them on the
Central Section's secondary passenger services by the less
costly Stirling 'B1' and 'F1' 4—4—0s, with their loss to the
Eastern Section being made good by transferring 'T9s' Nos.
300/1/4/7/10-4/36 to Battersea. Because of the less
generous Eastern Section load gauge, new stovepipe
chimneys with short capuchons were provided to reduce
the height by 1¾ in. to 13 ft., while to suit the short turntables of the smaller sheds, the 4,000 gallon double bogie
tenders were replaced by the 3,500 gallon six-wheel pattern
from the '700' class. Details are:-

300 (ex-No. 696) 5/1925		311 (ex-No. 315) 7/1925
301 (ex.No. 325) 7/1925		312 (ex-No. 306) 1/1925
304 (ex-No. 317) 2/1925		313 (ex-No. 308) 7/1925
307 (ex-No. 698) 7/1925		314 (ex-No. 368) 5/1925
310 (ex-No. 309) 1/1925		336 (ex-No. 697) 9/1925

The displaced double bogie tenders were transferred to
'L11' class Nos. 154, 438, 155/70, 156/71/2, 168, 148/67.

This complicated three-fold exchange was necessary
because the '700' class six-wheel tenders had a 13 ft. wheelbase, whereas those of similar capacity attached to most
'L11s' had a 14 ft. wheelbase. Therefore, to ensure that the
'T9s' could be accommodated by all Eastern Section turntables, they had to be provided with the shortest possible
tenders, likewise double bogie tenders would have restricted

'700' class availability, if a straight exchange had been made. As some 'L11s' had been built with double bogie tenders, their extended use with the class could create no problems. On the Eastern Section Nos. 300/1/4/7/10-4/36 were stationed at Battersea and given the same route availability as ex-SE & CR 'D1' and 'E1' 4—4—0s, therefore they could work the Holborn Viaduct, Sheerness, Margate (via Kent Coast line) and Dover (via Maidstone East) services. After the disastrous Sevenoaks derailment and the withdrawal of the 'River' 2—6—4 tanks, the severe restrictions placed on the Swanley-Otford-Maidstone East-Ashford line left the Eastern Section with few engines capable of working the heavy and smartly timed Continental expresses over that route and consequently the 'T9s' proved invaluable in the summer months and at other busy periods. There were only two booked duties in the July 1928 engine workings, both on Saturdays only, these being the 7.40 a.m. Victoria-Ramsgate, 11.20 a.m. return, this duty concluding with the 4.20 p.m. Victoria-Faversham, 8.53 p.m. return; and the 11.55 a.m. Victoria-Margate and 5.20 p.m. return. However, various 'D1' and 'E1' duties were also covered, while regular appearances were made on the 3.10 a.m. Victoria-Dover Marine via Tonbridge, seaside excursions and relief Continentals. Another regular duty was the 7.06

a.m. Holborn Viaduct-Ashford via Maidstone East, the 9.40 a.m. onwards to Dover Marine and the 11.53 a.m. Dover Marine-Charing Cross via Tonbridge, duties for which many crews preferred the class to the 'D1s' and 'E1s'. Many of the Sheerness trains were also worked, while most summer Sundays and bank holidays found two or three heading excursions from Denmark Hill and Crofton Park to Hastings via Tonbridge and Battle.

The easing of restrictions between Faversham and Ramsgate in mid-1932 permitted the use of 'King Arthurs' and other large classes on the Kent Coast services, leaving the Battersea 'T9s' available for other duties. From January 1933 they took over the down Eastbourne Pullman, which at the same time had the schedule accelerated to 80 minutes; engines recorded being Nos. 282, 300/1/3/4/7/11/4, 726. The summer weekday 10.45 a.m. to the same timing was also shared with the 'King Arthur' class, the loading being two Pullmans and up to ten carriages.

Most Eastern Section crews found their performance and coal consumption similar to the 'D1s' and 'E1s', with the result that they gained the same acclaim as these excellent Maunsell rebuilds. This is confirmed by the following table of 97 timings on Sole Street bank, which in the days of steam proved a reliable test of a class, for the long climb

Saturated 'T9' No. 286 in early Southern Railway green livery without the E-prefix or small cabside numberplates at Salisbury on 30th July 1925.

H. C. Casserley

'T9' class No. E304 with a six-wheeled tender, short capuchon stove-pipe chimney and Maunsell superheater, on 19th August 1929.

H. C. Casserley

from Rochester Bridge had to commence at 25 to 30 mph and therefore all the initial impetus had been lost by Cuxton Road box. As a result, the average speed over the succeeding four miles to Sole Street station offered an excellent comparison of the effort sustained by various classes. Details are:-

Class	T9	L12	D1	E1	L	L1
No. of runs	24	7	21	17	17	11
Av. speed (mph)	32.6	31.8	31.4	32.0	28.9	31.2
Av. load (tons)	234	293	225	230	265	257
Best Runs	m s	m s	m s	m s	m s	m s
Time (min/sec)	7 01	6 48	7 08	6 27	7 08	7 13
Av. Speed (mph)	34.2	34.8	33.6	37.2	33.6	33.3
Load (tons)	287	314	280	285	289	278

Some of these recordings were made after the stringent Kent Coast weight restrictions had been lifted in mid-1932, but the general pattern of performance remained the same as when the 'T9s' were first transferred to the Eastern Section.

In mid-1928 Nos. 281/2, 303, 704/26/9 were transferred to Brighton for service on the Central Section, although the reason for this is not readily apparent for the early Grouping motive power shortage had been overcome and there was an adequate supply of secondary passenger engines. A possible explanation was a temporary imbalance of dual-braked ex-LB & SCR engines and the imported vacuum braked Southern and ex-LSWR corridor sets, which necessitated the provision of more vacuum fitted engines for the summer service.

No. 281 reached Brighton on 8th June 1928 and immediately commenced working the Portsmouth services. Early the following month it was joined by Nos. 282, 303, 704/29, with No. 726 appearing on 3rd September. All were fitted with 3,500 gallon six-wheel tenders and stove-pipe chimneys having short capuchons. Dates of fitting are:-

281 — 5/1928; 282 — 7/1928; 303 — 7/1928; 704 — 7/1928; 726 — 8/1928; 729 — 7/1928.

The tenders were obtained from 'K10s' Nos. 382, 144, 391/2, 135 and 380, which in return received the displaced 4,000 gallon pattern.

At Christmas 1928 Nos. 281, 303 and 729 worked van trains to Hastings, Eastbourne, Tunbridge Wells and Redhill, while No. 726 was noted at Ashford on 23rd December, but otherwise they were mainly restricted to the Brighton-Portsmouth services until mid-1929, when regular workings commenced over the Mid-Sussex line in partnership with 'L12s', and occasional appearances were made on the Brighton-London services. Nos. 281, 303 and 726 were stored at Hove for the winter and in April 1930 were transferred with No. 282 to Battersea. Some months earlier No. 729 had gone to Salisbury, leaving No. 704 to share the through trains with 'L12s' Nos. 417/21/5.

In mid-1934 the amalgamation of the two Battersea sheds brought a great increase of Central Section work, particularly over the Mid-Sussex line, where assistance was especially valuable following the tightening of restrictions. As a result, the class became all-year performers on such trains as the 9.05 a.m. Victoria-Portsmouth Harbour and the 2.55 p.m. return, while in summer they appeared all over the section, with Bognor and Littlehampton sheds abounding with them on Sunday afternoons awaiting return excursions.

For some reason the Central Section was more restrictive than the Eastern Section and it was not until the wartime easement that use was permissible south of Hurst Green on the Eridge line. Consequently there were few Oxted line appearances, although the high summer spate of Sunday school outings invariably found several heading rakes of ancient stock from Oxted, Lingfield etc. to Littlehampton or Bognor via Haywards Heath. Needless to say, a few illegal workings occurred, including No. 726 on the 11.08

a.m. Victoria-Eastbourne via Heathfield on 15th July 1937 and No. 729 on the 4.50 p.m. Victoria-Brighton via Uckfield on 28th October 1938.

In 1936-7 Nos. 304/10/3 were stationed at Brighton for the Portsmouth, Bournemouth and Salisbury services, but in summer they also worked the Wednesday and Sunday Margate and Deal excursions. At this period those stationed at Battersea appeared more frequently on the Tonbridge line, with the 6.22 a.m. Cannon Street-Dover being a regular duty, while most summer Sundays found several heading excursions to Hastings, Folkestone, Deal and Ramsgate from Denmark Hill, Crofton Park, Bromley South and other suburban stations.

By 1935 many of the four-coupled passenger tender classes taken into stock at Grouping had been withdrawn or were working out their mileage on light duties. On the Western Section all the early Adams 4-4-0s and 'Jubilees' had gone while inroads were being made into the 'C8s', the later 'Jubilees' and classes 'X2', 'T3', 'X6' and 'T6'. Fortunately, the 'T9s' did not fall in that category and they remained in demand, although new boilers were required for which no funds were available. So once again resort had to be made to refurbishing the Drummond barrels with new fireboxes, tubeplates, tubes and superheaters. Indeed, the metamorphosis was so complete that Eastleigh Works allotted new boiler numbers and engines returned to traffic in as good order as when first superheated.

Since Grouping the average mileage worked between successive general repairs had progressively increased and if not bettering the modern Maunsell classes were nevertheless most respectable by 1936. Details are:-

Period	Intermediate Repair		General Repair	
	Miles	Months	Miles	Months
1923-6	29,685	16.2	57,641	27.3
1932-6	37,014	19.6	74,016	31.4

In 1932-4 the cost of intermediate repairs averaged £259 and general repairs £647.

The 1932-6 'T9' mileages compared favourably with those of the Eastern and Central Sections' 4-4-0s, details being:

Class	Intermediate Repairs		General Repairs	
	Miles	Months	Miles	Months
D	21,225	19	71,890	34
E	23,603	18	73,118	32
D1	28,670	19	69,865	29
E1	24,130	17	65,470	27
L	24,885	16	73,340	26
L1	29,663	18	76,479	31
B4X	19,428	25	61,781	39

Despite the cramped erecting shop and obsolescent equipment at Ashford Works, the standard of workmanship was as high as that of Eastleigh Works, while the costs in

'T9' class No. 729 at Bognor in June 1936 in post-1931 Maunsell livery with no E-prefix, the splasher sandboxes replaced by containers between the frames, a plain stove-pipe chimney, fluted coupling rods and a six-wheeled tender, the last mentioned for service on the Central Section.

P. Ransome Wallis, courtesy National Railway Museum

May 1936 were 8% less. Eastleigh's advantage was the marginally shorter time repairs took to complete.

As No. 119 was frequently rostered for royal and other important specials, it was given VIP treatment in mid-1935 to make it more suitable for such work. This included a beautifully applied green livery with lined wheels, black shaded gilt lettering and numerals, chromium-plated snifting valve caps, highly burnished piping, coupling rods and footplate controls and an organ pipe whistle. When actually engaged on royal duties, plaques of the royal coat-of-arms were mounted on the leading splashers. Shortly after

returning to service, the special conveying King George V to the Silver Jubilee Naval Review at Spithead was worked on 2nd July 1935.

The Portsmouth line electrification of July 1937 surprisingly had little effect on the remainder of the Western Section for apart from a number of transfers and a few withdrawals, the duty pattern was unchanged. As far as the 'T9s' were concerned, any loss of work over the Portsmouth line was made good by additional duties elsewhere. Details for mid-1939 are:-

Shed	Engine Nos.	Duties
Nine Elms	119, 705	No booked duties, but No. 705 often worked early morning vans to Reading and No. 119 was available for specials and Sunday excursions.
Guildford	714/30	No weekday duties, but two on Sundays: 7.12 a.m. Woking-Portsmouth via Alton and 6.07 p.m. return to Alton; 10.56 a.m. Alton-Portsmouth and 9.08 p.m. return to Aldershot.
Eastleigh	302/5/37, 706-8/24/5/31	Five weekday duties: A two day turn in stages to Weymouth via Bournemouth, returning the following morning; two passenger and van turns to Bournemouth and return; Local passenger, Portsmouth-Reading and return to Southampton Terminus.
Fratton	114/5/8/20/1, 287, 338, 702/12/21	Eight weekday duties: Mostly Portsmouth-Salisbury, but also Portsmouth-Basingstoke-Southampton Terminus and Portsmouth-Netley-Southampton-Salisbury; Vans to Waterloo and back on 3.20 a.m. newspapers.
Bournemouth	113, 719/28	One daily duty: Bournemouth-Salisbury locals and 3.25 a.m. newspapers to Wimborne, a two day turn shared with a Salisbury 'T9'. Saturdays only: Through Poole-Sheffield to Basingstoke and return. The class also used as reliefs on the Swanage and Weymouth services.
Dorchester	284/6	One duty: Dorchester-Weymouth, to Bournemouth and return, to Portland and return, and a second return trip to Bournemouth. The spare engine often deputised for 'K10s' Nos. 381/7 or 'L11' No. 410 on the shed's mixed traffic duties.
Salisbury	117/22, 285/8, 713/5/8/27	Three duties: Bournemouth locals; a two day turn alternating with a Bournemouth 'T9' on Salisbury-Bournemouth locals and 3.25 a.m. Wimborne newspapers; Salisbury-Yeovil Junction, goods piloting and return to Salisbury.
Exmouth Junction	283, 709/16/7/22/33	Three duties: A two day turn to Salisbury and return, 7.50 p.m. goods to Eastleigh, goods to Salisbury, goods to Templecombe and 5.20 p.m. Templecombe-Exeter; Exeter-Bude and return, Saturdays only: Exmouth Junction-Tavistock goods, then passenger Tavistock-Plymouth, Plymouth-Okehampton, Okehampton-Padstow and return to Exeter; Exeter-Plymouth and return; Exeter-Bude and return.
Okehampton	723	Mondays-Fridays: Padstow passenger; Saturdays: goods to Bude, passenger Bude-Exeter, Exeter-Plymouth and return to Okehampton.
Launceston	732	Padstow-Okehampton passenger.
Wadebridge	703/10	One daily duty to Okehampton and return; Saturdays: Exeter and return; Piloting Atlantic Coast Express to Exeter, returning on a passenger to Wadebridge.
Plymouth	116, 280/9, 711	Weekdays two duties: Both Plymouth-Exeter and return. Saturdays: Four return turns to Exeter.

'T9' class No. 302 at Weymouth in July 1938 with lengthened and angled sand container filler pipes and smokebox door lamp brackets.
Author

On Sundays there were a number of interesting duties, including Bournemouth's 10.00 a.m. Poole-Brighton and the 7.58 p.m. return, Dorchester's 10.05 a.m. Portland-Portsmouth excursion and Salisbury's 2.00 p.m. milk train to Waterloo, returning on the 6.54 p.m. semi-fast. There was also a Salisbury-Brighton excursion, which on fine Sundays had to be run in two or three parts.

At Battersea Nos. 281/2, 300/1/3/4/7/10-4/36, 704/26/9 still had few booked duties, but nevertheless were kept fully occupied working excursions to Brighton, Eastbourne, Bognor Regis, Ramsgate, Margate, Deal and Hastings. Use was also made of the class on the Saturday through trains to the LMS, Victoria-Margate reliefs and hop-picking specials.

The Bulleid livery changes did not affect the class until mid-1939, details being:-

Maunsell green, light green and yellow lining, tender numerals: No. 285 (May 1939).
Maunsell green, black and yellow lining, tender numerals: Nos. 116, 311 (July 1939), 722 (June 1939).
Maunsell green, unlined, tender numerals: Nos. 705/13/4/25 (October 1939).
Olive green, black and white lining, Bulleid lettering, cabside numerals: No. 119 (June 1939).
Maunsell green, unlined, Bulleid lettering, cabside numerals: Nos. 121, 708 (November 1939), 717 (December 1939), Nos. 287, 730 (January 1940), 120, 284, 707/28 (May 1940), 113/4, 731 (June 1940), 117, 723 (July 1940), 305/7, 719 (August 1940), 122, 703/9 (September 1940), Nos. 711 (January 1941), 336 (February 1941), 702 (March 1941).
Malachite green, unlined, Bulleid lettering, cabside numerals: Nos. 115, 716 (November 1940), 310, 704 (December 1940), Nos. 302, 722 (January 1941).

All later repaints, commencing with No. 721 on 19th March 1941, were plain black with Bulleid lettering and cabside numerals.

All heavy repairs were received at Eastleigh Works until mid-1942, when Nos. 300, 705/31 were dealt with at Ashford Works. After completion of repairs they were run-in on the Tonbridge or Hastings slows before returning to the Western Section via Brighton.

After the outbreak of the Second World War in September 1939, the drastically reduced passenger timetable made it unnecessary to retain so many 'T9s' at Battersea, therefore in October Nos. 282, 300/1 were transferred to Exmouth Junction and Nos. 310/2/4 to Salisbury. All kept the 3,500 gallon six-wheel tenders fitted for service on the Eastern and Central Sections. Nos. 282, 300/1, with the assistance of Nos. 721/4/5/30/1, replaced 'U1' class 2—6—0s Nos. 1890-9 on the Exeter-Plymouth, North Devon and North Cornwall services. Nos. 281, 303/4/7/11/3/36, 704/26/9, retained by Battersea, were mainly employed working vans, troop specials and odd Central Section duties until January 1940, when the 6.05 a.m. Holborn Viaduct-Ramsgate via Maidstone East and Canterbury West became a regular duty. The return was on the 11.18 a.m. Ramsgate-Folkestone-Tonbridge, the 7.10 p.m. Tonbridge-Ashford and the 9.32 p.m. Ashford-Swanley. However, the reign on this interesting and taxing duty was only brief for in April 1940 the class was displaced by 'D1' class 4—4—0s and transferred to the Western Section, with Nos. 281, 303/4/7/11, 729 going to Nine Elms, Nos. 313/36 to Eastleigh and Nos. 704/26 to Guildford. At the last two sheds they were mainly employed on van trains and local goods, with No. 704 being noted on several occasions at Midhurst.

Because of this concentration on the Western Section, the class was not seriously affected by the Dunkirk evacuation, the only known involvement being the loan of Nos. 704/14/6/29 to Redhill for piloting heavy Reading branch trains and working empty stock, van and short ambulance trains eastwards to Ashford and Folkestone Junction. However, the demand for 4—6—0s at this period was so great that on several occasions in June 1940 Bournemouth had to turn out No. 337 for the ten carriage 3.05 p.m. Bournemouth West-Waterloo.

'T9' class No. 114 as an oil-burner, at Eastleigh on 26th April 1948, with tubular ladders at rear of tender, electric lighting, no smokebox snifting valves and painted plain black.
Author

At Grouping, motive power on the Somerset & Dorset Joint Railway became the responsibility of the LMS and visits by Southern engines were mainly restricted to the southern end of the line. However, the increased Midland Division goods traffic in September 1941 necessitated the LMS recalling most of its engines and requesting assistance from the Southern, who replaced the '2P' 4–4–0s and '4F' 0–6–0s with 'S11s' Nos. 396/8, 400-4 and 'T9s' Nos. 303/4/7/12 from the Western Section. Of the latter, Nos. 303/7 were replaced by 'S11s' Nos. 397/9 in December 1941 and No. 312 by No. 395 in February 1942, but No. 304 remained on loan until May 1945. It was classified '2P' and was stationed at Templecombe for working stoppers to Bournemouth West and Bath or piloting heavy expresses or troop specials. On the Western Section wartime loads brought increased demands for piloting main line expresses, especially between Salisbury and Exeter, where the principal services regularly loaded to 14 or 15 corridors. Occasionally both train and pilot engines were 'T9s', usually when a Merchant Navy Pacific had failed. In May 1942, as part of a series of interchange duties introduced in the West of England to make more economic use of engines and crews, Exmouth Junction 'T9s', often Nos. 709/21/4, commenced working between Exeter and Yeovil via Taunton and Martock. On a mileage basis, the Great Western's balancing working was from Exeter Central to Barnstaple and Ilfracombe, for which '43XX' 2–6–0s were used.

Many local and pick-up goods were also worked and it was while so engaged on 29th November 1942 that No. 120 with the 6.00 a.m. Brockenhurst-Dorchester goods was attacked between Wool and Moreton by a single enemy fighter. Two low level attacks with 20mm cannon fire were made, but failed to cause serious damage and, after the fireman and guard had attended to the driver's minor injuries, the train was taken on to Moreton. On inspection at Dorchester, No. 120 was found to have the tender side sheeting, outer firebox casing and two superheater elements holed, a lubricating pipe severed and both lookout windows shattered. Later the same day No. 728 was shot up on Bournemouth shed and also escaped serious damage. Other 'T9s' in trouble during the war years included No. 288 on Fratton shed, No. 704 on Pokesdown bank and No. 733 at Eastleigh, the last mentioned falling into a bomb crater in the blackout. All were repaired and returned to service.

High mileages were worked during the war; consequently by VE day many were badly run down, with a sizeable proportion requiring new fireboxes and cylinders. Nos. 336/7 were fitted with Flaman speed recorders in September 1945 and transferred to Bournemouth for the Poole-Victoria British Overseas Airways specials. These ceased running at the end of April 1946, with the speed recorders being removed from No. 336 in September 1946 and No. 337 in May 1947.

No. 119, while working the 4.54 p.m. Waterloo-Basingstoke semi-fast on 10th November 1945, was run into from the rear about half a mile on the London side of Woking station by No. 452 *Sir Meliagrance* and the 5.00 p.m. Waterloo-Exeter express. The latter, although not derailed, was considerably damaged, as were the last two carriages of the Basingstoke train, but No. 119 only suffered broken firebox stays. Nevertheless, it was not repaired by Nine Elms shed, but stored until called to Eastleigh Works for general repairs in March 1946, during which it was painted malachite green with black and white lining, had the safety valves, whistle, piping and window surrounds highly burnished and was fitted with a Loudaphone telephone for communication with the train crew for working royal and other specials. On returning to traffic, it was run-in on local passenger services from Eastleigh before being borrowed for several weeks by Bournemouth for working the through Birmingham train before being despatched to Nine Elms. The first special duty came in late November 1946, when a party of directors toured the system in a train composed of two 1st class saloons, two new sleeping cars, a restaurant car and a bogie van. The malachite green livery was renewed in May 1948, when the smokebox snifting valves were removed, a deep-toned hooter substituted for the standard whistle and the tender lettered 'British Railways'. The short capuchoned chimney was retained.

The abortive Government oil-burning scheme of 1947-8 involved fifteen members of the class, details being:

No.	Converted	Electric lighting	No.	Converted	Electric lighting
113	9/1947	11/1947	305	1/1947	2/1948
114	9/1947	2/1948	314	9/1947	11/1947
115	8/1947	12/1947	713	9/1947	10/1947
118	8/1947	2/1948	722	9/1947	1/1948
121	8/1947	1/1948	731	9/1947	2/1948
280	9/1947	11/1947	732	—	—
286	9/1947	12/1947	733	—	—
303	9/1947	2/1948			

No. 732/3 were stored at Eastleigh from May 1947 awaiting conversion, but had not been transferred to the Works when the scheme was abandoned.

All the tenders were of the 4,000 gallon double bogie pattern with 1,600 gallon oil fuel tanks fitted precariously in the coal space. Nos. 303/14, which entered Works with six-wheeled tenders, exchanged these for the larger variety from 'S11s' Nos. 395/6. All were run-in on local van and goods services by Eastleigh shed, when the allocation became: Fratton Nos. 113/4/5/8, 280, 303/5/14; Eastleigh Nos. 121, 286, 713/22/31. They were mainly employed on passenger, van and goods services in the Portsmouth-Bournemouth - Southampton - Eastleigh - Salisbury area, although occasionally Alton and Basingstoke were visited. As oil-burners they proved free-steaming and fully capable of performing these secondary duties, although having a tendency to set the sleepers alight in stations and sidings. When the scheme was abandoned in September 1948, they were laid aside in store until condemned in April and May 1951. The last at work was No. 30286 with a Portsmouth-Eastleigh local on 7th October 1948.

All entered British Railways stock at Nationalisation and, except for Nos. 113/4/6/8, 280, 303/5/14, 713/22/3/31, were renumbered into the 30,000 series. Two carried the temporary S-prefix: S282 from 7th February 1948 to 30 November 1951, and S285 from 7th February 1948 to 23rd December 1950.

The early repaints, Nos. S282/5, 30284/6, 30702/7/18 were plain black and No. 30119 malachite green, but with No. 30729 in December 1948 lined black became standard.

These dates and those for renumbering into the 30,000 series and the removal of the snifting valves are:-

No.	BR No.	Lined Black	Snifting valves off
114	—	—	9/1947
115	6/1948	—	6/1948
117	8/1949	12/1950	12/1947
119	5/1948	—	5/1948
120	1/1949	6/1950	6/1950
121	6/1948	—	6/1948
122	1/1949	—	—
280	—	—	9/1947
281	4/1949	—	—
282	12/1951	8/1952	2/1948
283	2/1949	2/1949	2/1949
284	7/1948	7/1949	7/1949
285	12/1950	12/1950	2/1948
286	5/1948	—	5/1948
287	1/1949	5/1950	5/1950
288	7/1949	11/1950	11/1950
289	2/1949	10/1950	10/1950
300	1/1950	1/1950	1/1950
301	9/1949	9/1949	9/1949
302	1/1949	—	1/1949
303	—	—	9/1947
304	9/1951	3/1953	11/1947
307	12/1949	12/1949	12/1949
310	10/1948	8/1950	8/1950
311	9/1951	—	9/1951
312	9/1949	—	9/1949
313	6/1949	6/1949	6/1949
314	—	—	9/1947
336	5/1950	5/1950	9/1946
337	12/1949	4/1953	12/1949
338	8/1950	8/1950	11/1947
702	8/1948	9/1952	8/1948
703	7/1949	7/1949	7/1949
704	3/1950	—	10/1947
705	5/1949	5/1949	5/1949
706	9/1949	9/1949	2/1948
707	5/1948	12/1949	11/1947
708	7/1948	3/1949	3/1949
709	5/1949	5/1950	5/1950
710	8/1949	8/1949	8/1949
711	5/1949	5/1949	5/1949
712	7/1949	4/1952	7/1949
713	—	—	9/1947
714	4/1949	—	11/1946
715	9/1948	3/1950	9/1948
716	3/1949	3/1949	12/1947
717	4/1949	4/1949	4/1949
718	4/1948	4/1953	4/1948
719	6/1949	6/1949	6/1949
721	7/1949	7/1949	7/1949
724	7/1949	7/1949	7/1949
725	7/1949	7/1949	7/1949
726	4/1949	4/1949	4/1949
727	2/1950	2/1950	2/1950
728	12/1950	12/1950	12/1947
729	12/1948	12/1948	12/1948
730	8/1949	8/1949	8/1949
731	—	—	9/1947
732	6/1948	9/1949	9/1949
733	7/1949	—	7/1949

Nos. 113/6/8, 281, 305, 722/3 retained snifting valves until withdrawal. All were renumbered and repainted by Eastleigh Works, but in 1952-6 Nos. 30120, 30285/8/9,

30300/13/38, 30707/12/7/9/21/5/7/32 received general repairs at Brighton Works. Thereafter all major repairs were received at Eastleigh Works, the last being No. 30707 in March 1959.

By 1948, with all wartime travel restrictions removed and little competition from cars or coaches, a mass summer exodus by rail was anticipated from the inland towns and cities to the South Coast resorts, so to ensure that the Eastern Section had sufficient motive power, six-wheel tender 'T9s' Nos. 281, 301/4/11/2, 704/26/9 were transferred to Battersea. They were mainly employed working Saturday reliefs to Dumpton Park, Margate and Ramsgate, Chatham-Dover Priory locals, Central Section excursions to Tunbridge Wells West via Oxted, and Sunday specials from Denmark Hill and Crofton Park to Hastings via Tonbridge, duties which, of course, ceased with the winter timetable, when Nos. 281, 301, 726/9 were despatched to store at Fratton and the other laid up at Battersea. However, apart from No. 704, which was replaced by No. S282, all were back on the Eastern Section for a final season in 1949, when No. 301 surprised lineside observers by heading a Charing Cross-New Romney relief.

Despite the war duty, changes on the Western Section were few, with most of the Portsmouth-Salisbury trains being worked, together with some of the Waterloo-Basingstoke-Salisbury semi-fasts. Only in the West of England had major changes occurred with most of the Exeter-Plymouth and Padstow services having been lost to the Bulleid light Pacifics. The mid-1948 allocation was: Nine Elms Nos. 30119, 30718; Basingstoke Nos. 307, 706; Guildford Nos. 30708/32; Eastleigh Nos. 120, 30121*, 30286*, 302/13/36, 705, 30707, 711/3*/22*/31*; Fratton Nos. 113*/4*, 30115*, 118*, 280*/7, 303*/5*/14*/38; Bournemouth Nos. 337, 719/28; Dorchester Nos. 30284, 300, 721; Salisbury Nos. 117/22, S285, 288/9, 709/15/27; Yeovil Nos. 310, 702/10/2/4/6; Exmouth Junction Nos. S282, 283, 723/4/5/30/3; Wadebridge Nos. 703/17; Plymouth No. 116; Battersea No. 281, 301/4/11/2, 704/26/9. (* = oil-burners.)

In 1949 there was only one booked duty from Waterloo, this being the 10.27 a.m. to Andover Junction, a Guildford turn usually entrusted to No. 30708, but there were regular appearances on reliefs and excursions. This increased the following summer, as with only two 'T14s' available, there were insufficient Pacifics and 4-6-0s to cover all the main line Saturday duties, and the class appeared regularly on the 10.38 a.m. Waterloo-Swanage, 2.38 p.m. Waterloo-Bournemouth West, 12.20 p.m. Bournemouth Central-Waterloo, 3.05 p.m. Bournemouth West-Waterloo, the Bournemouth-Newcastle, 1.05 p.m. Waterloo-Salisbury, and 11.39 a.m. Waterloo-Lymington Pier. The principal performers were Nos. 30302/12/36/7, 30712/8. Never again were 'T9s' to play such an important main line role, but in passing they certainly left their mark, for the running was so fine that it was difficult to appreciate their age and moderate dimensions, particularly in view of the frequent Pacific and 4-6-0 failures.

Unfortunately, this could not last, for in 1951 Nos. 116, 30122, 30281, 30704/14/6, 723 and the thirteen derelict oil-burners were condemned, with Nos. 30119, 30302/7/11/2, 30703/25/33 following in 1952. All had worked more than 1½ million miles, the highest being No. 30714 at 1,746,960.

The frames of No. 722 were salvaged and in December 1954 were set up in the erecting shop and fitted with a spare boiler and the cab, cylinders, motion, wheels, bogie etc. of No. 30732. With the latter's number, the amalgamation saw a further five years service.

Despite these withdrawals and the arrival of new BR class 4-6-0s from Swindon, 1953 proved a more hopeful year, for the closure of Winchester (WR) shed gave Eastleigh 'T9s' a regular turn to Newbury with the 10.22 a.m., returning at 12.25 p.m., while in the West Country Barnstaple (SR) shed acquired the 4.00 p.m. Barnstaple Junction-Taunton on summer Saturdays, returning at 9.10 p.m., for which No. 30710 had to be borrowed from Exmouth Junction. There were no booked duties over the Somerset & Dorset line but Bath was occasionally visited as replacements for failures at the south end of the line. The summer service also saw Nos. 30284/8/9, 30729 sharing the 10.35 a.m. (SO) Lymington Pier-Waterloo, which loaded to eight corridors and was booked 95 minutes non-stop from Southampton. The RCTS 25th Anniversary Special of 28th June 1953, from Waterloo to Exeter and back to Paddington, involved two Drummond engines, 'D15' No. 30464 to Salisbury and 'T9' No. 30711 onwards to Axminster, with 8 minutes being gained on the 64 minute schedule. After a tour of the Lyme Regis branch behind 0415 No. 30583 and Terrier No. 32662, No. 30711 took the special on to Exeter Central in 35½ minutes, a further gain of 1½ minutes and with the 86 mph recorded at Sherborne and the 83 mph after Whimple suggesting how the nickname 'Greyhounds' was gained.

No. 30282 was condemned in March 1954, but the others remained in demand, with Nine Elms employing Nos. 30718/9 on the Reading vans, while Eastleigh's Nos. 30283/7/9, 30310 gave rousing performances on the summer Saturday 10.35 a.m. up Lymington. The booked return was with empty carriage stock to Southampton, but frequently this was cancelled and the 4.00 p.m. Army special worked to Marchwood. At Basingstoke Nos. 30705/24, with their tenders piled high with coal, were strategically positioned to offer assistance or replacement to ailing engines of both up and down expresses. A call on 6th July 1954 found No. 30724 hurriedly substituted for failed main line diesel No. 10203 on the 4.30 p.m. Exeter-Waterloo, while on 14th August it replaced No. 30450 *King Arthur* on the Torrington portion of the up Atlantic Coast Express, loaded to twelve corridors and a restaurant car. Finally, on 8th September, No. 30724 completed an excellent season by working the special conveying Sir Brian Robertson and other BTC dignitaries non-stop from Portsmouth Harbour to Waterloo in 95½ minutes, a gain of 4½ minutes on schedule. Guildford's No. 30337 appeared regularly on the Redhill-Reading services, but it was a stranger, No. 30719, which had the unusual task on 26th November 1954 of working a 450 ton ballast train from Redhill to Woking, a task successfully accomplished by rushing the banks, a habit no doubt perfected by years of practice on the West of England line.

The 10.22 a.m. Newbury duty was lost to BR Class 4 2-6-0s in 1954, but in the following year Eastleigh's Nos. 30283/4/7/9, 30300/10, 30707/27 gained the 7.32 a.m. Southampton Terminus-Didcot, returning at 3.55 p.m. and the 7.05 a.m. Shawford-Reading via Newbury and

'T9' class No. 304 in post-World War 2 Eastern Section service at the head of the 3.35 p.m. Margate-Victoria on 31st July 1948.　　*Author*

Malachite green 'T9' No. 30119 in early British Railways livery at Eastleigh on 9th August 1952. Note the short capuchoned stove-pipe chimney and fluted coupling rods.　　*Author*

'T9' class No. 30726 in early British Railways lined black livery with plain tender sides, smokebox numberplate, no smokebox snifting valves, the Urie power classification below the cabside numerals and a six-wheeled tender.   *Author*

Theale, returning with the 3.45 p.m. to Didcot, the 5.52 p.m. to Newbury and finally the 7.25 p.m. to Southampton Terminus. In the West of England regular appearances were still being made on the Plymouth and Padstow services, making a welcome change from the West Country Pacifics.

An interesting detailed alteration in July 1955 was the replacement of No. 30707's double bogie tender by the six-wheel pattern from '700' class No. 30346.

From time to time brief appearances were made in films and TV commercials, but at Baynards on the Guildford-Horsham line in February 1957 No. 30310 and 'M7' No. 30026 became fully-fledged stars during the filming of scenes for 'The Railway Children' by the BBC. Both had all evidence of British Railways ownership painted out and were renumbered 10 and 26. Unusual care was taken to gain authenticity and when viewed on television the standard of production was exceptionally high, with No. 30310 exactly fulfilling its role.

Nos. 30283/4/5, 30307/37, 30705/8/12/21/7/30 were withdrawn in 1956-8 and in January 1959 the survivors' allocation was: Nine Elms Nos. 30338, 30718/9; Basingstoke No. 30724; Guildford No. 30732; Eastleigh Nos. 30117/20, 30287-9, 30300; Bournemouth Nos. 30310, 30706/7/29; Salisbury Nos. 30301/13; Exmouth Junction Nos. 30702/9-11//5/7/26.

From 5th January 1956, the Salisbury 'T9' off the 6.11 a.m. Salisbury-Andover Junction-Eastleigh was booked to work the 12.08 p.m. Eastleigh-Didcot and the 3.35 p.m. back, before returning to Salisbury at 7.38 p.m. At Eastleigh there were daily duties to Bournemouth, Weymouth, Wimborne, Portsmouth, Andover Junction and

Salisbury, while in June and July No. 30287 replaced 'U' class 2—6—0s on the eight carriage Littlehampton. At Nine Elms the Reading vans, empty carriage stock and local goods duties kept Nos. 30338 and 30718/9 fully occupied until replaced by 'L1s' Nos. 31754/85/9 in mid-year, when they were transferred to Exmouth Junction as substitutes for withdrawn Nos. 30710/1/26. No. 30718 travelled westward light engine but on 17th June 1959 Nos. 30338 and 30719 double-headed an eight carriage troop special, empty from Clapham Junction to Farnborough and loaded thence to Yeovil from where they made their own way to Exmouth Junction. This departure for the first time in sixty years left the London area without the regular sight of the class, although No. 30732, officially transferred to Eastleigh, remained working from Guildford on the Reading-Redhill services. It was finally released in late August, but performed little work before being laid aside in October 1959 with a mileage of 1,910,328.

At Exmouth Junction Nos. 30313 (ex-Salisbury), 30338, 30709/15/7-9 spent little time in the vicinity of Exeter as their four-day duty diagrams involved three being out-stabled at Okehampton and one each at Wadebridge and Launceston for the Plymouth, Bude and Padstow services. Several of these duties were smartly timed and necessitated speedy descents of the banks, a 'T9' speciality and doubtless the reason why precedence was gained over the more powerful 'N' class 2—6—0s.

After a lapse of several years, Ashford Works again accepted the class for breaking up, and if those concerned were 'runners', use was made of their availability to work the Sunday 8.30 a.m. Southampton docks-Brighton banana vans, the 4.55 a.m. Brighton-Eastbourne newspapers, several Hailsham locals, the 4.20 p.m. Western Region through train to Hastings and the 6.17 p.m. vans to Ashford. Nos. 30711/26 are known to have been despatched in this manner and probably others not recorded.

After these withdrawals only fourteen remained in stock, Nos. 30117/20, 30287/8, 30300, 30707 at Eastleigh and Nos. 30313/38, 30709/15/7-9/29 at Exmouth Junction. Most of those at Eastleigh were in store, but No. 30120 was specially prepared on 2nd January 1960 in preparation for working an enthusiasts special from Southampton to Swindon via Reading the following day, while the same engine worked the last down passenger train, the 5.55 p.m. Didcot-Eastleigh, over the Didcot, Newbury and Southampton line on Saturday 5th March 1960. After some carriage piloting the following morning, it returned to store, so the survival of No. 30719 sent to Eastleigh Works by Exmouth Junction appeared unlikely. However, repaired it was, and before returning west, several days were spent working the 10.48 a.m. Eastleigh-Southampton docks

goods, the 10.57 a.m. Salisbury-Portsmouth vans (from Southampton Terminus) and the 7.18 p.m. vans back to Eastleigh.

At the beginning of the summer service, these Eastleigh van duties were taken over by No. 30707 until August 1960, when it replaced ailing 'U' class No. 31794 on the 5.45 p.m. Portsmouth-Cardiff and worked the seven corridors and two bogie vans to Salisbury without further loss of time. It returned on the 7.25 p.m. Bristol-Portsmouth and on the following day had charge of the nine corridor Portsmouth-Cardiff as far as Salisbury. On 24th August, a return was made to the Portsmouth van duties, which were worked on most days until relieved by ex-SE & CR No. 31735 in late February 1961. However, this did not prove a popular substitution and in April 1961 it was supplanted by No. 30117, which had been taken out of store some weeks earlier for a London area railtour. Unfortunately, after a promising beginning, its stay on these duties proved equally brief, for in May 1961 they became Basingstoke's responsibility and No. 30117 was relegated to local goods

'T9' class No. 30729 in British Railways lined black and attached to a six-wheeled tender, at Brockenhurst on 8th September 1953.

R. C. Riley

'T9' class No. 30285 in British Railways lined black livery with smokebox number and shed plates, small tender totem and 3P power classification above the cabside numerals, at Eastleigh on 11th May 1957.

E. W. Fry

duties, carriage piloting and the Botley soft fruit specials until failing with a fractured motionplate on 24th June 1961.

At Exmouth Junction Nos. 30313/38, 30709/15/7-9/29 remained in charge of the Okehampton cyclic duties throughout 1960, but in the following year 'N' class 2—6—0s played the major role, especially after the fireboxes of Nos. 30338, 30718/9/29 failed to pass the boiler smith in March-April 1961. However, with the assistance of No. 30120 transferred from Eastleigh, a presence was retained at Okehampton until mid-year when this engine and Nos. 30313, 30709/15/7 were called to Eastleigh Works for scrapping, a fate which No. 30120 evaded, when the original candidates for preservation, Nos. 30117 and 30288, could not be economically repaired and it was substituted. After a period in store, Eastleigh Works were entered in October 1961 for a heavy casual repair, the provision of a capuchoned stovepipe chimney and painting in South Western Urie livery. It was ex-works on 3rd March 1962 and for the next ten days carriage piloted at Eastleigh before re-entering revenue earning service on 26th March with the 8.50 a.m. Eastleigh-Portsmouth vans. Later several appearances were made on the Bournemouth slows before working a 4-CEP electric set to London in readiness for the 'Sussex Coast Limited' railtour of 24th January 1962. Before returning to Eastleigh, the 12.42 p.m. (S.O.) Waterloo-Basingstoke was worked on several occasions in June and July 1962, but thereafter it was mainly restricted to special duties until withdrawn in July 1963. However, before entering store, forces were joined with Caledonian single No. 123 on 15th September 1963 to work a Bluebell Railway special, while the following month 'U' class 2—6—0 No. 31790 was partnered on the 'Thames, Avon and Severn' railtour.

On 11th January 1964 it was steamed and run to Fratton to await preservation. This proved a lengthy process and involved moves to Stratford, Tyseley, York and finally the Mid-Hants Railway, where it was displayed for a time at Alresford before being called to Ropley Works for repair and repainting. This was completed in May 1983, when as British Railways No. 30120 and painted lined black, it entered service between Alresford and Ropley, extended to Alton two years later.

ENGINE SUMMARY

No.	Date	Order No.	Superheated		Withdrawn
			Eastleigh	Maunsell	
113	6/1899	G9	—	11/1925	5/1951
114	6/1899	G9	—	11/1927	5/1951
115	7/1899	G9	—	8/1927	5/1951
116	7/1899	G9	—	8/1925	4/1951
117	7/1899	G9	—	11/1927	7/1961
118	7/1899	G9	—	6/1928	5/1951
119	8/1899	G9	9/1923	10/1925	12/1952
120	8/1899	G9	—	5/1927	7/1963
121	9/1899	G9	2/1924	2/1927	4/1951
122	9/1899	G9	—	4/1926	3/1951
280	10/1899	K9	—	7/1927	5/1951
281	11/1899	K9	—	6/1928	10/1951
282	11/1899	K9	12/1923	4/1925	3/1954
283	12/1899	K9	—	10/1025	12/1957
284	12/1899	K9	7/1923	3/1926	4/1958
295	1/1900	O2	—	1/1926	6/1958
286	1/1900	O2	—	6/1926	4/1951
287	1/1900	O2	12/1923	7/1925	8/1961
288	2/1900	O2	—	2/1926	12/1960
289	2/1900	O2	—	12/1927	11/1959
300	12/1900	T9	10/1922	6/1925	3/1961
301	12/1900	T9	1/1923	7/1925	8/1959
302	12/1900	T9	11/1925	11/1925	9/1952
303	12/1900	T9	4/1923	1/1926	6/1951
304	12/1900	T9	6/1922	2/1925	9/1957
305	2/1901	X9	7/1922	8/1925	4/1951
307	2/1901	X9	8/1924	7/1925	12/1952
310	4/1901	X9	2/1923	1/1925	5/1959
311	4/1901	X9	12/1922	5/1925	7/1952
312	5/1901	X9	—	2/1925	1/1952
313	9/1901	G10	7/1922	8/1925	7/1961
314	9/1901	G10	4/1922	1/1925	5/1951
336	10/1901	G10	3/1923˙	7/1925	2/1953
337	10/1901	G10	—	5/1925	12/1958
338	10/1901	G10	1/1923	9/1925	4/1961
702	1/1899	—	5/1923	10/1925	10/1959
703	1/1899	—	—	9/1926	9/1952
704	1/1899	—	6/1923	5/1925	10/1951
705	1/1899	—	5/1924	10/1925	1/1958
706	1/1899	—	—	9/1925	5/1959
707	6/1899	—	—	10/1924	3/1961
708	6/1899	—	—	5/1927	12/1957
709	6/1899	—	5/1923	10/1925	7/1961
710	6/1899	—	—	7/1929	3/1959
711	6/1899	—	—	8/1927	8/1959
712	6/1899	—	—	3/1928	11/1958
713	6/1899	—	—	7/1925	4/1951
714	6/1899	—	2/1924	9/1925	3/1951
715	6/1899	—	12/1923	7/1925	7/1961
716	6/1899	—	—	7/1927	10/1951
717	9/1899	—	—	9/1927	7/1961
718	9/1899	—	—	9/1928	3/1961
719	9/1899	—	—	8/1926	3/1961
721	9/1899	—	8/1923	12/1925	7/1958
722	9/1899	—	10/1923	5/1928	4/1951
723	9/1899	—	—	2/1928	6/1951
724	9/1899	—	5/1923	3/1926	5/1959
725	10/1899	—	—	2/1926	12/1952
726	10/1899	—	2/1924	3/1926	8/1959
727	10/1899	—	—	5/1925	9/1958
728	12/1899	—	—	1/1926	9/1956
729	12/1899	—	8/1923	8/1927	3/1961
730	12/1899	—	—	12/1927	8/1957
731	12/1899	—	—	1/1927	5/1951
732	12/1899	—	—	3/1927	10/1959
773/733	11/1901	—	—	3/1925	4/1952

All built by Nine Elms Works, except Nos. 702-19/21-33 by Dübs & Co. (Works Nos. 3746-75, 4038). No. 773 was renumbered 733 in 12/1924. Disposal: Nos. 119, 282, 301/2/7/11/2, 702/3/11/25/33 broken up at Ashford Works, Nos. 304, 705/21 at Brighton Works and the remainder at Eastleigh Works. The tender tops of Nos. 113/6/9/22, 314, 703/25/33 were salvaged and fitted to the frames of a similar number of ex-LB & SCR 'C2X' class tenders. Final mileages: Nos. 117 − 1,982,396; 119 − 1,543,560; 120 − 1,713,304; 287 − 1,927,593; 301 − 1,819,562; 338 − 1,879,273; 711 − 1,896,489; 714 − 1,746,960; 717 − 2,064,698; 733 − 1,506,947.

'L12' class 4—4—0 No. 430 at Nine Elms on 22nd May 1906 with a balanced crank axle, Duplex feed pumps between the coupled wheels, firebox water tubes and a double bogie tender.

J. B. Ashford

THE LATER EXPRESS 4-4-0s

The introduction of heavier, steam-heated rolling stock and the tightening of schedules after the turn of the century, ended much of the 'T9s' reserve power and this led to Drummond providing a 5 ft boiler for his standard 4—4—0 chassis in 1904, a modification which undoubtedly enhanced the steam supply, but, with an unchanged grate and only marginal cylinder enlargement, the combination offered little extra power and was but a stop gap until 4—6—0s could be designed and built. Unfortunately, the latter did not prove an unqualified success; consequently when further construction was necessary for the Bournemouth services in 1911, Drummond reverted to 4—4—0s, the 'D15' class, in which the standard layout was extended to accept piston valves, a sloping grate, longer boiler and enlarged firebox. Success was immediate and the class did much to bolster Drummond's somewhat tarnished reputation.

'L12' Class

The Drummond 5 ft boiler, introduced on the 'S11' mixed traffic 4—4—0s in 1903, appeared on the express series in February 1904, when 'L12' class Nos. 415-34 were ordered from Nine Elms Works for the Bournemouth and West of England services. They were completed between June 1904 and March 1905 at a cost of £2,560 each and had the following dimensions:

Cylinders	19″ x 26″
Bogie wheels	3′ 7″
Driving wheels	6′ 7″
Wheelbase	6′ 6″ + 6′ 9″ + 10′ 0″ = 23′ 3″
Boiler diameter	5′ 0″
Boiler length	10′ 6″ (Tubeplates 10′ 9 3/8″)
Firebox	7′ 4″
Heating surfaces:	
Tubes (247 x 1¾″)	1,222 sq. ft.
Firebox	163 sq. ft.
Crosswater tubes (61 x 2¾″)	165 sq. ft.
Total	1,550 sq. ft.
Working pressure	175 lb.
Grate area	24 sq. ft.
Weights in working order:	
Bogie wheels	16T 17C
Leading coupled wheels	19T 2C
Trailing coupled wheels	18T 0C
Engine total	53T 19C
Tender	44T 17C
Engine & Tender	98T 16C

The bogie, cylinders, motion, wheelbase, boiler and tender were standard with the 'S11' class, while the chassis was similar to the 1900-1 'T9' series. The 5 ft diameter boiler and shorter mountings gave the appearance of being considerably larger and more capable than the 'T9s', although in reality the class was only marginally more powerful.

The 4,000 gallon double bogie tender was equipped with exhaust steam heating and fed the boiler by means of Duplex pumps and clackboxes at the base of the front tubeplate. On Nos. 415-9 these pumps were mounted below the footplate, but Nos. 420-34 had them positioned outside the frames between the coupled wheels. Like the 'S11' class, the crank axle was balanced and the driving wheels without balance weights.

When new, Nos. 415-9/26/30-4 were stationed at Nine Elms, Nos. 421/3/5/9 at Salisbury, Nos. 420/2/4 at Bournemouth and Nos. 427/8 at Fratton, but by March 1906 the last mentioned were also working from Nine Elms. In the days before transatlantic air travel, the only means of journeying between Western Europe and North America was by sea. At the turn of the century a number of British, French, German and Dutch shipping companies were competing vigorously for this prestigious and lucrative traffic, with each in turn attempting to gain ascendancy by placing in service larger, faster and more luxuriously appointed liners, factors which obviously influenced most prospective travellers, although politicians and businessmen probably placed most emphasis on the time taken by the crossings, which was unfortunate for at the time the maximum speed of commercial shipping was restricted to 20 knots. As a result, the journey time could only be materially shortened by reducing the distance travelled by sea, this the America Line (successor of the Inman Line) decided could most advantageously be accomplished east bound by calling briefly at Plymouth to land passengers and mail by tender, thereby saving a day by completing the journey to London by rail.

The Great Western and London & South Western Railways both served Plymouth; therefore to avoid needless and expensive competition it was agreed that the Post Office mails should be conveyed by the former, while the South Western accommodated the passengers. The first of these specials ran on 9th April 1904 and was booked non-stop from Devonport to Waterloo, except for a momentary enforced stop at Exeter St. David's and a hasty engine change at Templecombe. The first section of the journey was worked by 'S11' class No. 399, which had the misfortune to run into a permanent way trolley between Broad Clyst and Whimple, causing a delay of seven minutes while the engine was inspected and the wreckage removed from the line. As a result, the train was taken over 11 minutes late at Templecombe by No. 336, which by fast running regained 8 minutes to Waterloo, giving a journey time of 4 hrs 23 mins as against the 4 hrs 17 mins of the Great Western. The timings of the next four specials were:-

		Schedule	
		South Western	Great Western
Date		*4 hrs 20 mins*	*4 hrs 15 mins*
23/4/1904	Actual	4 hrs 01 mins	4 hrs 14 mins
30/4/1904	″	4 hrs 00 mins	3 hrs 54 mins
7/5/1904	″	3 hrs 59 mins	3 hrs 59 mins
14/5/1904	″	4 hrs 02 mins	4 hrs 01 mins

These timings and those of later specials were known to South Western crews, who obviously wished to better the Great Western; consequently some very fast running was

'L12' class No. 416 in original condition.

J. E. Kite Collection

recorded, so fast that Drummond found it necessary to remind crews of the 30 mph speed restriction through Salisbury station, apparently to little effect for in October 1904 the schedule was revised to give an extra minute between Templecombe and Hampton Court Junction, the overall timing remaining 4 hours 20 minutes. Before time Waterloo arrivals were not officially encouraged, but no objections were raised providing this was achieved surreptitiously with all speed restrictions being meticulously observed and no complaints of rough riding received from the passengers or head guard.

This means of operation was absolutely dependent on the experience, skill and judgement of drivers, but nevertheless not the faintest suspicion of danger arose before the fatal night of 30th June 1906, when Stonehouse Pool was left with passengers and baggage off RMS *New York*. The special consisted of brake van No. 17, 1st class eagle saloons Nos. 38, 47, 84 and kitchen car/brake No. 492, all eight-wheelers of modern construction and having a gross weight of 120 tons. 'T9' No. 288 had charge to Templecombe, which was reached a minute early at 1.22 a.m., where engines were changed, with 'L12' No. 421 crewed by driver W. J. Robins and fireman A. Gadd coming on. For some unknown reason the restart was exceptionally slow, so tardy in fact that the head guard anticipated an engine change being demanded at Salisbury, but thereafter according to entries in the guard's and signalmen's journals, Robins ran from Dinton to Wilton at approximately 70 mph, which was unusually fast, although giving no cause for alarm. However, there certainly was at the Salisbury distant, past which the 'L12' roared with prolonged whistling towards the station and the notorious ten chain curve without the slightest reduction in speed or apparent attempt at braking. Signalman Mundy at Salisbury West box estimated the speed of passing as fully 60 mph and was horrified by the sight, but absolutely helpless to do anything to stop the impending disaster. At the

London end of the station, Beattie double frame goods No. 0351 was standing on Fisherton Street bridge in the Bournemouth bay while a down milk train was slowly negotiating the station approach. Notwithstanding the boat special's grossly excessive speed, nothing untoward occurred before the sharp Fisherton Street bridge curve, when No. 421 lurched violently and made contact with the milk train, causing it to veer across the tracks and crash into No. 0351 with a shuddering crunch heard throughout the city. The full weight of the special was taken by No. 421's tender which jack-knifed against the cab, killing Robins and his fireman instantly, while all the carriages except the kitchen car were shattered by the tender or the bridge girders. Twenty-four passengers were killed and seven seriously injured. Only one passenger escaped unscathed, he fortunately having fallen asleep in the kitchen car after illegally playing cards with the staff. Also killed were No. 0351's fireman, the guard of the milk train and an unfortunate passer-by. The East box signalman booked the crash at 1.57 a.m. and immediately despatched the line obstructed danger signal, but as such occurrences were virtually unknown on the South Western, Waterloo demanded confirmation before accepting the dreadful truth.

When inspecting the wreckage, Drummond discovered No. 421's regulator firmly closed and the vacuum brake in the running position, suggesting that Robins had no intimation of his grossly excessive speed or imminent danger. Not unexpectedly, the Board of Trade inquiry did little to solve the problem, though a number of interesting facts were revealed, including:-

Plymouth Boat Specials Schedule

	mins
Devonport	00
Tavistock	20
Meldon Junction	40
Cowley Junction	69
St. David's	71

Queen Street	74	
Sidmouth Junction	87½	
Seaton Junction	101	
Yeovil Junction	129	(pass at 20 mph)
Templecombe (117½ miles)	141 to 145	(changing engines)
Dinton	165	
Salisbury West Box	174	(pass at 30 mph)
Salisbury East Box	175	(pass at 30 mph)
Andover Junction	193	
Basingstoke	212	
Woking	234	
Hampton Court Junction	244	
Wimbledon	250	
Clapham Junction	254	(pass at 40 mph)
Waterloo (229½ miles)	260	

Average speed: To Templecombe (117½ mls) 50.0 mph
After Templecombe (112 mls) 58.4 mph

R.M.S. New York Special	Distance between Signal boxes ml ch		Booked time mins	Booked speed mph	Actual time mins	Actual speed mph
Templecombe	0	00	0	0	0	0
Gillingham	6	50½	–	–	9½	42.7
Semley	4	12¾	–	–	15	45.4
Tisbury	4	75¾	–	–	20	59.3
Dinton	4	23½	20	63.6	24	64.4
Wilton	5	66½	25½		29	70.0
Salisbury West Box	2	25¼	29	39.7	31	69.4
Salisbury East Box	0	34½	30	25.7	–	–

Average speed (actual) Dinton to derailment (8.4 mls) 72 mph

It was reported that Robins had not previously worked one of the boat specials and therefore probably had no experience of passing through Salisbury station at speed, while No. 421 was not his regular engine, this being 'T9' class No. 283. Possibly with its lower centre of gravity, the latter might just have escaped derailment. It was also divulged that there had been heated discussions in the enginemen's lobbies as to the maximum speed that Salisbury station could be traversed; the consensus was 45 mph. Possibly Robins and his fireman were attempting to discover the answer. This will never be known and probably the company's own inquiry offers the best solution — excessive speed. The costs of the disaster were: No. 421 £350; No. 0351 £96; rolling stock £4,400; track and station £608; Compensation: passengers £32,854, staff £350; Total £38,658.

On being returned to the track by the Nine Elms and Eastleigh breakdown cranes, No. 421 proved to be surprisingly little damaged and could be towed away to Nine Elms Works, but its tender had to be conveyed away on a flat wagon. When stripped down, the crank axle of the 'L12' was found fractured and was replaced by one of conventional pattern and consequently required driving wheel balance weights. On returning to traffic, it was diplomatically transferred to Bournemouth, where crewing by Salisbury men was unlikely, while the boat special schedule

'L12' class No. 432 at Waterloo with a train for Plymouth.   *J. E. Kite Collection*

'L12' class No. 427 at the head of a heavy West of England restaurant car express in mid-1918.

F. E. Mackay

Superheated 'L12' No. 421 ex-works in July 1915, with an extended smokebox, Urie smokebox door, lipped chimney without a capuchon, boiler barrel clackboxes, injectors and fluted coupling rods.   *F. Burtt*

was increased to 268 minutes, with stops of 3 minutes for engine changing at Exeter and Salisbury.

Incidentally, by Grouping, Nos. 415/23/30/1 and 'S11s' Nos. 395/8, 400 were also fitted with unbalanced crank axles. For over a decade no spare boilers were available for the 'L12s' and 'S11s', but this was remedied when three were ordered from Eastleigh Works at a cost of £1,055 each in 1914 and fitted to Nos. 417 (October 1914), 418 (May 1915) and 420 (December 1914). Apart from having fireboxes without cross water tubes, Urie smokebox doors and boiler barrel clackboxes, they were similar to the original series. A fourth boiler was completed in July 1918 and fitted to No. 429. Around the same period the Duplex feed pumps were replaced by hot water injectors, Nos. 423/4/34 received fireboxes without cross water tubes and the clackboxes were repositioned on the boiler barrel.

During the First World War the L12s' wide route availability and relatively high power proved particularly useful and by March 1915 all had been concentrated at Nine Elms for working the many troop, ambulance and van specials required to cover the needs of the Western Front armies. Later, Nos. 415-7/22 were reported stationed at Basingstoke for the Oxford-Southampton docks specials, while after the introduction of armoured vehicles use was made of 'S11s' and 'L12s' to head long trains of them from Salisbury Plain and Aldershot. It was while so employed on 4th January 1917 that No. 431 broke a crank axle approaching Winchester Junction, fortunately without casualties.

Urie strongly advocated superheating and on 24th April 1914 ordered the material for 'T14s' Nos. 443-5/58, 'D15s' Nos. 464-6/72 and 'L12' No. 415. The last mentioned

entered Eastleigh Works for heavy repairs in July 1914, but for some reason was returned to traffic still saturated and it was No. 421 in July 1915 which was the first to be superheated. On trial the performance and coal consumption was markedly improved, particularly on the Portsmouth services; consequently on 22nd November 1917 instructions were issued for the remainder of the class to be similarly modernised at a cost of £685 each. Details are:-

415	10/1920	420	3/1932	425	10/1920	430	1/1919
416	12/1918	421	7/1915	426	4/1919	431	9/1921
417	3/1921	422	8/1920	427	1/1922	432	2/1920
418	10/1919	423	6/1919	428	3/1920	433	6/1919
419	2/1919	424	10/1918	429	2/1922	434	6/1922

The changed dimensions were:-
Heating surfaces:

Tubes, small (138 x 1¾")	682 sq. ft.
large (21 x 5¼")	311 sq. ft.
Firebox	161 sq. ft.
Total evaporative	1,154 sq. ft.
Superheater	195 sq. ft.
Total	1,349 sq. ft.

Weights in working order:

	LSWR	Southern (1927)
Bogie	18T 2C	18T 14C
Leading coupled wheels	18T 4C	19T 0C
Trailing coupled wheels	16T 18C	17T 11C
Total	53T 4C	55T 5C

New fittings included an extended smokebox and saddle, tube cleaning apparatus, a Detroit four-feed sight lubricator and a Urie lipped chimney. Except on No. 421, the last mentioned had a short capuchon. The slide valves and the tender exhaust steam heating tubes were retained.

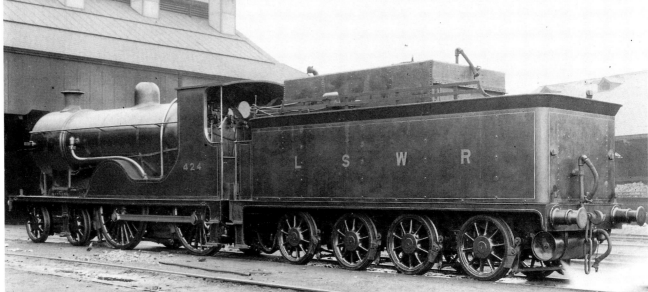

Two views of superheated 'L12' No. 424 as an oil-burner in 1921 at Eastleigh and Nine Elms respectively.

J. E. Kite Collection
and H. C. Casserley

In 1921 when good quality steam coal was in short supply, Nos. 415/23/4 were converted to oil-burning, details being:-

No.	System	To oil-burning	To coal-burning
415	Scarab	25/6/1921	14/9/1921
423	Scarab	25/6/1921	5/10/1921
424	Holden	18/6/1921	24/10/1921

During this period all were extensively employed by Eastleigh on the Portsmouth-Salisbury and Eastleigh-Bournemouth services, with No. 424, the most successful conversion, running 13,697 miles. After the Urie 'N15' class 4–6–0s Nos. 736-45 entered traffic in 1918-9, most of the 'L12s' were transferred to the provincial sheds and by March 1920 the allocation was: Nine Elms Nos. 415-20/30/1/4; Eastleigh Nos. 421/2/5/8; Fratton Nos. 424/7/9/32; Basingstoke Nos. 423/6/33.

As the class shared with the mixed traffic 'S11s' the distinction of being the largest South Western passenger engines having almost universal route availability, the 'L12s' retained an important role, especially in the summer months, when many holiday reliefs were routed by Wimborne, Fordingbridge, Alton and the Meon Valley line.

At Grouping all entered Southern Railway stock to be painted Maunsell green and receive the E-prefix, details being:-

No.	Southern Livery	E-prefix Removed	No.	Southern Livery	E-prefix Removed
415	8/1924	11/1933	425	2/1925	7/1931
416	6/1925	5/1932	426	2/1924	3/1933
417	8/1925	7/1931	427	2/1924	3/1933
418	6/1924	1/1932	428	10/1925	5/1933
419	2/1925	3/1932	429	5/1924	7/1931
420	12/1923	12/1932	430	3/1925	9/1931
421	12/1924	7/1931	431	12/1923	10/1931
422	7/1925	1/1932	432	9/1924	7/1931
423	6/1924	8/1931	433	5/1925	5/1933
424	11/1923	5/1932	434	12/1923	1/1933

In early July 1924 the class was passed for running over the Mid-Sussex line and at once commenced working Saturday reliefs from Waterloo-Portsmouth Harbour via Raynes Park, Epsom and Horsham. Although these services failed to survive after 1925, Fratton regularly rostered the class for the Victoria and London Bridge services via Three Bridges and Sutton, while those at Nine Elms fulfilled a heavy programme of summer Sunday and bank holiday excursions from Clapham Junction, Wimbledon, Surbiton and other Western Section suburban stations to Worthing, Bognor Regis and Littlehampton via Epsom.

By mid-1925 the availability of 'H15s' Nos. 330-4, 473-8, 521-4 and King Arthurs Nos. 448-57, 773-8 had created an embarrassing surplus of superheated passenger engines on the Western Section. Therefore when the ex-SE & CR 'L' class 4−4−0s had difficulty maintaining time with the 80 minute Charing Cross-Folkestone expresses, ten 'L12s' could be spared for the Eastern Section. Because of the stricter load gauge and small turntables, it was necessary to fit short stovepipe chimneys, lower the safety valve columns and provide 3,500 gallon six-wheel tenders. Details are:-

416 (from No. 406) 9/1925		424 (from No. 168) 8/1925
417 (from No. 405) 8/1925		425 (from No. 170) 5/1925
419 (from No. 438) 5/1925		430 (from No. 163) 7/1925
421 (from No. 161) 5/1925		431 (from No. 171) 6/1925
422 (from No. 437) 7/1925		433 (from No. 442) 5/1925

Their double bogie tenders were transferred to 'L11s' Nos. 163, 158, 406, 161, 442, 165, 159/73, 386 ('K10') and 134.

Whilst *en route* to Bricklayers Arms via Brighton, No. 421 was commandeered by that shed for several weeks to work the Portsmouth services and the Sunny South Express to and from Willesden.

On the Eastern Section Nos. 416/7/21/2/5/33 were stationed at Bricklayers Arms and Nos. 419/24/30/1 at Deal. On arrival all had notices stating — Restriction as for the Eastern Section L class, except for the Tonbridge-Hastings branch — posted in the cab interiors. Little difficulty was met maintaining time with the Folkestone expresses, although the stress and strain of doing so took its toll, for all ten required attention at Ashford Works to the coupled boxes between July 1925 and April 1926, when they were relieved by the newly built 'L1' class 4−4−0s Nos. A753-8/82-9, This was a most fortuitous relief as the delayed delivery of the Central Section's King Arthurs had created a minor emergency because, in anticipation of their availability, five sets of Southern and three sets of ex-LSWR vacuum braked corridor stock had been drafted in. As a result, Nos. 416/7/9/21/2/5/31/3 were despatched to Brighton to tide over the main line services until all fourteen King Arthurs, Nos. 793-806, had arrived from Eastleigh Works. Then Nos. 417/9/25/31/3 were transferred to Battersea, leaving Nos. 416/21/2 at Brighton for the Bournemouth, Plymouth and Cardiff through trains. Those at Battersea were mainly employed on the Victoria-Margate services, though regular appearances were also made on the Bognor Regis and Portsmouth trains, and the 10.45 a.m. Eastbourne Sunday Pullman.

During the 1926 General Strike resort was again made to oil-burning, details being:-

No.	To Oil-burning	To Coal-burning
415	2/1926	12/1926
420	6/1926	12/1926
424	6/1926	12/1926

All employed the Mexican trough system and gave reliable service after the grate had been raised above the foundation ring. For the duration No. 424 was re-attached to a double bogie tender and returned to the Western Section. At first employment was mainly on van, goods and ECS trains, but later they shared the Southampton-Alton-Waterloo services. A return was made to coal-burning in December 1926.

Another emergency occurred in August 1927, when the sudden withdrawal of the 'River' class 2−6−4 tanks from traffic following the disastrous Sevenoaks derailment left the Reading line denuded of motive power. At first ex-SE & CR 'E' class 4−4−0s were drafted in, but proved inadequate and in September 1927 'L12s' Nos. 417/9/24/5/30/1/3 were sent to the rescue. They were mainly rostered for the London Bridge and Charing Cross commuter services, the Birkenhead and Wolverhampton through trains between Redhill and Reading, the Waterloo vans and the Reading branch slows, duties which were successfully performed until September 1928, when the arrival of 'U' class 2−6−0s Nos. A800-4 (tender rebuilds of the 'River' class) permitted their return to Battersea, where useful service was given on relief Continental expresses via Maidstone East. This route was often used at busy periods to relieve the Tonbridge line, but prohibited to heavy engines following the Bearsted derailment. Use was also made of them on the Kent Coast expresses, including the important 3.15 p.m. Granville Express. On summer Sundays and bank holidays regular appearances were also made on Central and Eastern Section excursions.

As with other classes fitted with Eastleigh superheaters, there was a gradual replacement by the less expensive Maunsell pattern with a 215 sq. ft. heating surface and smokebox top snifting valves. Details are:-

415	4/1927	420	1/1926	425	5/1925	430	3/1925
416	6/1925	421	5/1925	426	8/1926	431	6/1925
417	8/1925	422	7/1925	427	12/1925	432	11/1925
418	6/1929	423	9/1926	428	10/1925	433	5/1925
419	2/1925	424	8/1925	429	5/1927	434	11/1928

Around the same period the stovepipe chimneys of Nos. 416/7/9/21/2/4/5/30/1/3 had the prominent capuchons removed, while Nos. 415/8/20/3/6-9/32/4 commenced receiving handsome, waisted chimneys, also without capuchons.

In June 1929 Nos. 417/21/5 were transferred to Redhill for the Reading services and the fast 60 minute 7.50 a.m. Gomshall-London Bridge and 5.23 p.m. return commuter trains. The Ashford 2−6−0s often had trouble working the up trains, but No. 421 in particular found little difficulty keeping time. Nevertheless, by March 1930 the class was no longer required by the Eastern Section and for the summer timetable the allocation was adjusted to: Nine Elms Nos. 415/20/6/7; Basingstoke Nos. 423/8/32/4; Fratton Nos. 416/9/22/4/9/30/1/3; Bournemouth No. 418; Brighton Nos. 417/21/5. Those with six-wheel tenders were shared between Fratton and Brighton.

'L12' class No. 431 at Eastleigh in October 1931 with a Maunsell superheater, snifting valves, a capuchoned stove-pipe chimney, Urie power classification on the platform valance and a six-wheeled tender.
Author's collection

Those stationed at Brighton immediately took over the heavy through Bournemouth, Plymouth and Cardiff trains, while Fratton employed its allocation on the Salisbury services and over the Central Section to Victoria, London Bridge, Bognor Regis and Eastbourne.

As with other Western Section engines, the E-prefix was discarded from mid-1931 as the class passed through Eastleigh Works for intermediate and general repairs, while commencing with No. 429 in December 1936, the lamp brackets were transferred from the smokebox front plate to the door, thereby bringing the class in line with engines fitted with smoke deflectors. This modification was also applied to other Drummond classes, including the 'M7s'.

The inauguration of Southampton as the terminal for the Imperial Airways Empire flying-boats in May 1937 necessitated the provision of smartly timed connections with London. At first four carriage specials headed by 'T9s' or 'L12s' were run, but these proved uneconomic and were replaced by carriages and Pullman cars attached to the rear of the 7.30 p.m. Waterloo-Bournemouth West express as far as Eastleigh, where they were detached and worked onwards to Southampton Terminus by any convenient engine, often 'M7s' or 'Jubilees'. Up specials were attached to the rear of the 'Bournemouth Belle'. Occasionally bad weather delayed arrivals or departures, when separate trains were provided headed by 'T3s', 'T9s' and 'L12s'. In June 1939 Victoria replaced Waterloo as the London terminal for the flying boat passengers and separate trains were again provided, often worked by 'L12' No. 415.

During the early months of 1938, Bognor shed had the misfortune to have three of its 'H2' class Atlantics under repair and was forced to borrow Nos. 421/2/9 from Brighton and Fratton for the London services. Nos. 422/9 had no sooner returned to Fratton when most of its 'L12s'

were made redundant by the Mid-Sussex electrification of July 1938. As a result, Nos. 416/9/22/30/1/3 were transferred immediately to Battersea, while at the end of the year No. 424 went to Brighton for the through trains and No. 429 to Basingstoke. Later other transfers occurred until by May 1939 the allocation was:-

Shed	Nos.	Duties
Nine Elms	415/20/7/9/32/4	One daily booked duty, 1.54 p.m. Waterloo-Basingstoke and 5.37 p.m. return, but there were six daily special duties shared with 'S11s' and 'L11s' between Waterloo and Bramshot Halt for workmen constructing an army camp. On 22/6/1936 these were headed by Nos. 415/27/9/32, 'L11' No. 411 and 'S11' No. 395. Saturdays: Lymington Pier reliefs and Waterloo-Salisbury semi-fasts.
Basingstoke	418/23/6/8	Three daily duties, East end carriage pilot from 5.30 a.m. to 12.30 a.m. (next day); 3.25 a.m. fish vans to Eastleigh, then passenger trains to Southampton, Reading, Portsmouth via Eastleigh and return; 11.51 a.m. Basingstoke-Portsmouth Harbour (through Wolverhampton) on Mondays and Fridays, no booked return. Saturdays: 11.34 a.m. Basingstoke-Portsmouth Harbour and 2.45 p.m. return (through Wolverhampton). Sundays: three duties, East end station pilot; Basingstoke-Waterloo and return; slow passenger Basingstoke-Eastleigh, Eastleigh-Southampton, Southampton-Basingstoke, Basingstoke-Waterloo and Waterloo-Basingstoke.
Brighton	417/21/4/5/31	Four daily duties, 9.42 a.m. Bournemouth West and 1.48 p.m. return; 11.00 a.m. Fareham and 4.35 p.m. return (through Cardiff); 12.00 p.m. Salisbury and 4.00 p.m. return (through Plymouth); 5.02 a.m. Brighton-Littlehampton, 10.02 Bognor-London Bridge fruit vans and 10.40 p.m. London Bridge-Brighton vans. Sundays: excursions to Bournemouth, Weymouth and Salisbury.
Battersea	416/9/22/30/3	Mainly employed on Victoria-Margate semi-fasts and Victoria-Maidstone East-Ashford-Dover services, but in the summer months also appeared regularly on specials from the Midlands to Brighton and Eastbourne, and excursions to the Sussex coastal resorts. Occasionally on August Saturdays one or two passed through Tonbridge on Charing Cross-Deal or continental reliefs.

'L12' class No. 424 at Brighton in August 1937 in post-1931 Maunsell livery with a plain stove-pipe chimney and a six-wheeled tender.

O. J. Morris

'L12' class No. 424 at Willesden Junction on 30th May 1936 with a through train for Brighton and Eastbourne.

K. Nichols

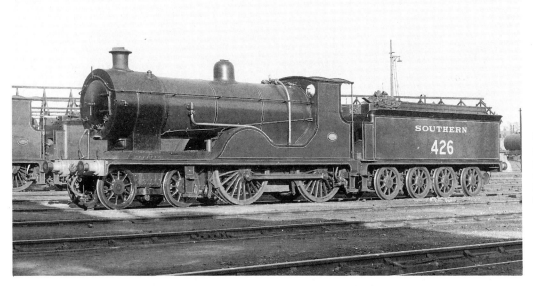

'L12' class No. 426, one of the Western Section allocated members of the class with full height lipped chimney and dome cover and a double bogie tender.
W. Beckerlegge

The Bulleid livery changes first affected the class in August 1939, details being:-

Maunsell green, black and yellow lining, tender numerals: Nos. 416 (September 1939), 431 (August 1939).
Maunsell green, unlined, cabside numerals, Bulleid lettering: No. 420 (December 1939), Nos. 415 (March 1940), 419 (July 1940), 423 (October 1940), 430 (June 1940), 434 (January 1940).
Malachite green, unlined, cabside numerals, Bulleid lettering: No. 429 (December 1940).

All later Southern repaints, commencing with No. 427 in April 1941, were plain black with cabside numerals and Bulleid lettering. No. 429 was given a general repair at Ashford Works in August 1944 and No. 434 minor attention at Brighton Works in January 1945, but otherwise all repairs remained with Eastleigh Works.

Around this period short stovepipe chimneys of the same pattern as classes 'H16' and 'G16' appeared on those having double bogie tenders, details being:-

415 — 3/1940; 418 — 5/1947; 420 — 12/1939; 426 — 10/1949; 428 — 9/1948; 429 — 6/1948; 432 — 5/1950; 434 — 3/1950; Nos. 423/7 retained lipped chimneys to withdrawal.

After the outbreak of war, Nos. 424/32 and 'S11s' Nos. 396/7, 402/4 were transferred to Feltham for London area goods duties, while at the end of the year Nos. 425/31 moved from Brighton to Nine Elms. Other transfers followed in mid-1940 when the Battersea series returned to the Western Section and, with those already there, were distributed as follows: Nine Elms Nos. 416/9/22/30/3/4; Feltham Nos. 415/32; Guildford Nos. 420/7/9; Basingstoke Nos. 418/23/6/8; Fratton Nos. 417/21/4/5/31. The last Eastern Section recorded work was No. 419, which passed up through Tonbridge with a short train of Red Cross carriages on 10th June 1940. During the Dunkirk evacuation Nos. 417/20/4/9/34 were loaned to Redhill for working troop specials up the Reading branch in partnership with 'D15s' Nos. 466/8/70 and 'S11s' Nos. 398, 404. On 2nd June 1940 No. 434 and 'L1' No. 1756 formed an unusual combination as they entered Reading (Great Western) shortly

after dawn at the head of sixteen LNER green and cream carriages overflowing with RAF personnel. Both worked on to Oxford and returned later in the day with twenty empty LMS carriages bound for Redhill. Other special workings around this period included Channel Island evacuation trains from Southampton docks to Reading headed by Nos. 416/8/30/4, 'T14' No. 461, 'N15s' Nos. 749/51/4 and 'T9s' Nos. 303/14.

In November 1940 Nos. 415/20/9 were transferred to Bournemouth and Nos. 421/32 to Salisbury, while after the arrival of Eastern Section 'Ds' Nos. 1731/4 and 'D1s' Nos. 1145, 1247, 1492/4, 1739 at Nine Elms in September 1941, Nos. 416/9/22/33/4 were moved to Guildford and No. 427 to Basingstoke. For the remainder of the war the class was mainly employed on mixed traffic duties.

After the cessation of hostilities and in time for the winter timetable of October 1945, Nos. 423/8/30 were transferred to Brighton for the Bournemouth and Plymouth through trains. The Cardiff remained on Eastleigh 'D15' class duty. However, their stay on these trains was not prolonged for 'Schools' Nos. 928-30 became available in November 1946 and, when the fuel crisis caused the cancellation of the Bournemouth and Cardiff services in early 1947, they were transferred to Eastleigh.

British Railways stock was entered at Nationalisation, when all except No. 430 were renumbered into the 30,000 series and Nos. 30415/6/9/26-8/32-4 were painted lined black. Around the same period the snifting valves were removed and these dates, together with those of renumbering and receiving the lined black livery, are:-

No.	BR No.	Lined Black	Snifting Valves Removed
415	1/1950	1/1950	1/1950
416	5/1949	5/1959	5/1949
417	7/1948	(a)	7/1948
418	9/1949	—	—
419	10/1948	10/1948	10/1948
420	7/1948	(a)	7/1948

No.	BR No.	Lined Black	Snifting Valves Removed
421	6/1949	—	7/1946
422	9/1950	—	11/1947
423	11/1948	—	11/1948
424	7/1950	—	—
425	8/1948	(a)	8/1948
426	10/1949	10/1949	10/1949
427	10/1949	10/1949	10/1949
428	9/1948	9/1948	9/1948
429	6/1948	(a)	6/1948
430	—	—	11/1947
431	5/1948	(a)	5/1948
432	5/1948	3/1949	9/1948
433	8/1950	8/1950	8/1947
434	12/1948	3/1950	3/1950

(a) Nos. 417/20/5/9/31 were painted BR unlined black in May-August 1948.

By mid-1949 the Western Section was so well provided with Pacifics and 4—6—0s that the number of duties booked for the 'L12s' was greatly reduced and Nos. 30417, 422, 30425/8/9, 430, 30431, 433 were rusticating in store at Eastleigh and Fratton. Of those remaining active, Nine Elms regularly rostered No. 427 on Saturdays for vans to Woking via Ascot, 11.18 a.m. Woking-Andover Junction, light engine to Farnborough, a goods to Woking and vans to Waterloo. At Guildford Nos. 30416/9/20/34 were mainly employed working the Reading-Redhill services, local goods to Aldershot, Alton, Fareham and Gosport or vans from Woking to Alton, while Nos. 418/26 at Basingstoke were usually restricted to the Overton goods or carriage piloting, while Bournemouth's No. 415 worked the Salisbury services or piloted at the West station. Salisbury also employed No. 30421 on the Bournemouth-Fordingbridge-Salisbury locals, while at Dorchester and Eastleigh Nos. 421, 30423/32 were only steamed on Saturdays. Therefore, it came as no surprise that the entire class, except the recently repaired Nos. 30415/34, was condemned in March-November 1951.

In May 1951 No. 30415 was transferred to Fratton and for the next twelve months, between periods of store, was mainly employed on the Meon Valley goods services and Portsmouth-Eastleigh locals or vans. However, on 10th June 1952 light Pacific No. 34035 *Ottery St. Mary* failed on the Brighton-Plymouth and had to be replaced. The only available substitute was No. 30415, so it was hastily commandeered and worked the nine carriage train onwards

'L12' class No. 30432 in early British Railways livery, with smokebox numberplate, plain tender sides, the snifting valves removed, a lipped chimney without a capuchon and a double bogie tender, at Eastleigh on 27th March 1949.

W. Gilburt

'L12' class No. 30415 in British Railways lined black livery, with a large tender totem, Urie power classification below the cabside numerals and a stove-pipe chimney, at Bournemouth Central on 26th August 1950.   *Author*

to Salisbury with the loss of only 3 minutes. The return train was also successfully worked and because Brighton's other Pacifics, Nos. 34046-8, were also under repair, it continued with the through Cardiff on 11th June and the Bournemouth on the following day, when it was replaced by 'U' class No. 31805 on loan from Salisbury. Withdrawal came in January 1953, mileage 1,593,614.

No. 30434 remained working from Guildford, usually sharing the 6.35 a.m. to Reading, 11.05 a.m. Reading-Redhill, 3.04 p.m. Redhill-Reading and the 8.05 p.m. home with the last 'S11', No. 30400. In March 1952 a brief visit was made to Eastleigh Works for attention to the motion, boxes and brake gear and to have the leaking double bogie tender replaced by the six-wheel pattern from 'K10' class No. 329, while minor firebox attention was necessary in February 1953, but otherwise it was in steam daily, interspersing the Reading-Redhill passenger duties with goods to Fareham and Gosport, the Woking-Alton vans and carriage piloting at Woking. It was while so engaged on 31st July 1954 that 'S15' class No. 30499 failed on a down Channel Islands boat express and had to be hurriedly replaced by No. 30434, which successfully worked the train on to Basingstoke. This was the final main line appearance, although on several occasions in September and October 1954 trains of empty ballast hoppers were worked from Redhill to Woking. The end came in February 1955 with a mileage of 1,490,604.

ENGINE SUMMARY

No.	Date	Order No.	Superheated Eastleigh	Maunsell	Withdrawn
415	6/1904	L12	10/1920	4/1927	1/1953
416	6/1904	L12	12/1918	6/1925	6/1951
417	6/1904	L12	3/1921	8/1925	10/1951
418	7/1904	L12	10/1919	6/1929	6/1951
419	7/1904	L12	2/1919	5/1925	10/1951
420	10/1904	O12	3/1922	1/1926	8/1951
421	10/1904	O12	7/1915	5/1925	8/1951
422	11/1904	O12	8/1920	7/1925	8/1951
423	11/1904	O12	6/1919	9/1926	7/1951
424	11/1904	O12	10/1918	8/1925	7/1951
425	12/1904	R12	10/1920	5/1925	8/1951
426	12/1904	R12	4/1919	8/1926	10/1951
427	12/1904	R12	1/1922	12/1925	10/1951
428	1/1905	R12	3/1920	10/1925	4/1951
429	1/1905	R12	2/1922	5/1927	9/1951
430	2/1905	T12	1/1919	7/1925	2/1951
431	2/1905	T12	9/1921	6/1925	9/1951
432	2/1905	T12	1/1920	11/1925	9/1951
433	3/1905	T12	6/1919	5/1925	11/1951
434	3/1905	T12	6/1922	11/1928	2/1955

All built by Nine Elms Works. Disposal: Nos. 419/28 broken up at Brighton Works, Nos. 415-8/20-7/9-34 at Eastleigh Works. Mileages: Nos. 415 – 1,593,614; 420 – 1,396,943; 425 – 1,500,143; 430 – 1,506,432; 434 – 1,490,604.

'D15' Class

As excellent and well-liked as the 'T9s' and 'L12s' proved in express service, Drummond appreciated that the heavier and faster trains of the future would demand larger and more powerful engines; therefore he forsook 4−4−0s in 1905 for several classes of massively constructed multi-cylinder 4−6−0s. Unfortunately, the earliest performed so dismally that their use on the best services had to be hastily curtailed, while those built later seldom excelled the 4−4−0s. As a result, when more express engines were required for the Bournemouth services in 1911, Drummond had to decide whether to persevere with his 4−6−0s in the hope of some improvement or to update and enlarge his standard 4−4−0.

No decision had been reached by March 1911, when, holidaying in Scotland, he took the opportunity of observing the local railway scene as offered by the Caledonian and Glasgow & South Western, both of which employed recently built 4−6−0s. Whatever thoughts Drummond gained of Scottish railways without his guidance can only be imagined, although they were probably profound, for on returning south, he ordered five large 4−4−0s from Eastleigh Works. Could this have been the outcome of finding that the latest Scottish 4−6−0s performed little better than his own?

Classified 'D15' and numbered 463-7, these impressive 4−4−0s were completed at a cost of £3,065 each between March and August 1912. The dimensions were as follows:-

Cylinders	19½" x 26"
Bogie wheels	3' 7"
Coupled wheels	6' 7"
Wheelbase	6' 6" + 8' 3" + 10' 0" = 24' 9"
Boiler diameter	5' 0"
Boiler length	12' 0" (Tubeplates 12' 5")
Firebox length	8' 4"

'D15' class No. 469 shortly after completion at Eastleigh.

J. E. Kite Collection

'D15' class 4—4—0 No. 465, with firebox water tubes, Duplex feed pumps, fluted coupling rods and a 4,500 gallon double bogie tender, standing outside Eastleigh Works on 9th July 1912.   *Author's collection*

'D15' class No. 465 at Waterloo with a special train for Plymouth.   *Lens of Sutton*

'D15' class No. 467, showing the high-roofed spacious cab, smokebox wingplates and the layout, painting and lining of the double bogie tender.
Author's collection

Heating surfaces:

Tubes	1,406 sq. ft.
Firebox	148 sq. ft.
Cross water tubes	170 sq. ft.
Total evaporative	1,724 sq. ft.
Steam drier	62 sq. ft.
Working pressure	200 lb.
Grate area	27 sq. ft.

Weights in working order:

Bogie	20T 15C
Leading coupled wheels	19T 10C
Trailing coupled wheels	19T 10C
Engine total	59T 15C
Tender	49T 0C
Engine & Tender	108T 15C

Five more, Nos. 468-72, were ordered from Eastleigh Works in October 1911 and completed at a cost of £3,045 each between September 1912 and February 1913, some after Drummond's death.

The main consideration when designing the class was how to expand and advance the standard 4−4−0 to accept 19½ inch cylinders, piston valves and a larger firebox without restricting the bearing surfaces or cramp the grate and ashpan, for experience with the 4−6−0s had highlighted the folly of gaining space by injudicious contraction. Consequently, all the standard features found incapable of enlargement or strengthening without endangering reliability and performance were discarded. Therefore, when it proved impractical to retain steam chests between the cylinders, they were resited above, while Walschaert's valve gear replaced Stephenson's to halve the number of eccentrics and permit the use of 22 inch cylinder centres, 5 inch crank

webs and 9 inch bearings, dimensions and details which virtually ensured free-steaming, fast-running and reliability.

The crank axle was of massive proportions and constructed to the patent of W. & G. Drummond, whereby the reciprocating masses were wholly balanced by crank extensions and removed the necessity of driving wheel balance weights. This gave smooth riding, although imposing greater unsprung weight on the permanent way and underbridges, much to the displeasure of the engineer.

The Walschaert's valve gear was robustly constructed and differed from standard practice by not having the eccentric rods attached to the expansion links, but working drop arms from short rocking shafts, at the outer extremity of which the links were attached, a layout which had the advantage of transferring the motion from the plane of the eccentrics to that of the valves without the use of 'donkey-legs'. The motionplate was at the centre of the slide bars, but because the crosshead arm depended from the crosshead face, the usual Drummond trough bars could not be accommodated and a two bar style was substituted. The large valve spindle bearings were housed in pedestals cast on top of the motionplate, while the radius arms were forked and embraced these bearings.

Drummond favoured large diameter piston valves, thus for the 4−6−0's 15 in. cylinders the size was 9 in. and this was increased to 10 in. for the 19½ in. cylinders of the 'D15s', with outside admission and free exhaust to the blast pipe. The wheelbase at 24 ft. 9 in. was 18 in. longer than standard from the rear of bogie wheels to the driving wheels and this necessitated lengthening the connecting rods to 7 ft.

'D15' class No. 471, fitted with indicator shelter, at Bournemouth Central on 5th May 1913.

J. E. Kite Collection

The boiler was based on that fitted to No. 720 in 1905, the barrel and tube layout being similar, but to accept the 8 ft. 4 in. firebox, the pitch was raised 3 in. and the grate sloped to clear the trailing axle. Like No. 720 and the Drummond 4–6–0s, the entire firebox roof was sling stayed for greater flexibility, while the usual cross water tubes were fitted. The intention was that all ten engines should be equipped with steam driers, but on Urie's instructions after Drummond's death they were omitted from Nos. 471/2.

5,800 gallon double bogie tenders were built with the class, but not attached for they were transferred to the 'thirsty' 'T14s' and replaced by their 4,500 gallon pattern. The contents were exhaust steam heated and transferred to the boiler by means of Duplex pumps and front tubeplate clackboxes.

In service the provision of outside admission valves, unrestricted exhaust passages and a sloping grate was a winning combination for the 'D15s' proved economical, free-steaming and fast-running, all the attributes missing from the 4–6–0s. Hot boxes were practically unknown, there only being one occurrence, No. 468 in August 1916, recorded by the Repair Register between entering traffic and 31st December 1917. During the same period classes 'H15', 'T14' and 'G14'/'P14' required attention on 13, 12 and 5 occasions. The mileages worked to the first general

repair were marginally better than the 'L12s' and 'T9s', details being:

No.	Date	Mileage	No.	Date	Mileage
463	3/1914	74,946	468	8/1916	139,427
464	9/1914	79,165	469	1/1917	141,016
465	1/1915	81,643	470	10/1915	96,713
466	6/1914	72,114	471	1/1915	78,249
467	3/1914	71,594	472	9/1915	93,740

When new the allocation was Nine Elms Nos. 463-6/9-71, Bournemouth Nos. 467/8 and Salisbury No. 472, with the best Bournemouth and Salisbury services being shared with the 'T14s'. No. 472 occasionally worked to Exeter, but could usually be found on the 12.15 p.m. Salisbury-Waterloo and the 5.50 p.m. return. At Bournemouth Nos. 467/8 worked up to Waterloo daily with the 8.00 and 9.08 a.m. expresses, the latter being booked non-stop in 130 minutes, the return workings being at 2.00 and 4.10 p.m. By March 1913 No. 472 had been transferred to Nine Elms.

Although well satisfied with the class, Urie considered that the performance would be improved by superheating, therefore on 24th April 1914 he ordered the necessary fittings for Nos. 464-6/72. The first, No. 464, returned to traffic with an Eastleigh superheater in May 1915 and gave such an excellent account of itself on trial that on 7th October 1915 instructions were issued for the remainder of the class to be similarly modernised. Apart from the superheater, the main alterations were an extended smokebox carried by a saddle, a conventional firebox, 20 in. cylinders of Urie pattern, 180 lb working pressure and a Detroit four-feed lubricator. No. 464 retained its Drummond chimney, but the others were provided with a marginally shorter pattern having a capuchon. Although losing some of their distinctive Drummond features, the class appeared even more imposing and many considered it the best proportioned of the later South Western 4—4—0s. The changed dimensions were:-

Heating surfaces:

Small tubes (138 x 1 3/8")	782 sq. ft.
Large tubes (21 x 5¼")	357 sq. ft.
Firebox	145 sq. ft.
Total evaporative	1,284 sq. ft.
Superheater	231 sq. ft.
Total	1,515 sq. ft.

Weights in working order:

Bogie	21T 13C
Leading coupled wheels	20T 0C
Trailing coupled wheels	19T 8C
Total	61T 1C

Dates of superheating:

463	10/1916	464	5/1915	465	9/1915	466	3/1916
467	3/1917	468	7/1916	469	11/1916	470	5/1917
471	9/1917	472	1/1916				

No. 463 retained its distinctive deep-toned Caledonian hooter whistle.

During the First World War the class remained on the best Bournemouth and Salisbury expresses until mid-1917, when Nos. 466/7/9 went to Eastleigh for working the many troop, ambulance, leave and explosives van specials running to and from Southampton docks. Of the others, Nos. 463-5/71/2 were stationed at Nine Elms for the Bournemouth and Salisbury expresses and Nos. 468/70 at Bournemouth for the Waterloo services. On the morning of 14th November 1917 No. 466 hauled Great Northern 0—6—0s Nos. 150A and 1087 from Clapham Junction to Eastleigh while on 20th November 1917 GNR No. 312 assisted No. 470 to work a troop special off the Midland Railway to Southampton docks. These 'foreigners' formed part of a batch of 0—6—0s loaned by the Great Northern and Midland Railways to partially offset the sale of Adams '0395s' to the Government for service in the Middle East.

By early 1920 the Urie 'N15s' had charge of the Waterloo-Salisbury expresses, but the 'D15s' worked most of the Bournemouth services as well as many of the ocean liner specials. During the 1921 coal strike No. 470 was converted to oil-burning (Scarab system) on 3rd September. It was stationed at Eastleigh and after brief local trials worked two return Bournemouth-Waterloo services daily until reconverted to coal-burning on 29th October 1921.

All entered Southern Railway stock at Grouping to be painted Maunsell green and receive the E-prefix, details being:-

463	5/1924	464	2/1925	465	7/1924	466	11/1923
467	4/1924	468	8/1924	469	3/1924	470	8/1925
471	6/1924	472	8/1924				

For some months No. 466 ran without the small cabside numberplates.

Newly superheated, 'D15' class No. 464 in Eastleigh Works yard in May 1915.

J. E. Kite Collection

Superheated 'D15' No. 467 in post-World War 1 livery, with an extended smokebox, boiler barrel clackboxes, a conventional firebox and a capuchon-topped lipped chimney, at Eastleigh Works in March 1917.   *Author's collection*

The next change occurred in March 1925 when the 4,500 gallon double bogie tender of No. 472 was replaced by the 3,500 gallon six-wheel (13 ft wheelbase) pattern of '700' goods No. 692, so that it could be transferred to Fratton for working the Waterloo expresses. The small tender was necessary to permit use of the short Fratton shed turntable. As was to be expected, No. 472 proved much superior to the 'L12s' on these difficult services and later in the year it was joined by Nos. 466/7/9/70, with Nos. 463-5/8/71 following in 1926. All were similarly equipped with 3,500 gallon tenders, details being:-

463 (from No. 690)	2/1926	468 (from No. 693)	2/1926
464 (from No. 355)	4/1926	469 (from No. 689)	12/1925
465 (from No. 691)	9/1926	470 (from No. 695)	8/1925
466 (from No. 327)	12/1925	471 (from No. 350)	5/1926
467 (from No. 352)	8/1925	472 (from No. 692)	3/1925

The discarded 4,500 gallon tenders were transferred to 'L11s' Nos. 166, 439, 157/69, 405/37, 436, 164, 414 and 435, while the '700s' received the 3,500 gallon (14 ft. wheelbase) tenders removed from that class.

The complicated three-fold exchange was necessary because the Fratton shed turntable could only accommodate a 'D15' coupled to a 13 ft wheelbase tender, while a double bogie tender would have created problems for the '700' class in the smaller goods yards and at some provincial shed turntables.

The Portsmouth services were not smartly timed, but nevertheless the difficult route demanded lengthy periods of sustained hard steaming if the 73½ miles were to be run non-stop with loads of 300 to 350 tons in 98 minutes. Time was lost, but generally the running was excellent, with

engines accepting the heavy pounding until relieved by the newly built Ashford 'U1' class three-cylinder 2–6–0s Nos. A891-A900 in early 1931, when Nos. 463-6 were transferred to Eastleigh. Nos. 467-72 remained at Fratton for the Salisbury and Basingstoke services. Unfortunately, Ford bridge forbade their employment on the heavy Brighton-Bournemouth, Cardiff and Plymouth through trains on which they could have usefully replaced the 'L12s'.

A spare boiler was not provided by the South Western, a deficiency remedied in March 1925, when Maunsell authorised one being constructed by Eastleigh Works at a cost of £1,185. It was fitted to No. 469 in December 1925 and generally was similar to those carried by classes 'G16' and 'H16', with a closed dome, two lock-up safety valves over the firebox and a Maunsell superheater. The heating surfaces were:-

Tubes	1,280 sq. ft.
Firebox	139 sq. ft.
Superheater	252 sq. ft.
Total	1,671 sq. ft.
Weight in working order: 60T 19C	

In course of time this boiler was also carried by:-

No.	Fitted	Removed
467	4/1934	12/1935
468	4/1936	8/1938
470	11/1938	6/1941
471	9/1941	2/1944
469	11/1945	To withdrawal

The boiler was broken up with No. 469 at Ashford Works in January 1952. Like other Eastleigh replacement boilers, it was not considered as free-steaming as the original pattern.

No. 470 ran again as an oil-burner between 10th June and 29th November 1926. At first it was restricted to the 12.00 p.m. Eastleigh-Basingstoke-Staines-Clapham Junction vans and the 7.50 p.m. Nine Elms Yard-Southampton docks fitted goods, but later it had charge of the 11.30 a.m. Waterloo-Bournemouth. Just prior to reconversion to coal-burning, brief trials were held with No. 472, details being:-

No.	Distance miles	Average Load tons	Fuel	Fuel burnt per mile lbs	Cost per mile
470	423	208	Oil	23¾	17.7 d
472	479	214	Coal	36¼	12.5 d

In 1925-6 the Eastleigh superheaters were replaced by the Maunsell pattern (252 sq. ft.), while from 1931 the E-prefix was discarded, dates being:-

No.	Maunsell Superheater	E-prefix discarded	No.	Maunsell Superheater	E-prefix Discarded
463	2/1926	12/1931	468	2/1926	1/1932
464	4/1926	2/1933	469	12/1925	2/1934
465	9/1926	8/1932	470	8/1925	7/1933
466	2/1926	4/1933	471	5/1926	12/1932
467	8/1925	1/1932	472	6/1926	9/1932

Other modifications in the 1930s included chimneys without capuchons, the transfer of the smokebox front plate lamp brackets to the door and the filling-in of the lower cab openings to improve footplate comfort.

'D15' class No. 463 in post-1931 Southern livery, with a Maunsell superheater, snifting valves, a lipped chimney without a capuchon, a hooter whistle and a 3,500 gallon six-wheeled tender, about to leave Waterloo for Bournemouth in July 1932.

P. Ransome Wallis, courtesy National Railway Museum

'D15' class No. 468 in post-1931 Southern livery, with the spare Urie pattern boiler, at the head of a Portsmouth express in June 1936.

O. J. Morris

In December 1931 Nos. 470-2 were replaced at Fratton by 'T9s' Nos. 115/9, 707 and transferred to Salisbury for the through workings to Bristol and the Portsmouth services. Occasionally Exeter was also reached with semi-fasts and vans. Nos. 467-9 remained at Fratton until March 1935, when they were sent to Bournemouth for the through Margate (as far as Guildford) and the Oxford services. Their stay, however, was only brief for in late May 1935 'U' class 2—6—0s Nos. 1627-9 arrived as replacements and they were transferred to Guildford, where they were joined by Nos. 463-6/70-2, which had been similarly displaced by 'Us' Nos. 1621-6. At Guildford they worked some of the Waterloo-Alton-Southampton Terminus services, several Waterloo-Portsmouth semi-fasts, the Haslemere-Waterloo commuter trains and the Margate-Bournemouth West through train west of Guildford via Havant, Fareham and Southampton Central. Most of these duties ceased on 4th July 1937 with the Portsmouth and Alton electrification, when the entire class was transferred to Eastleigh. On the last day of through Waterloo-Alton-Southampton Terminus services, No. 464 worked two return journeys.

At Eastleigh the following duties were worked:-

Duty No.	Details
281	9.44 a.m. Eastleigh-Waterloo, 5.09 p.m. Waterloo-Basingstoke and 7.33 p.m. Basingstoke-Eastleigh.
282	Fish vans to Portsmouth, passenger Portsmouth-Romsey-Eastleigh, 11.58 a.m. Eastleigh-Woking, 3.54 p.m. Waterloo-Basingstoke and 6.50 p.m. Basingstoke-Southampton Terminus.
283	7.34 a.m. Eastleigh-Romsey, 8.00 a.m. Romsey-Bournemouth Central, 11.45 a.m. Bournemouth-Brentford vans and 7.54 p.m. Waterloo-Salisbury.
288/9/90/1	Local passenger to Southampton, Totton, Portsmouth and Salisbury, goods Salisbury-Eastleigh and Fratton-Eastleigh.

On Sundays there were four booked duties:-

281	7.10 a.m. Southampton-Waterloo boat express, 10.45 a.m. Waterloo-Eastleigh, 3.48 p.m. Eastleigh-Waterloo and ECS to Eastleigh.
283	9.50 a.m. Eastleigh-Bournemouth West, 4.07 p.m. Bournemouth Central-Waterloo and 9.54 p.m. Waterloo-Southampton Terminus.
299	Local passenger Eastleigh-Portsmouth-Basingstoke.
300	Eastleigh down side station pilot.

On 14th August 1939 the driver of No. 470 misread the signals at St. Denys while heading the 12.43 p.m. Salisbury-Portsmouth and ran into the protecting sand drag at about 30 mph. No one was injured and damage was superficial, but delays to following up services were severe until the carriages could be pulled clear and the culprit extricated by

'D15' class No. 463 as an oil-burner, with the fuel tank perched precariously on the six-wheeled tender, fitted with electric lighting and a short stove-pipe chimney, the snifting valves removed, and painted black, at Eastleigh on 3rd November 1948.   *Author*

'Jubilee' No. 630.

The class was first affected by the Bulleid livery changes in August 1939, details being:-

Maunsell green, black and yellow lining, tender numerals: No. 469 (August 1939).
Maunsell green, unlined, tender numerals: No. 463 (October 1939), organ pipe whistle replaced by standard pattern.
Maunsell green, unlined, Bulleid lettering, cabside numerals: Nos. 464/72 (May 1940), 467 (June 1940), 468 (October 1940).
Malachite green, unlined, Bulleid numerals, cabside numerals: Nos. 465 (June 1941), 466 (April 1941), 470 (July 1941), 471 (September 1941).

Commencing with Nos. 464/9 in November 1942, later repaints were plain black with Bulleid lettering and cabside numerals.

No. 469 was also the first to have the handsome lipped chimney replaced by a short stovepipe of similar pattern to those carried by classes 'G16' and 'H16', details being:-

463	5/1943	464	3/1945	465	2/1944	466	10/1950
467	2/1947	468	4/1948	469	11/1942	470	8/1944
471	4/1947	472	11/1949				

The reduced passenger timetable of the early war months led to Nos. 463/5/6/9/70/2 being placed in store, the first three in the goods yard at Guildford and Nos. 470/2 at Petersfield. Most returned to traffic for the Christmas period, when No. 471 worked a van special from Reading to Redhill on Christmas Eve and next morning was standing on Tonbridge shed, where it remained for several days before being steamed to tow 'Schools' class No. 903 *Charterhouse* to Eastleigh Works via Redhill, Guildford and Alton. The Dunkirk evacuation found Nos. 466/8/70, together with 'L12s' Nos. 417/20/4/9/34, working over the Reading-Redhill line, while No. 463 was at Paddock Wood on the evening of 3rd June, but once the BEF was safely home the class returned to Eastleigh and the Portsmouth, Salisbury, Bournemouth and Waterloo duties. Occasionally

pick-up goods were also worked, including those to Southampton, Alton and Andover Junction, while following the removal of the Ford bridge restriction in February 1942, the Brighton-Plymouth through train was added to the itinerary. The first recorded working was by No. 470 on 14th February, when for the first time for some months no time was lost. Normally only the Brighton-Salisbury section was worked, but because of a shortage of motive power at Exmouth Junction in June and July 1942, the train was worked throughout, with the down engine stabling overnight to head the up service next day. These trains were well patronised by the public and armed forces, and occasionally loaded to twelve corridors and, although not smartly timed, nevertheless presented a difficult task under wartime conditions. Time was lost, but mainly because parties of sailors travelling between Portsmouth and Plymouth insisted on leaving the trains at Salisbury in search of liquid refreshment and only reboarding when their needs had been satisfied. As the station master and staff had no desire for their prolonged presence, the departures were delayed until all had been shepherded aboard and the station could relax for twenty-four hours.

All ten survived hostilities and remained working from Eastleigh. In September 1947 No. 463 was converted to oil-firing (Mexican trough system), while in December 1947 a steam turbo-generator was fitted to supply electricity for cab illumination and the route code lights. As an oil-burner, it proved free-steaming and popular with crews and performed well on the Portsmouth-Salisbury and Eastleigh-Bournemouth-Weymouth services. When oil-firing was abandoned because of lack of foreign currency in October 1948, it was laid aside at Eastleigh until withdrawn with a mileage of 1,384,163 in November 1951.

The class remained a familiar sight on the Brighton through trains, at first the Plymouth and later the Cardiff, until November 1946, when 'Schools' Nos. 928-30 were transferred from Bournemouth for these services.

'D15' class No. 30467 in British Railways lined black livery with small tender totems and the Urie power classification below the cabside
numerals, leaving Southampton Central with a Bournemouth local in July 1953.   *P. Ransome Wallis, courtesy National Railway Museum*

The class entered British Railways stock at Nationalisation, when all except No. 463 were renumbered into the 30,000 series, while Nos. 464/5/7/8/70-2 also received the lined black secondary passenger livery. These dates and those for the removal of the snifting valves are:-

No.	BR No.	Lined Black Livery	Snifting valves Removed
463	—	—	9/1947
464	4/1950	4/1950	1/1948
465	5/1950 (a)	5/1950	2/1948
466	9/1949	—	10/1947
467	5/1949	10/1950	5/1947
468	4/1948	3/1950	4/1948
469	6/1948	—	6/1948
470	6/1948	9/1950	6/1948
471	11/1948	3/1950	3/1950
472	1/1949	11/1949	11/1949

(a) No. 465 carried the temporary S-prefix from
7th February 1948 to 19th May 1950.

No. 463 was not returned to coal-burning and remained in store, but the other nine were actively employed on the Eastleigh-Bournemouth, Portsmouth-Salisbury and Eastleigh-Woking passenger services and the Eastleigh-Clapham Junction vans until 1951-2, when Nos. 30466/8/9/70/2 were withdrawn. Few anticipated that the survivors would ever return to regular main line service, but fortunately the abysmal performance of 'U1' class 2—6—0s Nos. 31907/9/10 on the summer Saturday Waterloo-Lymington Pier trains led to their replacement in 1953 by Nos. 30464/5/7, an exchange well received by the crews and although time was occasionally lost, it was usually caused by signal or station delays and not poor running.

On 28th June 1953 the RCTS ran a special train from Waterloo to Lyme Regis and thence back to Paddington via Exeter and Bristol. From Waterloo to Salisbury No. 30464

was in charge and, despite a slow departure over the Windsor line to Clapham Junction, the net time for the 83¾ miles was 90 minutes, with 78 mph being attained at mile post 62½ and again near Porton. The load was seven carriages weighing 245 tons full.

The 1954 summer saw Nos. 30464/5/7 again in charge of the Lymington services, but the following year they were replaced by 'U' class 2—6—0s Nos. 31621/34 (fitted with BR blast pipes and new pattern cylinders), although No. 30465 did gain a final fling on the 8.45 a.m. ex-Waterloo on the first Saturday, 18th June. Thereafter it could usually be found heading the 12.42 p.m. Waterloo-Basingstoke, from where the 1.24 p.m. ex-Waterloo was taken on to Salisbury, while No. 30467, the only other active survivor, was mainly employed on ECS duties. The latter was condemned with a mileage of 1,497,699 in August 1955, but No. 30465 remained working ECS, vans and local goods until the New Year.

ENGINE SUMMARY

No.	Date	Order No.	Superheated Eastleigh	Maunsell	Withdrawn
463	3/1912	D15	10/1916	2/1926	11/1951
464	5/1912	D15	5/1915	4/1926	9/1954
465	6/1912	D15	9/1915	9/1926	1/1956
466	7/1912	D15	3/1916	2/1926	9/1952
467	8/1912	D15	3/1917	8/1925	8/1955
468	9/1912	G15	7/1916	2/1926	1/1952
469	10/1912	G15	11/1916	12/1925	12/1951
470	12/1912	G15	5/1917	8/1925	12/1952
471	1/1913	G15	9/1917	5/1926	2/1954
472	2/1913	G15	1/1916	6/1926	1/1952

All built by Eastleigh Works. Disposal: Nos. 463/71 broken up at Eastleigh Works, Nos. 464/6-70/2 at Ashford Works and No. 465 at Brighton Works. Mileages: Nos. 463 — 1,384,163; 465 — 1,553,885; 467 — 1,497,699; 472 — 1,299,693.

'K10' class mixed traffic 4—4—0 No. 329, with smokebox sand containers, firebox water tubes, numberplates and a 3,500 gallon six-wheeled tender, at Nine Elms on 11th October 1902.

J. B. Ashford

THE MIXED TRAFFIC 4-4-0s

Most railways in the 19th century assigned 0—6—0s or obsolescent passenger engines for mixed traffic duties, but a few, including the South Western, provided specially designed classes for this role. This practice, commenced by Nine Elms in 1851 with Joseph Beattie's 'Hercules' class 5 ft. 6 in. 2—4—0s, must have proved beneficial since Adams in later years built no less than ninety 'Jubilee' 0—4—2s for these duties, while after the turn of the century, a similar number of small-wheel 4—4—0s were provided by Drummond.

The 'C8' class 6 ft. 7 in. 4—4—0s may have proved inadequate express engines, but in a secondary role gave useful main line passenger service, particularly on excursions and ocean liner specials. As a result, when additional mixed traffic engines became necessary in 1900, Drummond modified the design to accept 5 ft. 7 in. coupled wheels and ordered the 'K10' class from Nine Elms Works. With the subsequent 'L11' class, the obvious means of enhancing the performance was taken by lengthening the coupled wheelbase to accommodate the larger 'T9' firebox. The final Drummond engines of this type, the 'S11s' of 1903, were much larger and more powerful for they were intended for service in the West of England and over the difficult Portsmouth line.

'K10' Class

Numbered 135-46/9/50-3, 329/40-7/80-94, the forty 'K10s' were ordered from Nine Elms Works in March 1900 and delivered at an average cost of £2,085 each between November 1901 and January 1903. Unofficially they became known as the *Hoppers*, adjusted to the *Small Hoppers* after the larger 'L11' class entered traffic in 1903-7. The dimensions were as follows:-

Cylinders	18½″ x 26″
Bogie wheels	3′ 7″
Coupled wheels	5′ 7″
Wheelbase	6′ 6″ + 6′ 9″ + 9′ 0″ = 22′ 3″
Boiler diameter	4′ 5″
Boiler length	10′ 6″ (tubeplates 10′ 9½″)
Firebox length	6′ 4″

The smokebox layout of 'K10' class No. 343 while carrying the experimental water tube boiler.

C. H. Eden

Heating surfaces:

Tubes (216 x 1¾″)	1,068 sq. ft.
Firebox	124 sq. ft.
Cross water tubes	100 sq. ft.
Total	1,292 sq. ft.

Working pressure 175 lb.
Grate area 20.4 sq. ft.

Weights in working order:

Bogie	14T 2C
Leading coupled wheels	17T 10C
Trailing coupled wheels	15T 2C
Engine total	46T 14C
Tender	39T 12C
Engine & tender	86T 6C

The boiler, except for the firebox cross water tubes, was similar to that of classes 'C8', 'M7' and '700', while the cylinders and motion were interchangeable with most other Drummond inside cylinder engines. The bogie was also of standard design, while the cab and splashers were of the wide pattern introduced on the final Nine Elms-built 'T9s'. All entered traffic with smokebox sand containers, these being steam operated and depositing sand between the bogie wheels, where it must have served little practical purpose. Replenishing the containers necessitated a ladder and a specially designed funnel, as access was by means of small brass-covered openings high up the smokebox. At the first general repair gravity sanding from sandboxes inside the frames and feeding the leading coupled wheels was substituted. New 3,500 gallon six-wheel tenders with a 14 ft wheelbase and weighing 40 tons 14 cwt were built with Nos. 329/40-5/7/93/4, but Nos. 135-46/9/50-3, 380-92 received similar tenders second-hand from 'C8s' Nos. 291/4 and 'T9s' Nos. 114/7/8/21/2, 282/6-9, 702/5/6/8/10-4/7/9/25-9/31/2. Those from the Dübs-built 'T9s' were marginally lighter at 39 tons 4 cwt.

No. 343, completed in December 1901 at a cost of £2,520, differed by having an experimental water tube boiler. Externally little difference was noticeable, but internally the 216 fire tubes were replaced by a single 2 ft. 8 in. diameter flue across which short water tubes were fitted in pods of fives, with the various pods being set at different angles. There were also 18 conventional fire tubes distributed around the outside of the flue, while the firebox cross water tubes, working pressure and grate were standard with the remainder of the class. The heating surfaces were:-

Circular flue	427 sq. ft.
Fire tubes	86 sq. ft.
Firebox	124 sq. ft.
Cross water tubes	100 sq. ft.
Total	737 sq. ft.

Drummond claimed that steam could be raised from cold in 1½ hours and that despite the smaller heating surface, the evaporative rate was at least equal to that of

The experimental water tube boiler fitted to 'K10' class No. 343 when built.

C. H. Eden

'K10' class No. 345 passing over Kent Road bridge, Swaythling with a Waterloo-Alton-Southampton Terminus on 9th July 1902. *Dr. Sellon*

the standard 'K10' boiler. In practice, steam-raising was quicker, but fractured flues, leaking tubes and priming severely disrupted evaporation and little revenue-earning service was possible, while several potentially serious blow-backs occurred. One test run was completed between Clapham Junction and Andover Junction on 12th January 1902, but the return run had to be abandoned at Overton, while a second run on 13th February 1902 terminated at Grateley. Later several trial journeys were successfully accomplished and in March-April 1902 the Reading vans were worked regularly. In a report dated July 1902, Drummond stated that the boiler performed well in a stationary capacity, but the jolting and vibration inevitable with railway usage caused flue fracturing and leaking tubes, which could only be attended to by lifting the boiler. In December 1902, with a mileage of 4,641, these fittings were removed and No. 343 returned to traffic as a standard 'K10'.

A second 'K10', No. 341, was also subject to a boiler experiment, when it was fitted in June 1905 with a modified smokebox spark arrester before being involved in a series of performance and fuel consumption trials. Unfortunately, like the earlier Drummond system, the steaming was adversely affected and the equipment was removed in October 1905.

Unlike most new South Western classes, the 'K10s' were stationed at the provincial sheds, where numerous light passenger and local goods duties were available. However, when the more powerful 'L11' class became available in 1903-4, Nos. 135-9/41/2/5 were transferred to Nine Elms, while the others were stationed at: Strawberry Hill Nos. 140, 342/7/86/8; Guildford Nos. 143/6, 382; Fratton Nos. 340/4/92; Basingstoke Nos. 329/91/4; Eastleigh Nos. 144/9/50/1, 393; Salisbury Nos. 343/80/4; Bournemouth Nos. 345/87; Dorchester No. 381; Yeovil No. 390; Exmouth Junction Nos. 152/3, 383/5/9.

At Guildford Nos. 143/6, 382 shared the Woking-Alton-Gosport goods during the week and the Woking-Portsmouth vans on Sundays.

The class proved very useful for excursion, light passenger and local goods duties, but when called to main line service on summer Saturdays, the small firebox proved wanting and time was almost invariably lost, with delays to other trains.

The Southern District coal returns of August 1911 offer interesting comparisons between the Drummond and Adams mixed traffic classes. Details are:-

No.	Class	Mileage Worked		Coal burnt per mile	Duties
		Passenger	Goods		
149	K10	4,260	647	39.9 lb	
382	K10	2,868	1,028	39.0 lb	Eastleigh, Dorchester,
530	A12	1,417	2,098	33.5 lb	Portsmouth and
537	A12	1,652	1,422	36.7 lb	Woking passenger and
551	A12	1,198	1,299	37.6 lb	goods

'K10' class No. 149 in post-World War 1 livery, with transfer numerals, a Urie smokebox door, conventional firebox, gravity sanding from containers between the frames, boiler barrel clackboxes and a six-wheeled tender, at Brockenhurst with a Bournemouth pick-up goods in July 1922.

Courtesy National Railway Museum

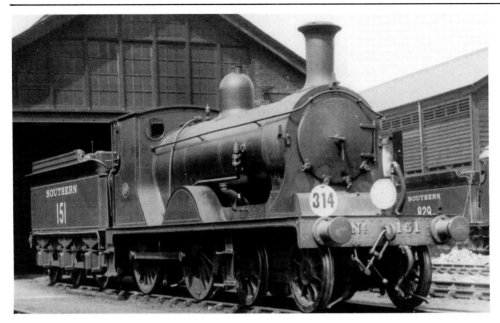

'K10' class No. 151 in post-1931 Southern livery with fluted coupling rods and angled sandbox filler pipes, at Salisbury on 20th March 1935.
H. C. Casserley

647	A12	1,059	2,527	35.3 lb	
343	K10	3,406	380	32.5 lb	
345	K10	2,658	—	34.1 lb	Bournemouth, Salisbury,
155	L11	3,954	20	33.6 lb	Swanage, Eastleigh and
407	L11	2,896	59	34.1 lb	Weymouth passenger and
635	A12	2,286	870	33.4 lb	goods.
645	A12	2,121	1,877	31.6 lb	

These figures suggest that as mixed traffic engines, the Adams 'Jubilee' 0—4—2s were not only equally as capable as the more modern small-wheeled Drummond 4—4—0s, but also considerably more economical to operate.

No spare boilers were available until 1913, when four were constructed at Eastleigh Works and fitted to:-

139 6/1913   387 7/1913   389 4/1913   391 2/1913

There were no dimensional changes, but the fireboxes were without cross water tubes, the clackboxes repositioned on the sides of the barrel and Urie pattern smokebox doors fitted, features which in time appeared on the remainder of the class, although because of a shortage of copper caused by the war, it was 1921-2 before Nos. 153, 329/47/94 lost their Drummond fireboxes. With the removal of the cross water tubes, the 'K10' boiler became interchangeable with classes 'C8', 'M7' (except No. 126) and '700' (saturated).

Nos. 344/7/93 were transferred to Guildford after the outbreak of war for working army stores, horse-box, ammunition and ambulance trains from the Aldershot area to Redhill (SE & CR), while from mid-1915 Nos. 135/44, 380/91 were sub-shedded at Reading (SE & CR) for use on ammunition trains from the Midlands to Portsmouth docks via Alton and the West Meon Valley line. Four, Nos. 149/53, 329/41, were loaned to the Somerset & Dorset Joint Railway from September 1914 to October 1915, while Nos. 135/9, 342/84 were hired by the Midland & South Western Junction Railway in October 1914 for working troop and horse-box specials. No. 342 was returned to Eastleigh Works in November 1915 for attention to a 'burnt' firebox. Nos. 342/84 were released to the South Western in

July 1917 and Nos. 135/9 in March 1919, with the M & SWJR being surcharged £131 11s. 7d. for damage to No. 342's firebox.

All entered Southern Railway stock at Grouping to be painted Maunsell green and receive the E-prefix, details being:-

No.	Southern Livery	E-prefix Removed	No.	Southern Livery	E-prefix Removed
135	11/1924	5/1932	342	2/1924	3/1934
136	1/1924	1/1933	343	11/1925	4/1932
137	7/1925	6/1932	344	4/1926	10/1934
138	6/1925	8/1931	345	7/1925	9/1934
139	8/1924	1/1935	347	11/1924	6/1934
140	6/1925	1/1932	380	8/1925	11/1934
141	4/1925	8/1931	381	3/1924	7/1932
142	2/1924	4/1932	382	9/1925	9/1931
143	5/1924	10/1932	383	2/1924	8/1934
144	4/1926	9/1934	384	12/1924	4/1934
145	7/1926	1/1934	385	11/1924	8/1931
146	3/1926	3/1933	386	10/1926	12/1932
149	10/1924	5/1934	387	8/1926	10/1932
150	7/1925	3/1933	388	7/1925	1/1933
151	11/1924	3/1935	389	11/1925	9/1934
152	12/1924	10/1935	390	5/1924	11/1934
153	3/1924	10/1931	391	4/1926	2/1934
329	2/1924	6/1933	392	11/1925	11/1934
340	12/1924	2/1934	393	12/1924	8/1932
341	12/1924	8/1933	394	4/1925	4/1935

There were no major duty changes until June 1925, when Nos. 137/8/40/1/50, 345/84/8/93/4 were fitted with stovepipe chimneys, reducing the height by 2¾ in. to 13 ft, and transferred to Gillingham to replace withdrawn ex-LC & DR 'M3' class 4—4—0s on the Eastern Section Victoria and Dover stopping services. Unlike the 'T9s' and 'L12s', they did not prove popular; consequently they were ousted by Stirling 'F1s' in April 1926 and sent to Reading for the Waterloo and Redhill services. They also worked the Wednesday Guildford-Redhill-Charing Cross excursions and occasionally piloted the heavy through Birkenhead. At this period the remainder of the class were stationed at: Nine Elms Nos. 142/9, 347/80/6; Feltham Nos. 153, 344/85; Guildford Nos. 343/83; Basingstoke Nos. 341/91; Eastleigh Nos. 139/44/51, 342/81/90; Fratton No. 329; Salisbury Nos. 382/9; Yeovil Nos. 143/5, 340/87; Bournemouth No. 152; Dorchester Nos. 136/46; Exmouth Junction Nos. 135, 392.

In 1925-8 numerous tender exchanges occurred on the Western Section, but only Nos. 135/44, 380/2/91/2 of this class were involved, their 3,500 gallon six-wheeled tenders being transferred to 'T9s' Nos. 726, 282, 729, 281, 303 and 704 in May-September 1928 to permit the latter's use on the Central Section. In exchange the 'K10s' received the 'T9s' double bogie 4,000 gallon tenders.

Around the same period the sandboxes were fitted with tall filler pipes, these being angled outwards over the frames to ease replenishing and avoid spillage of sand on the motion, while some years later, commencing with No. 385 in May 1939, the smokebox wing plates were removed from all except Nos. 138/49/53, 393/4. Drummond pattern chimneys also reappeared on Nos. 137 (January 1946), 140 (November 1946), 345 (September 1934) and 388 (September 1944).

During the 1930s there was gradual reduction in duties until by mid-1939 only a handful remained in the London area, details being:-

Shed	Engine Nos.	Duties
Nine Elms	142/9, 347/80/6	Two booked goods duties: To Guildford via Hampton Court and Cobham; to Chertsey and Walton. Spare engines often substituted for 'L11s' on London area goods.
Feltham	137/9/40/4/53, 383/5	Three booked duties: Local goods to Teddington and Brentford; Early morning workmen's train Waterloo-Winchfield, spending the day on Basingstoke shed and returning to Waterloo in the early evening; Yard shunting at Twickenham and the 4.30 p.m. grammar school special Hampton Court-Twickenham, known to successive generations of patrons as the *Grid*.
Guildford	141, 343/91	One booked duty: Woking-Clapham Junction vans via Staines, Feltham and Kingston (on Wednesdays, Thursdays and Fridays only).
Eastleigh	138/50/1, 341/93/4	No booked duties, but substituted for 'L11s' on local passenger turns and the Dorchester goods. Special duties: Soft fruit vans to Salisbury and Basingstoke; Eastleigh-Newbury race trains.
Andover Junction	342/90	One booked duty: 6.52 a.m. passenger to Southampton, 8.49 a.m. return, 11.27 a.m. to Eastleigh, 3.26 p.m. to Portsmouth and 6.48 p.m. to Romsey.
Fratton	135, 329/88	A two day goods duty to Petersfield, Midhurst, Guildford, Woking and Godalming (shared with 'L11' class).

'K10' class No. 383 at Feltham in July 1937 for London goods and shunting duties. *P. Ransome Wallis, courtesy National Railway Museum*

Salisbury	382/9	No booked duties, but substituted for 'T9s' on the Bournemouth locals and '0395s' on local shunting and transfer goods to Milford Yard.
Bournemouth	136, 345	No booked duties, but appeared regularly on the Swanage branch and the Salisbury locals. Also banked up expresses from Poole to Branksome.
Dorchester	146, 381/7	Two booked duties: 4.55 a.m. Wimborne-Dorchester newspapers, passenger to Broadstone and return, goods to Wareham and 9.27 p.m. Bournemouth Central-Weymouth; Goods to Hamworthy Junction, Ringwood and Bevois Park (two day duty, alternating with an Eastleigh 'L11').
Yeovil	143/5/52, 340/4	Three booked duties: shunting the Town and Junction yards with a return midday Town-Pen Mill passenger; Templecombe and Chard goods; shunting at the junction, goods to Pen Mill and Templecombe, a lengthy spell of shunting at Templecombe and a goods to Yeovil (two day duty).
Exmouth Junction	384/92	No booked duties, but one often sub-shedded at Okehampton for local shunting.

At Poole the banker assisted heavy up trains by buffering against the last carriage and pushing hard to the top of Branksome bank, where it fell away and stopped by the signal box awaiting permission to cross over to the down line and return to wait for the next train. This policy occasionally led to difficulties such as when No. 865 *Sir John Hawkins* accelerated so rapidly away from Poole with the 1.30 p.m. Weymouth-Waterloo on 6th August 1938 that the driver of No. 345 was caught unawares and fell 10 yards behind the last carriage. Then deciding not to risk reconnection, he trundled along the embankment bordering Poole Park looking extremely foolish. Obviously *Sir John Hawkins* did not require assistance, but unfortunately its gigantic effort had repercussions for the Kylchap blast pipe sprayed the embankment and cutting sides with fiery cinders and quickly had the grass ablaze for several hundred yards, delaying other services until the flames could be doused by the local fire brigade.

The Bulleid livery changes first affected the class in May 1939, details being:-

Maunsell green, green and yellow lining, tender numerals: Nos. 345/94 (May 1939).

Maunsell green, black and yellow lining, tender numerals: Nos. 136, 381 (July 1939).

Maunsell green, unlined, Bulleid lettering cabside numerals: Nos. 143, 391 (December 1939); Nos. 386 (February 1940), 138, 343 (March 1940), 137 (April 1940), 140/1 (July 1940), 388 (August 1940).

Malachite green, unlined, Bulleid lettering, cabside numerals: Nos. 153, 389 (January 1941).

All later repaints, commencing with No. 135 in April 1941, were plain black with Bulleid lettering and cabside numerals.

'K10' class No. 136 under repair at Eastleigh Works on 30th July 1939. Because of the works holiday and the outbreak of World War 2, it was one of the last secondary engines to be fully lined.

H. C. Casserley

'K10' class No. 384 with stovepipe chimney and wingplates at Barnstaple Junction in the late 1930s.   *D. H. Wakeley*

In November 1941 Nos. 135/7/8, 388/9 were loaned to the LMS (Midland Division), with Nos. 135, 388/9 being stationed at Bristol and Nos. 137/8 at Gloucester. Classified '2P', they were usually employed shunting at Cheltenham (Lansdown), Evesham, Gloucester and Ashchurch or working pick-up goods, including those to Avonmouth, Tewkesbury, Nailsworth, Yate, Thornbury and Bath. All were repaired at Derby in 1943-4, when No. 388's stove-pipe chimney was replaced by a Drummond pattern procured from Eastleigh Works. In August 1944 Nos. 135/7/8 were transferred to Nottingham and employed working local passenger and goods to Peterborough until returned to the Southern at the end of the year. Nos. 135/8 arrived reclassified '2F', but No. 137 was still '2P'. Nos. 388/9, in surprisingly good condition, remained at Bristol, usually working local goods, until March 1945. No. 394 was also commandeered from September 1941 to August 1942, at first shunting for the War Department at Bulford and later working on the Longmoor Military Railway.

The repair of Western Section engines was the responsibility of Eastleigh Works, but during the war assistance had to be sought from Ashford Works. Ideally, the transfers should have been restricted to two or three classes, but this proved impractical and a full range of engines had to be assigned, including 'K10s' Nos. 143/53, 341/84/93/4. On returning to traffic, they were run-in on the Tonbridge and Hastings slows, local goods and van trains. The journey to and from the Western Section was via Tonbridge, Redhill, Guildford, Alton and the Watercress line. On reaching

Ashford Works, No. 394 was found to have fractured frames and worn out cylinders, so withdrawal was proposed, but this was refused by Eastleigh. Incidentally, it entered works with a stovepipe chimney, smokebox wing plates, red coupling rods and painted Maunsell green.

At this period the mileages worked between heavy repairs were high for such elderly 4−4−0s, details being:

No.	From	To	Mileage
137	4/1940	11/1945	102,449
140	7/1940	10/1946	93,763
142	10/1944	6/1946	97,799
143	12/1939	12/1944	113,395
329	9/1937	11/1945	115,317
386	2/1940	11/1945	120,480
387	9/1938	9/1944	123,908
394	5/1939	1/1946	136,875

On 25th February 1946 there was a violent collision in Eastleigh goods yard between No. 151 and 'S15' No. 827, the latter having lost control of a 47 wagon Micheldever-Bournemouth goods and been diverted into the sidings, where the unfortunate 'K10' happened to be standing on the same line. It was thrown over onto its side and severely battered, but surprisingly was repaired and returned to traffic.

In 1947 Nos. 136/8/49, 342/4/7/81/7/8 were laid aside, leaving 31 to enter British Railways stock at Nationalisation, when withdrawal was so rapid that only one, No. 382, was renumbered in the 30,000 series. Nos. 384/9 were the last

'K10' class No. 137 in wartime black livery, and still carrying the stove-pipe chimney fitted for service on the Eastern Section in 1925, at Exeter on 31st August 1945. Note the removal of the smokebox wingplates. *H. C. Casserley*

in service, the former shunting at Wimbledon and working the Sunningdale goods from Feltham until sent to join No. 389 at Yeovil in April 1951. The two then shared the Templecombe goods until No. 389 failed in July 1951. Officially No. 384 had already been condemned, but, remaining serviceable, the Yeovil shedmaster saw no reason for rustication and surreptitiously rostered it for the Town-Junction services or the Templecombe and Blandford goods before obeying the summons for breaking up in mid-August 1951.

ENGINE SUMMARY

No.	Date	Order No.	Withdrawn
135	9/1902	V10	5/1949
136	9/1902	V10	1/1947
137	9/1902	A11	8/1949
138	10/1902	A11	1/1947
139	10/1902	A11	10/1948
140	10/1902	A11	1/1950
141	11/1902	A11	10/1949
142	11/1902	C11	1/1950
143	11/1902	C11	9/1948
144	11/1902	C11	7/1949
145	12/1902	C11	10/1948
146	12/1902	C11	2/1948
149	12/1902	E11	1/1947
150	12/1902	E11	2/1948
151	12/1902	E11	2/1950
152	12/1902	E11	2/1949

No.	Date	Order No.	Withdrawn
153	1/1903	E11	2/1949
329	11/1901	K10	4/1950
340	11/1901	K10	6/1948
341	12/1901	K10	12/1949
342	12/1901	K10	1/1947
343	12/1901	K10	1/1948
344	1/1902	L10	1/1947
345	2/1902	L10	9/1949
347	3/1902	L10	1/1947
380	4/1902	P10	6/1949
381	4/1902	P10	6/1947
382	5/1902	P10	8/1950
383	5/1902	P10	6/1949
384	5/1902	P10	6/1951
385	5/1902	S10	1/1949
386	6/1902	S10	8/1949
387	6/1902	S10	3/1947
388	6/1902	S10	4/1947
389	6/1902	S10	7/1951
390	6/1902	V10	10/1950
391	7/1902	V10	10/1949
392	7/1902	V10	10/1948
393	4/1902	L10	1/1949
394	4/1902	L10	5/1949

All built at Nine Elms Works. Disposal: Nos. 137/40/2/4/51, 341/5/86 broken up at Horley, Nos. 136/8/49, 342/4/81/7/8 at Dinton and the remainder at Eastleigh Works. Mileages: Nos. 135 — 1,116,768; 153 — 1,206,747; 329 — 1,268,493; 382 — 1,249,769; 387 — 1,190,164; 394 — 1,226,531.

'L11' class mixed traffic 4—4—0 No. 166 as built with transfer numerals, firebox water tubes, conventional gravity sanding and a 3,500 gallon six-wheeled tender, at Nine Elms in May 1904.

F. Burtt

'L11' Class

As mixed traffic engines the 'K10s' gave adequate, if unpretentious service, but failed dismally as main line reliefs in the busy summer months for even skilled firing failed to supply sufficient steam, and delays to following services were common. As a result, when more small-wheeled 4—4—0s were required in 1903, Drummond lengthened the coupled wheelbase by 1 ft and fitted the larger and more capable 'T9' class boiler. Known as the 'L11' class, forty of these 'stretched' mixed traffic engines were constructed by Nine Elms Works at an average cost of £2,200 each between May 1903 and June 1907. Numbered 134/48/54-9/61/3-75, 405-14/35-42, they had the following dimensions:

Cylinders	18½″ x 26″
Bogie wheels	3′ 7″
Coupled wheels	5′ 7″
Wheelbase	6′ 6″ + 6′ 9″ + 10′ 0″ = 23′ 3″
Boiler diameter	4′ 5″
Boiler length	10′ 6″ (Tubeplates 10′ 9 ³⁄₈″)
Firebox length	7′ 4″
Heating surfaces:	
Tubes (280 x 1½″)	1,187 sq. ft.
Firebox	148 sq. ft.
Crosswater tubes	165 sq. ft.
Total	1,500 sq. ft.

Working pressure	175 lb.
Grate area	24 sq. ft.
Weights in working order:	
Bogie	15T 2C
Leading coupled wheels	18T 10C
Trailing coupled wheels	16T 19C
Engine total	50T 11C
Tender (3,500 gallons)	39T 12C
Engine & tender	90T 3C

Forty double bogie 4,000 gallon tenders weighing 44 tons 17 cwt were ordered and built for the class, but only nine, Nos. 174/5 and 407-13, were actually attached to them, the remainder of the class being allotted second-hand six-wheel 3,500 gallon tenders weighing 39 tons 12 cwt. Details of the latter are:- Nos. 155/7/64/9/71, 405/38/41 from 'C8' class Nos. 290/2/3/5-9; Nos. 134/48/54/6/8/9/61/3/5-8/70/2/3, 406/14/35-7/9/40/2 from 'T9' class Nos. 113/5/6/9/20, 280/1/3-5, 703/4/7/9/15/6/8/21-4/30/73.

The new double bogie tenders provided for Nos. 174/5, 407-13 were equipped with exhaust steam heating and consequently these engines were fitted with Duplex pumps instead of injectors. By this date Drummond had abandoned numberplates and steam sanding, so all entered traffic with cabside transfer numerals and gravity sanding, while the

'L11' class No. 158 as built.

'L11' class No. 168 showing the standard Drummond 14 ft wheelbase six-wheeled tender with coal rails, toolboxes, carriage heating and vacuum brake hoses, rear panelling, buffer beam numerals and three link coupling.   *F. Burtt*

crank axles of the 1904-7 'F12', 'K13', 'M13', 'P13' and 'S13' series were balanced.

In traffic the class proved as great an advance on the 'K10s' as the 'T9s' had over the 'C8s'; consequently they performed considerably more secondary main line passenger, excursion and relief duties than their predecessors. There was also a tendency to concentrate the class at the larger running sheds, the mid-1907 allocation being: Nine Elms Nos. 154/6/7/70/2, 407-9/11/3/39/42; Strawberry Hill Nos. 405/35/6/40; Eastleigh Nos. 169, 406/14; Salisbury Nos. 148/61/3/5/6; Exmouth Junction Nos. 159/71/4/5, 437/8; Fratton Nos. 164/8, 441; Bournemouth Nos. 410/2; in Nine Elms Works (repair) Nos. 134/55/8/67/73. To distinguish the class from the 'K10s', the men referred to them as the 'Large Hoppers'.

Despite the intense rivalry, there was a regular interchange of traffic with the LB & SCR and since that company employed the air brake, it was necessary for the South Western to provide a number of dual-braked engines. At first these duties were performed by 'Jubilees' Nos. 529/38/54-6, but as the number and loadings of these exchange workings increased, they were augmented by 'T9s' Nos. 337/8 in October 1901 and 'L11s' Nos. 440/1 in March 1910. On the latter the air pump was attached to the left side of the smokebox. These fittings were removed from No. 440 in August 1934 and No. 441 in September 1937.

Like the Stanier 'Black 5s' in later years, the 'L11s' before the First World War could be found working every type of train, except the best expresses and the heaviest main line goods. Nine Elms regularly rostered the class for the Waterloo-Alton-Southampton services, the Portsmouth and Basingstoke semi-fasts, race specials, ocean liner expresses, milk trains and London area goods, while in the West Country, they worked most of the North Cornwall, North Devon and Plymouth stopping passenger and goods services as well as the Exmouth Junction-Nine Elms fish specials.

After Urie took office, the Duplex pumps of Nos. 174/5, 407-13 were replaced by hot water injectors, while all received that engineer's smokebox door and boiler barrel clackboxes. When firebox renewal became necessary from March 1916, the replacements were without the cross water tubes, but because of the war this proved a lengthy process with Nos. 157/64/9, 406/10-2/36-8 still retaining the Drummond pattern at Grouping. It finally disappeared from No. 410 in February 1926.

In October 1922 Urie authorised the superheating of Nos. 174/5, 407-13/40-1, the 4,000 gallon tender or dual-braked series, when next in Eastleigh Works for heavy boiler attention, but this was cancelled by Maunsell, who reasoned that the expense could not be justified in view of their secondary duties.

All entered Southern Railway stock at Grouping to be painted Maunsell green and receive the E-prefix, while in 1925-7 those having 3,500 gallon six-wheel tenders, except dual-braked Nos. 440/1, had them replaced by the 4,000

'L11' class No. 441 in post-World War 1 livery with a Urie smokebox door, conventional firebox and the Westinghouse brake, at Nine Elms on 21st April 1923.

H. C. Casserley

'L11' class No. 169 in Urie livery with boiler barrel clackboxes, but still retaining firebox water tubes at Eastleigh on 19th May 1923.

H. C. Casserley

'L11' class No. 437 in early Southern livery, without the E-prefix or small cabside numerals, at Plymouth on 12th July 1924.

H. C. Casserley

gallon double bogie pattern. The dates when this occurred and when the E-prefix was discarded are:-

No.	Southern Livery	E-prefix Discarded	Double Bogie Tender
134	2/1928	5/1934	10/1925 (b)
148	11/1923	8/1932	1/1925 (d)
154	2/1925	7/1931	5/1925 (d)
155	1/1925	4/1932	11/1925 (d)
156	1/1925	7/1933	1/1925 (d)
157	7/1925	7/1933	8/1925 (c)
158	2/1926	9/1933	9/1925 (b)
159	5/1924	7/1933	10/1925 (b)
161	12/1924	12/1931	5/1925 (b)
163	10/1925	10/1932	6/1925 (b)
164	1/1926	12/1931	11/1925 (c)
165	4/1925	8/1933	8/1925 (b)
166	9/1924	5/1935	3/1927 (c)
167	3/1924	10/1931	7/1925 (d)
168	7/1924	11/1933	8/1925 (d)
169	11/1923	9/1933	9/1926 (c)
170	11/1923	5/1934	7/1925 (d)
171	1/1927	9/1932	7/1925 (d)
172	1/1925	1/1935	2/1925 (d)
173	12/1923	10/1932	7/1925 (b)
174	10/1927	11/1933	when built
175	12/1924	7/1934	when built
405	11/1925	7/1934	11/1925 (c)
406	7/1925	10/1933	6/1925 (b)
407	10/1924	6/1931	when built
408	3/1926	12/1934	when built
409	12/1924	5/1934	when built
410	2/1926	10/1932	when built
411	6/1924	8/1934	when built
412	7/1926	7/1932	when built
413	11/1924	7/1934	when built
414	7/1924	11/1932	9/1926 (c)
435	6/1926	7/1931	6/1925 (c)
436	1/1926	3/1932	11/1926 (c)
437	11/1923	10/1933	7/1926 (c)
438	6/1925	8/1931	7/1925 (d)
439	9/1924	7/1933	4/1926 (c)
440	11/1924	8/1934	(a)
441	4/1926	6/1934	(a)
442	7/1925	1/1935	7/1925 (b)

(a) Retained 3,500 gallon six-wheel tenders.

(b) Nos. 134/58/9/61/3/5/73, 406/42 received 4,000 gallon tenders from 'L12s' Nos. 416/7/9/21/2/4/5/30/3, when the latter were provided with 3,500 gallon six-wheel tenders for service on the Eastern Section in mid-1925.

(c) Nos. 157/64/6/9, 405/14/35-7/9 received 4,500 gallon double bogie tenders from 'D15s' Nos. 463-72 in 1925-6, when the latter were fitted with 13 ft wheelbase 3,500 gallon six-wheel tenders from the '700' goods prior to being transferred to Fratton for the Portsmouth-Waterloo services. The capacity of the tenders fitted to Nos. 169, 414/36/7 was reduced to 4,000 gallons by the removal of the well in 1930-2. During the Second World War the tenders of Nos. 157/64/6, 405/35/9 were similarly modified.

(d) Nos. 148/54-6/67/8/70-2, 438 received their 4,000 gallon tenders from 'T9s' Nos. 300/1/4/7/10-4/36, when the latter were transferred to the Eastern Section in 1925.

'L11' class No. E410 in Southern Railway livery, passing Clapham Junction with a Southampton boat express in April 1926.

H. Gordon Tidey

After receiving Southern livery, Nos. 134/71 exchanged tenders with LSWR liveried 'L12' No. 433 and 'T9' No. 311, which left the 'L11s' with small cabside numberplates and tenders without numerals, a deficiency which Eastleigh Works ingeniously overcame by adding LSWR style numerals to the cab sidesheets. No. 134 regained full Southern livery in February 1928 and No. 171 in January 1927.

Around the same period all, except No. 169, had tall filler pipes fitted to the sand containers, these being angled outwards over the frames to ease replenishment and avoid spillage on the motion. Some years later, commencing with No. 166 in June 1939, the smokebox wingplates were removed; again one engine, No. 174, escaped modification.

In June 1939 the allocation and duties were:-

Shed	Engine Nos.	Duties
Nine Elms	154-6/68, 409/11/3/4/35	Weekdays: Five booked duties, almost entirely local goods and shunting in the area bounded by Staines, Epsom and Chessington. Saturdays: 11.57 a.m. Waterloo-Brockenhurst (for Lymington Pier). Specials: Waterloo-Bramshot Halt workmen's trains (for Lindsay & Parkinson Ltd. constructing an army camp).
Feltham	158/67, 412/39/42	Weekdays: Three goods turns to Sunningdale, Guildford via Chertsey and Hounslow Loop. Spare engines often relieved the '0395' class in Feltham yard or on transfer goods. Saturdays: Two main line passenger turns, 1.24 p.m. Waterloo - Basingstoke and 4.52 p.m. return; 2.52 p.m. Waterloo - Basingstoke vans and 7.40 p.m. semi-fast. Sundays: 9.54 a.m. and 12.24 p.m. Waterloo-Basingstoke, returning at 1.44 p.m. and 6.40 p.m. respectively.
Basingstoke	407	'L11' or Adams 'T6', Farnborough pick-up goods.
Fratton	164/6/72, 441	Two goods duties, one covering Fareham and Gosport, the other Midhurst and Guildford. Saturdays: 2.05 p.m. Portsmouth Harbour-Basingstoke (through Birmingham, returning at 6.00 p.m.)
Eastleigh	148/57/9/71/4, 408/40	Six weekday turns, mainly passenger to Portsmouth, Fawley and Andover, also to Reading on Mondays only and a long goods turn to Dorchester. Saturdays: A passenger to Bournemouth and back with vans to Basingstoke. Sundays: 9.42 a.m. Fareham-Bournemouth and 5.35 p.m. Bournemouth West-Eastleigh.
Andover	169	Weekdays: 'L11' or 'Jubilee', Test Valley goods. Sundays: Three return passenger trips to Eastleigh.
Bournemouth	165/73, 438	Weekdays: Poole-Ringwood-Brockenhurst goods. Saturdays: Working through trains over the Lymington branch. Sundays: 8.05 a.m. Bournemouth Central-Eastleigh, returning on 5.45 p.m. Southampton Terminus-Bournemouth West.
Dorchester	410	No booked duty, but often substituted for 'K10s' on the Eastleigh goods or Wimborne-Dorchester newspapers.
Salisbury	405/37	Two duties: One passenger to Portsmouth and back to Southampton, then Eastleigh-Salisbury goods, the other a goods to Wimborne, returning on milk vans.
Yeovil	134/63, 436	One booked duty: Shunting at Yeovil Junction, pick-up goods to Sidmouth Junction, light engine to Chard for milk van shunting and light back to Yeovil (sometimes worked by 'S11' class). Spare engines employed piloting up stone ballast trains to Salisbury or Woking.
Exmouth Junction	161/70/5	Three booked duties: Goods to Torrington and return; goods to Barnstaple and back on 5.20 p.m. Exeter passenger; goods to the Barnstaple-Bideford area and some local passenger trains, including the 8.22 a.m. Eggesford-Barnstaple (a two day duty alternating with a Barnstaple 'N' class 2—6—0).
Okehampton	406	Local shunting and carriage piloting (a former '0395' class duty).

The Bulleid livery changes first affected the class in May 1939, details being:-

Maunsell green, light green and yellow lining, tender numerals: No. 173 (May 1939).

Maunsell green, black and yellow lining, tender numerals: Nos. 166 (June 1939), 407 (August 1939), 439 (July 1939).

Maunsell green, black and yellow lining, Bulleid lettering, cabside numerals: No. 174 (September 1939).

Maunsell green, unlined, Bulleid lettering, cabside numerals: Nos. 406/37/40 (November 1939); Nos. 409 (January 1940), 148 (February 1940), 161/75 (April 1940), 165 (July 1940), 171 (August 1940), 408/35 (September 1940); Nos. 157/8, 441 (February 1941), 164 (March 1941).

Malachite green, unlined, Bulleid lettering, cabside numerals: Nos. 170 (November 1940), 410 (October 1940), 169 (December 1940).

All later repaints, commencing with Nos. 134, 414 in April 1941, were plain black until after Nationalisation.

During the war years, with many 4—6—0s and the 'S11' 4—4—0s away on loan, the class was kept extremely busy, not only working secondary passenger, local goods and van services, but also troop and ambulance specials, main line goods and relief expresses, while west of Exeter the Ilfracombe services were practically monopolised. On 17th November 1940 No. 440 had a lucky escape when heading the 5.35 p.m. Portsmouth-Salisbury (Cardiff through train) into Woolston for without warning a German fighter-bomber suddenly appeared and dropped a 250 lb bomb on the train, destroying the leading carriage and killing one passenger. Later the same month Nos. 409/14 were badly scorched by incendiaries at Nine Elms and No. 412 was strafed by a fighter near Pokesdown on 1st June 1941, but otherwise the class escaped hostilities unscathed. For such elderly 4—4—0s the mileages worked between general repairs were high, instances being:-

No.	From	To	Mileage
168	9/1939	5/1945	126,513
173	5/1939	1/1945	128,327
175	4/1940	7/1945	129,539
406	11/1939	1/1945	101,554
407	8/1939	12/1945	139,390
410	10/1940	5/1945	104,995

All repairs were normally received at Eastleigh Works, but during the war this was not always possible and Nos. 164 (August 1945), 174 (November 1944), 407 (January 1946) and 408 (September 1945) had to be sent to Ashford Works, while intermediate repairs were given by Nine Elms, Bournemouth, Guildford and Exmouth Junction sheds.

After VE day an acute shortage of steam coal caused the Government to grant funds for the conversion of 110 Southern Railway tender engines, including 'L11s' Nos. 148/54/5/7/66/8/70/2, 407/8/10/1/3/4/37, to oil-burning, but before the programme could be fully implemented the lack of foreign currency severely curtailed oil imports and caused the scheme's abandonment. As a result only Nos. 148/54/5/7/70/2, 411/37 saw service as oil-burners, details being:-

No.	Date	Electric Lighting
148	9/1947	11/1947
154	10/1947	10/1947
155	10/1947	10/1947

'L11' class No. 30442 in early British Railways lined black livery with lettered double bogie tender, unlined splashers, smokebox number-plate, angled sand container filler pipes and the Urie power classification below the cabside numerals, at Eastleigh on 9th October 1948. *Author*

No.	Date	Electric Lighting
157	10/1947	10/1947
170	10/1947	1/1948
172	9/1947	3/1948
411	8/1947	3/1948
437	7/1947	1/1948

All retained double bogie tenders, upon which the cumbersome rectangular oil tanks were perched precariously. At the rear of these tanks and on the tender sides the steps were fabricated from steel tubing similar to the Bulleid classes, while the electric generator was mounted on the left-hand platform alongside the firebox.

Most were stationed at Eastleigh and employed on that shed's passenger, van and goods duties to Portsmouth, Andover Junction, Salisbury, Fawley, Bournemouth and Alton. Nos. 170/2 were shedded at Fratton for local goods and yard piloting. By late September 1948 a shortage of oil fuel had caused all to be laid aside in store, never to be steamed again. No. 411, noted at Brockenhurst with vans on 30th November, was probably the last in service.

'L11' class No. 172 as an oil-burner with a double bogie tender, pre-fabricated laddering, electric lighting, fluted coupling rods, the smoke-box wingplates removed and painted black, at Eastleigh in August 1951. *P. Ransome Wallis, courtesy National Railway Museum*

'L11' class No. 30164 heading a lengthy goods at Feltham on 22nd March 1951, in wartime black livery with BR numberplate and Southern lettered double bogie tender.
J. F. Russell-Smith courtesy NRM

All entered British Railways stock at Nationalisation, when sixteen were renumbered into the 30,000 series and Nos. 30171/5, 30438/42 painted lined black. Details are:-

No.	Date	No.	Date
134	11/1948	174	1/1951
156	6/1948 (a)	175	12/1948 (c)
159	5/1948 (a)	405	2/1949
163	12/1949	406	10/1948
164	9/1949	407	5/1948
166	8/1948	409	2/1949
171	5/1949 (c)	438	1/1949 (c)
173	5/1948	442	9/1948 (b)

(a) Nos. 30156/9 painted plain black with the tender lettered 'British Railways'. (b) No. 30442 painted lined black with the tender lettered 'British Railways'. (c) Nos. 30171/5, 30438 painted lined black, tender unlettered and without totems.

The allocation of the 32 coal-burners in mid-1948 was:- Nine Elms Nos. 406/35/42; Feltham Nos. 158/67/74; Guildford Nos. 165/8, 438; Basingstoke No. 30407; Eastleigh Nos. 30159, 169/71/5; Bournemouth No. 30173; Fratton Nos. 164/6, 413/4/41; Dorchester Nos. 161, 410/40; Salisbury No. 405; Yeovil Nos. 134/63, 412; Exmouth Junction Nos. 30156, 408/9/36/9. By this date there was an appreciable reduction in duties, with few involving passenger trains. Nine Elms had two booked goods, one covering the Chessington branch and the other serving Hampton Court and Cobham, while at Feltham only the Windsor, Twickenham and Kington goods remained. Away

from the London area, Eastleigh still employed the class on local goods to Southampton, Fawley and Andover Junction, while No. 159 was sub-shedded at Andover for the Test Valley and Longparish goods, a reduced activity which led to Nos. 439/40 being withdrawn in May 1949 and heavy repairs ceasing with No. 30171 the same month.

Nos. 408 and 30409 were the last working in the West of England, the former being sub-shedded at Okehampton for local shunting while No. 30409 usually had charge of the Barnstaple goods. Probably the final passenger working occurred on 18th September 1950, when No. 408 piloted No. 34010 *Sidmouth* on the 8.42 a.m. Exeter-Plymouth. It was laid aside at Exmouth Junction on 11th January 1951 and despatched to Eastleigh Works for breaking up on 13th February, but No. 30409 remained working local goods, ballasting and shunting at Okehampton until withdrawn with a mileage of 1,261,984 on 14th June 1951.

Nos. 30171/5, 30442 were the last to work from Eastleigh, the only booked duty being the Fawley goods, although occasionally they travelled further afield with specials, one of which took No. 30175 to Salisbury with empty ballast hoppers on 28th October 1951 and thence to Templecombe with coal empties, where a day was spent shunting before piloting a goods to Bath to collect vans for Eastleigh, which were worked home over the Somerset and Dorset line. No. 30442's last working is equally worthy of note for after being officially condemned on 15th November 1951, it was observed heading the 3.15 p.m.

'L11' class No. 30171 at Eastleigh on 11th June 1949 in early British Railways lined black livery, with plain tender sides.   *Author*

goods to Andover Junction on 22nd November, yet at 11.30 a.m. next day it was being stripped at the rear of Eastleigh Works in preparation for breaking up. The class was now extinct, except for the derelict oil-burners Nos. 148/57/70/2, 411/37, which through oversight were not condemned until the following year. This hurried withdrawal and that of the 'S11s' left Eastleigh with insufficient mixed traffic motive power, so until the BR class '4' 2—6—0s and class '3' 2—6—2 tanks became available, use had to be made of 'Ls' and L1s' transferred from the Eastern Section.

ENGINE SUMMARY

No.	Date	Order No.	Withdrawn
134	4/1904	D12	2/1951
148	5/1904	D12	3/1952
154	5/1903	L11	3/1951
155	5/1903	L11	3/1951
156	6/1903	L11	4/1951
157	6/1903	L11	3/1952
158	6/1903	L11	11/1950
159	9/1903	O11	3/1951
161	9/1903	O11	2/1950
163	10/1903	O11	10/1951
164	10/1903	O11	9/1951
165	11/1903	O11	4/1951
166	4/1904	D12	7/1950
167	5/1904	D12	9/1949
168	5/1904	D12	2/1950

No.	Date	Order No.	Withdrawn
169	8/1904	F12	7/1949
170	8/1904	F12	6/1952
171	9/1904	F12	8/1951
172	9/1904	F12	6/1952
173	10/1904	F12	4/1951
174	5/1906	K13	7/1951
175	6/1906	K13	11/1951
405	9/1906	P13	1/1951
406	10/1906	P13	5/1951
407	5/1906	K13	10/1950
408	5/1906	K13	2/1951
409	6/1906	K13	6/1951
410	6/1906	M13	12/1949
411	6/1906	M13	6/1952
412	7/1906	M13	11/1950
413	8/1906	M13	2/1951
414	8/1906	M13	4/1951
435	11/1906	P13	11/1949
436	11/1906	P13	7/1951
437	12/1906	P13	6/1952
438	3/1907	S13	5/1951
439	3/1907	S13	5/1949
440	4/1907	S13	5/1949
441	5/1907	S13	4/1951
442	6/1907	S13	11/1951

All built at Nine Elms Works. Disposal: Nos. 148/57/70/2, 411/37 broken up at Ashford Works, No. 163 at Brighton Works, Nos. 167/8, 410/35 at Horley and the remainder at Eastleigh Works. Mileages: Nos. 134 — 1,264,114; 156 — 1,413,287; 175 — 1,364,814; 408 — 1,239,687; 438 — 1,112,948.

'S11' Class

The ten engines forming the class were intended for the Exeter-Plymouth services, the Waterloo-Portsmouth semifasts and the Exeter-Salisbury market goods, and therefore were provided with 6 ft. 1 in. coupled wheels, 5 ft. boilers and 19 in. cylinders. Numbered 395-404, they were completed by Nine Elms Works between June and December 1903 at a cost of £2,455 each and had the following dimensions:-

Cylinders	19″ x 26″
Bogie wheels	3′ 7″
Coupled wheels	6′ 1″
Wheelbase	6′ 6″ + 6′ 9″ + 10′ 0″ = 23′ 3″
Boiler diameter	5′ 0″
Boiler length	10′ 6″ (Tubeplates 10′ 9 3/8″)
Firebox length	7′ 4″
Heating surfaces:	
Tubes (247 x 1¾″)	1,222 sq. ft.
Firebox	163 sq. ft.
Cross water tubes	165 sq. ft.
Total	1,550 sq. ft.
Working pressure	175 lb.
Grate area	24 sq. ft.

Weights in working order:

Bogie	17T 0C
Leading coupled wheels	18T 0C
Trailing coupled wheels	17T 0C
Engine total	52T 0C
Tender	44T 17C
Engine & tender	96T 17C

The boiler and firebox lengths were similar to the 'T9s' and 'L11s', but the diameter was 7 in. greater which, together with the 9 in. higher pitching, necessitated the chimney and dome being considerably shorter than any previous Drummond class. The cab and splashers were of the wide pattern fitted to the final 'T9' series and the 'L11' class, while the firebox had sixty-one 2¾ in. cross water tubes, in pods of 36 and 25. The Webb pattern firebox door had a notched sector with a spring-loaded plunger at the top, enabling it to be fixed at any desired position. These fittings also held the door securely, but not inflexibly, a necessity with fireboxes containing cross water tubes for should a burst occur it was essential that the sudden change of pressure would snap the door shut before

'S11' class mixed traffic 4—4—0 under construction at Nine Elms Works in May 1903.

C. H. Eden

'S11' class No. 395 in shops grey outside Nine Elms Works on 27th June 1903.

'S11' class No. 397 leaving Waterloo with the 3.00 p.m. West of England express in 1904.

Lens of Sutton

the footplate became enveloped by scalding hot water and flames. Other Drummond classes having cross water tube fireboxes were similarly equipped. The steel crank shaft was balanced, the webs being extended to counteract the crank pins and thereby removing the need for driving wheel balance weights. The 4,000 gallon tender was without exhaust steam heating tubes, so the boiler feed was cold by means of injectors and clackboxes at the base of the front tubeplate.

Nos. 395/6, 400 went new to Exmouth Junction, Nos. 397/9 to Plymouth, No. 398 to Fratton, Nos. 401/2 to Nine Elms and Nos. 403/4 to Salisbury, but by March 1906 Nos. 397/8 had been transferred to Wadebridge and Nos. 403/4 to Fratton. Despite only differing from the 'L12s' by having smaller driving wheels, they were never considered their equal, while many crews preferred 'T9s' for passenger service. As a result, apart from those stationed at Fratton and Wadebridge, the class was mainly employed working van, milk and goods trains.

Because of this unpopularity and the often mundane duties, there was scant attention given by the railway journalists and observers of the period, consequently the Southern District coal returns of August 1911 are particularly important. Details are:-

FRATTON SHED PORTSMOUTH-WATERLOO PASSENGER

No.	Class	Mileage Worked	Coal burnt per mile	Remarks
396	S11	4,039	36.6 lb	Ex-Eastleigh Works 2/1911.
400	S11	–	–	In works, 80,039 miles since previous general repair.
402	S11	3,930	34.9 lb	Ex-Eastleigh Works 1/7/1911.
403	S11	3,912	42.5 lb	Mileage 72,634.
296	C8	3,927	37.2 lb	On loan for the summer traffic.
299	C8	4,003	36.0 lb	
713	T9	3,930	33.2 lb	Ex-Eastleigh Works 15/7/1911.
728	T9	4,112	31.8 lb	Ex-Eastleigh Works 3/6/1911.
558	T3	4,597	42.6 lb	Mileage 69,427.
659	X6	4,139	38.4 lb	Ex-Eastleigh Works 8/1910.

As expected, the two 'T9s' had the best coal consumption, but 'C8s' Nos. 296/7 and 'X6' No. 659 performed more than adequately over this difficult line.

No details are available for those stationed at Plymouth and Exmouth Junction, but in April 1912 Wadebridge's Nos. 397/8 featured in a report of that shed's passenger and goods mileages. Details are:-

'S11' class No. 399, photographed in 1909 in Eastleigh Works yard, with cross water tubes cover removed and stowed on the front platform.

J. E. Kite Collection

No.	Mileage worked			Coal burnt per mile (lb)		Oil & tallow used per 100 miles (lb)	
	Passenger	Goods	Total	Allowed	Actual	Allowed	Actual
397	2,164	1,009	3,173	38.0	43.7	4½	6.3
398	1,987	1,238	3,225	38.0	44.5	4½	6.8

Figures for 'Jubilees' employed on similar duties are:-

598	2,461	1,123	3,584	36.0	37.7	4½	5.1
647	2,502	964	3,466	36.0	38.1	4½	5.4

These details suggest why the Adams 'Jubilees' were more popular than the Drummond small-wheeled 4—4—0s.

No spare boilers were available for classes 'L12' and 'S11' until 1914, when three were built by Eastleigh Works and fitted to 'L12s' Nos. 417/8/20. They differed from the original series by having conventional fireboxes, five fewer tubes, barrel clackboxes and Urie pattern smokebox doors, changes which were made to the earlier boilers when heavy repairs became necessary.

During the First World War, with the 'H15s' and Drummond 4—6—0s mainly engaged working troop, van and goods specials for the Armed Forces, the 'S11s' returned to passenger service and with the 'L12s' played an extremely important role for they were the largest engines with almost universal route availability. Therefore both classes could work over all the main lines as well as the 'old road' to Weymouth, the Swanage and Lymington branches, and the secondary routes via Fordingbridge, the Meon Valley and Alresford over which the 'D15s' and 4—6—0s were banned.

As a result it is not surprising that Urie decided to superheat the 'S11s' instead of classes 'G14' and 'P14'. The order

was placed in November 1917, but, because of difficulties caused by the war, there was a lengthy delay before work could commence and it was May 1920 when the first, No. 399, left Eastleigh Works. In addition to the superheater, it was fitted with an extended smokebox, a lipped chimney with a capuchon and a Detroit four-feed lubricator. The changed dimensions were:-

Tubes, small (138 x 1¾")	682 sq. ft.
large (21 x 5¼")	311 sq. ft.
Firebox	161 sq. ft.
Total evaporative	1,154 sq. ft.
Superheater	195 sq. ft.
Total	1,349 sq. ft.
Weights in working order:	
Bogie	18T 2C
Leading coupled wheels	18T 10C
Trailing coupled wheels	17T 3C
Total	53T 15C

Details of superheating:-

395	7/1921	396	4/1922	397	8/1921	398	7/1922
399	5/1920	400	6/1921	401	2/1922	402	7/1922
403	10/1921	404	12/1921				

After superheating, No. 397 was transferred to Yeovil for the London milk vans, while the others were stationed at: Nine Elms Nos. 395, 402; Fratton No. 396, 400/1/3; Salisbury No. 398; Exmouth Junction Nos. 399, 404. Those at Fratton worked to both Waterloo and Salisbury, but Nine Elms restricted Nos. 395, 402 to the Portsmouth semi-fasts, leaving the best services to the 'L12s'. In mid-

1923 Nos. 396/9 were on loan to Bournemouth and employed on the Weymouth services and the through trains to Oxford, while No. 402 was recorded on the Waterloo-Weymouth Saturday extras via the 'old road'.

All entered Southern Railway stock at Grouping to be painted Maunsell green and receive the E-prefix, details being:-

395	10/1924	396	2/1924	397	3/1925	398	11/1924
399	9/1924	400	9/1924	401	6/1927	402	12/1924
403	3/1924	404	8/1924					

In mid-1924 the 'S11s' and 'L12s' were passed for use over the Mid-Sussex line and in July commenced working the Saturday Waterloo-Portsmouth Harbour reliefs via Raynes Park, Epsom and Horsham. At the same time Fratton began rostering both classes for the Victoria and London Bridge services via Three Bridges and Sutton. For some reason the Waterloo services failed to gain approval and were withdrawn after the 1926 season, but the latter lasted until the route was electrified. The 'L12s' and to a lesser degree the 'S11s', also appeared on the summer Sunday and bank holiday excursions from Wimbledon, Surbiton and other Western Section suburban stations to Littlehampton and Bognor via Epsom, services which proved so popular that on August bank holiday 1928 no less then seven were run, headed by Nos. 398, 415/20/6/8/32/3.

In 1925-6 the 'D15s' were fitted with six-wheel tenders and transferred to Fratton for the Waterloo services, thereby releasing Nos. 396/9, 401/3 to Exmouth Junction for the North Cornwall and Plymouth trains and No. 402 to Yeovil for a daily return duty to Portsmouth via Salisbury. Fratton retained Nos. 400/4 for the Portsmouth-Salisbury services and occasional Central Section duties. For several years No. 401 was sub-shedded at Wadebridge for working the through Waterloo carriages of the principal day express to Exeter. It could just be accommodated by the Padstow turntable, although the drop of the rear pair of tender wheels was clearly visible throughout the operation.

Commencing with No. 396 in November 1925, the Eastleigh superheaters were replaced by the Maunsell pattern and smokebox snifting valves fitted, while all new chimneys were without capuchons. Later in 1931-3 the E-prefix was discarded as engines passed through Eastleigh Works for heavy repairs. Dates for this and the superheater change are:-

No.	E-prefix removed	Maunsell superheater	No.	E-prefix removed	Maunsell superheater
395	9/1932	2/1930	400	3/1932	11/1931
396	9/1933	11/1925	401	11/1932	4/1930
397	9/1933	1/1931	402	7/1931	3/1929
398	3/1932	5/1930	403	11/1931	10/1929
399	6/1933	1/1931	404	8/1933	2/1931

Superheated 'S11' No. 401 entering Guildford with an up Portsmouth semi-fast on 16th May 1925.   *H. C. Casserley*

'S11' No. E397 about to leave Eastleigh Works after repair and a repaint on 25th August 1928.

S. Nash collection

In March 1932 Nos. 397/8 joined No. 402 at Yeovil, but their stay was brief for by mid-year they had been replaced by 'U' class 2—6—0s Nos. 1790-2 and sent away to Bournemouth where the summer months were spent working the through Brighton and Great Western trains. When the winter timetable commenced little regular work remained and Nos. 397/8 were placed in store while No. 402 became spare engine. As a result Nos. 397/8 were transferred to Basingstoke at the end of the year for the Waterloo semi-fasts and the Portsmouth services via Eastleigh, but again the stay was not prolonged for in September 1934 they returned to Yeovil, where later they were joined by No. 404. Apart from a daily Yeovil-Salisbury-Portsmouth turn, they were mainly employed on the Exeter and Salisbury stoppers or pick-up goods.

In the 1930s pigeon racing was considerably more popular than it is today and at weekends during the racing season it was not exceptional for ten specials to be booked over the Western Section, many originating on the LMS and being taken over at Templecombe or Willesden. Most were worked by 'S11s' or 'L11s' bound for such destinations as Portsmouth, Bournemouth and Weymouth.

Apart from being replaced in the West Country by 'N' class 2—6—0s, no major duty changes occurred until 1939, when the allocation and duties in mid-year were:-

Shed	Nos.	Duties
Feltham	396, 401/2	One booked daily duty: ECS Teddington-Waterloo, 7.42 a.m. Waterloo-Salisbury and 4.06 p.m. return, but there were regular special duties for workmen constructing an army camp at Bramshot Halt. On 18/8/1939 these were worked by Nos. 396, 402, 'L12s' Nos. 432/4 and 'L11s' Nos. 411/42. Saturdays: ECS Walton-Waterloo, 9.54 a.m. Waterloo-Basingstoke and 2.15 p.m. return.
Basingstoke	403/4	East End carriage piloting shared with the 'L12' class. Occasionally the 3.25 a.m. Eastleigh fish vans and Southampton-Reading, Reading-Portsmouth and return to Basingstoke duty worked.
Guildford	400	Weekdays: 8.50 a.m. Woking-Basingstoke, 12.02 p.m. to Waterloo and 6.09 p.m. return to Basingstoke, vans back to Woking. Sundays: 7.12 a.m. Woking-Portsmouth via Meon Valley line and 6.07 p.m. return to Alton, ECS to Guildford.
Bournemouth	395/7/9	Weekdays: 8.04 a.m. Bournemouth West-Brighton and 7.58 p.m. return. Saturdays: ECS Wareham-Swanage, 9.02 a.m. Swanage-Bournemouth Central (Waterloo train), 11.32 a.m. Bournemouth Central-Swanage and 1.55 p.m. return. Sundays: A double return trip to Eastleigh; carriage piloting at Bournemouth West. The Brighton duty was booked for a 'T9', but like weekdays it was usually worked by an 'S11'.
Yeovil	398	Yeovil Junction shunting, 8.11 a.m. goods to Sidmouth Junction, shunting, light engine to Chard for milk van shunting and light engine to Yeovil Town. Sundays: Excursion to Exeter (for Paignton).

'S11' class No. 395 circa 1935 with a Maunsell superheater, snifting valves and without the E-prefix.   *A. B. Macleod*

Another view of No. 395, circa 1935, at Littlehampton.   *S. Nash Collection*

Like other Western Section secondary passenger tender classes, the Bulleid livery changes did not immediately affect the 'S11s', all repaints being in standard Maunsell style until September 1939. Details are:-

Maunsell green, black and yellow lining, tender numerals: Nos. 401/4 (September 1939).
Maunsell green, unlined, tender numerals: No. 400 (October 1939).
Maunsell green, unlined, Bulleid lettering, cabside numerals: Nos. 398 (April 1940), 402 (June 1940).
All later repaints, commencing with No. 403 in June 1941, were plain black with Bulleid lettering and cabside numerals.

The war had little effect on the class until September 1941, when Nos. 396-404 were transferred to the Somerset & Dorset Joint line as replacements for LMS class '2P' 4–4–0s despatched to more important duties on the parent system. At the time No. 395 was under repair at Eastleigh Works and did not arrive until February 1942, its place meanwhile being filled by 'T9' class No. 302. They were classified '2P' and mainly employed working Bath-Evercreech locals, the Bournemouth slows or piloting heavy expresses and goods. Occasionally goods were worked to Gloucester or Bristol and van trains to the Midlands. In April 1942 Nos. 395/6, 402 were transferred to Saltley for local goods duties, for which the classification was changed in chalk to '2F'. The Somerset & Dorset shed at Branksome closed for the remainder of the war on 1st June 1942 and engines sent to Bournemouth Central for coaling and minor

maintenance. This led to the class being borrowed for the Weymouth slows, odd goods duties and the Swanage branch services. During this period the LMS was responsible for repairs and this led to No. 397 receiving casual attention at Bow Works in April 1943 and a general overhaul at Derby Works in December 1943, while this establishment also gave intermediate repairs to Nos. 400/1/3 in March-May 1943 and to Nos. 395/6 in February 1944. Spares, including short stovepipe chimneys for Nos. 401/3, were supplied by Eastleigh Works. Over the next two years various transfers occurred, including Nos. 395/6 to Burton in May 1943 for the Birmingham and Leicester locals, Nos. 395-7 to Peterborough in September 1944 for the Northampton passenger and goods services, and Nos. 403/4 to Saltley in November 1944 for local goods and shunting. Obviously all travelled widely, but probably none as far as No. 396, which was noted on a goods at Giggleswick on 19th March 1944. Nos. 403/4 were returned to the Southern in December 1944, No. 395-7 in January 1945 (all classified '2P 3F'), No. 402 in March 1945, Nos. 398, 401 in April 1945 and finally Nos. 399, 400 in May 1945. Their condition on arrival, both externally and mechanically, was so deplorable that Southern fitters were amazed that engines so neglected could perform a day's work.

After basic repairs, Nos. 395-7, 402-4 were stationed at Exmouth Junction, Nos. 398/9 at Bournemouth and Nos. 400/1 at Fratton. At this period the small Padstow turn-

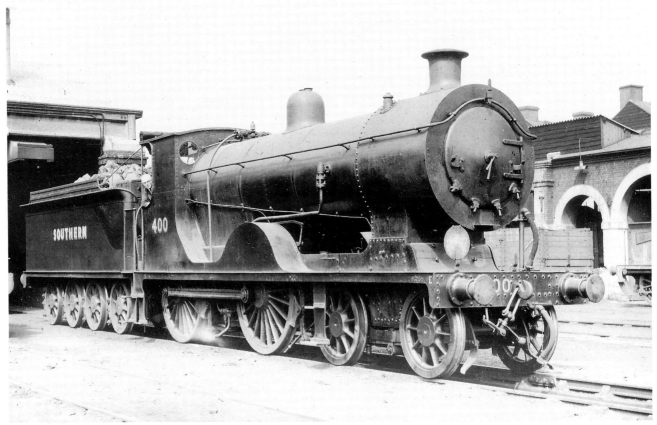

'S11' class No. 400 at Brighton in mid-1945, painted plain black with a lipped chimney and smokebox door lamp brackets.   *F. Burtt*

'S11' class No. 400 at Eastleigh on 26th September 1953, in British Railways lined black with large tender totems, short stove-pipe chimney, no snifting valves and fitted with smokebox number and shed plates.   *Author*

table forbade the use of West Country Pacifics, therefore Nos. 395-7, 402-4 spent most of their time working the North Cornwall line and only spasmodically reached Plymouth or Barnstaple. At Bournemouth Nos. 398/9 could usually be found on the Salisbury or Southampton slows, except on Saturdays when they shared the Swanage services. Occasional troop specials were also worked to Aldershot and Oxford. At Fratton Nos. 400/1 were found employment on local passenger and goods trips to Eastleigh, Romsey, Southampton and Salisbury.

The engines scheduled for conversion to oil-firing in 1946-7 did not include any 'S11s', nevertheless Nos. 396, 402-4 were despatched from Exmouth Junction to Fratton in October 1946 to await attention by Eastleigh Works. Their late inclusion in the scheme was probably caused by the provision of a turntable at Padstow capable of use by the Bulleid light Pacifics, thereby making the 'S11s' redundant in the West Country. In August 1947 Nos. 395/7 exchanged their double bogie 4,000 gallon tenders for the six-wheeled 3,500 gallon pattern of 'T9s' Nos. 303/14 in preparation for the latter's conversion to oil-burning. However, this proved to be the only involvement by the class, as before Nos. 396, 402-4 could be called to Eastleigh Works for conversion, the scheme had been abandoned and they re-entered traffic as coal-burners.

At Nationalisation the class entered British Railways stock, when all except Nos. 395 and 401 were renumbered into the 30,000 series, while Nos. 30396-8 and 30400/4 received the secondary passenger lined black livery. These

dates and those for the removal of the snifting valves and the fitting of stove pipe chimneys are:-

No.	BR No.	Lined black livery	Snifting valves removed	Stove pipe chimney
395	−	−	−	−
396	10/1948	10/1948	10/1948	10/1948
397	6/1949	6/1949	6/1949	12/1946
398	6/1949	5/1950	6/1949	−
399	6/1948	−	6/1948	6/1948
400	8/1948	2/1950	1/1949	1/1949
401	−	−	11/1947	4/1943
402	11/1950	−	10/1947	−
403	6/1949	−	−	5/1943
404	7/1950	7/1950	−	−

During the 1949 summer season Nos. 30396, 401 assisted 'D15s' with the Portsmouth-Salisbury services, but otherwise the class was mainly rostered for local passenger duties, light goods, van trains and empty coaching stock. In the winter months most rusticated in store, where Nos. 395, 30396/7, 30400, 401 remained in May 1950, when the allocation of the remainder was:- Fratton Nos. 30397, 402/4; Bournemouth Nos. 30398, 30403. Later Nos. 30396/7, 30400 were returned to traffic at Eastleigh for the South Hampshire soft fruit specials.

In February 1951 Nos. 30399, 30400, 401 were transferred to Guildford as replacements for 'L12s' Nos. 30420/5/8 sent to Eastleigh, while Basingstoke received Nos. 30397/8 in exchange for 'T9' No. 30302 and 'L12' No.

30426. At once those at Guildford commenced working the Reading-Redhill services, the Woking-Alton goods and the Sunday Woking-Portsmouth vans over the direct line, but at Basingstoke Nos. 30397/8, although well groomed, were usually restricted to carriage piloting and van trains. Only No. 30400 remained fully serviceable, therefore it came as no surprise when the other nine were withdrawn between February and November 1951.

No. 30400 remained at Guildford working the 6.35 a.m. Reading, 11.05 a.m. Reading-Redhill, 3.04 p.m. Redhill-Reading and the 8.05 p.m. home until despatched to Eastleigh Works on 29th June 1952. Few anticipated a return to traffic, but on 21st August it stood outside the erecting shop following an intermediate repair and a second application of BR lined black. After being run-in on the Bournemouth slows and Southampton-Portsmouth vans, a return was made to Guildford and the Reading-Redhill services in partnership with No. 30434, the last 'L12'.

On 12th June 1954 the nine carriage 12.39 p.m. Waterloo-Basingstoke semi-fast was worked, while the following morning probably saw its final appearance at Waterloo with the empty stock of the 11.30 a.m. Bournemouth. The end came on 11th September 1954, when called upon to work the 330 ton 7.00 p.m. North Camp-

Brighton return excursion. It was severely taxed by Gomshall bank and this undoubtedly caused the right-hand frame fracture, which led to withdrawal with a mileage of 1,336,661 a few days later. On 30th October 1954 No. 30400 was steamed for the last time and sent to Ashford Works for breaking up, which occurred on 23rd February 1955.

ENGINE SUMMARY

No.	Date	Order No.	Superheated Eastleigh	Maunsell	Withdrawn
395	6/1903	S11	7/1921	2/1930	9/1951
396	6/1903	S11	4/1922	11/1925	10/1951
397	7/1903	S11	8/1921	1/1931	11/1951
398	8/1903	S11	7/1922	5/1930	11/1951
399	8/1903	S11	5/1920	1/1931	11/1951
400	11/1903	V11	6/1921	11/1931	10/1954
401	11/1903	V11	2/1922	4/1930	8/1951
402	12/1903	V11	7/1922	3/1929	2/1951
403	12/1903	V11	10/1921	10/1931	9/1951
404	12/1903	V11	12/1921	2/1931	9/1951

All built at Nine Elms Works. Disposal: No. 400 broken up at Ashford Works, the remainder at Eastleigh Works. Mileages: Nos. 395 – 1,399,643; 396 – 1,401,231; 400 – 1,336,661; 402 – 1,426,592; 404 – 1,298,674.

Mr. Drummond's Car (The Bug)

Like most Victorian Scots obtaining high office, Drummond found life extremely serious, and as this also applied to his activities as locomotive superintendent, he toured the system frequently to ensure that these sentiments prevailed throughout his department. To this aim he persuaded the Locomotive Committee to authorise the construction of a private engine with attached saloon by Nine Elms Works at a cost of £1,535 in August 1898. Numbered 733 in the general list, it entered service in June 1899 and was a neat single-wheel outside cylinder tank engine having the small saloon carriage supported by an 8 ft. bogie. Officially it was known as Mr. Drummond's Car, but the men always irreverently referred to it as 'the Bug'. The dimensions were as follows:

Cylinders (outside)	11½" x 18"
Bogie wheels	2' 6"
Driving wheels	5' 7"
Wheelbase	5' 0" + 5' 7½" + 8' 9" + 8' 0" = 27' 4½"
Length over buffers	35' 9¼"
Boiler diameter	3' 4"
Boiler length	8' 10"
Firebox	3' 8"
Heating surfaces:	
Tubes	498 sq. ft.
Firebox	52 sq. ft.
Total	550 sq. ft.
Working pressure	175 lb
Grate area	11½ sq. ft.
Water capacity	600 gallons
Coal capacity	1 ton

Weights in working order:

Leading bogie	9T 3C
Driving wheels	13T 12C
Trailing bogie	14T 13C
Total	37T 8C

The rear bogie differed from standard Drummond practice by having inside frames and bearings with a swinging bolster, while the wheels of both bogies were provided with splashers.

The engine was painted royal green with the side tanks lettered 'LSWR', while the saloon was salmon pink above the waist and dark brown below, with the numerals '733' inscribed on the waistband above the company's coat-of-arms. The saloon was equipped with a table, several comfortable chairs, a buffet, lavatory, wash basin and a sliding panel via a porthole to the footplate. Lighting was by gas while an electric bell provided an alternative means of communication with the footplate, the code being: 1 ring — faster; 2 — as fast as possible; 3 — slow down; 4 — stop at once; 5 — sound the whistle; 6 — stop at the next station or signal box. According to William Eaton, sometime fireman of the Car, the bell saw little use as Drummond favoured the personal approach via the porthole, which could be disconcerting, if not frightening.

Drummond resided at Surbiton and therefore employed the Car for commuting daily to and from the company's workshops as well as for numerous unscheduled journeys for he was also Running Superintendent and preferred

Mr. Drummond's Car (The Bug) at Nine Elms between journeys on 23rd March 1905.   *J. B. Ashford*

seeing for himself than having to rely on reports. With this in mind, the apprehension of staff when the Car unexpectedly came in sight can readily be imagined. Some estimation of Drummond's travels can be ascertained from the 171,304 miles run between January 1900 and December 1912.

After his death the Locomotive and Running Departments were separated and with Urie seldom requiring private transportation, the Car was transferred to the Engineer's Department and stationed at Wimbledon. Steaming became spasmodic and when heavy repairs became necessary in October 1916, it was laid aside in store.

Southern Railway stock was entered at Grouping and in December 1924 it was transferred to service stock as No. 58S to permit the Glasgow Exhibition 'T9' to become 733 and thereby leaving its own number, 773, vacant for the new 'King Arthur' class 4—6—0.

Despite the renumbering, the Car remained in store until 6th January 1932, when the erecting shop was entered for repairs lasting until 17th February 1932. Then, following a series of trial runs to Alton, Micheldever and Portsmouth with a refurbished ex-SER six-wheel carriage, it was returned to the erecting shop to have a bogie frame fracture welded and Southern Railway livery applied. The Works were finally left on 14th March 1932, when the reason for the metamorphosis became apparent — it and the attached carriage were to be employed conveying officials and visitors around the construction works in Southampton New Docks.

At weekends stabling was with the contractors engines and not at the docks shed with the Marine Department 'B4s'. On completion of the docks, it remained in use carrying parties of school children around the various quays and

'The Bug' at Hounslow.   *Lens of Sutton*

dry docks and in December 1936 was transferred to the Marine Department. Unfortunately, the firebox failed in March 1937, when it was laid aside with Beyer Peacock 0—6—0 saddle tank No. 0334 and IWR 2—4—0 tank *Ryde* in the Eastleigh paint shop. All three would probably have been preserved but for the Second World War, when the Car was stripped to the frames and, with driving wheels removed, was used for conveying heavy loads around the shops. The saloon was set up in the carriage works and provided comfortable accommodation for the timber inspector until early 1974.

ENGINE SUMMARY

No.	Date	Order No.	To Service Stock	Withdrawn
733	6/1899	F9	58S 12/1924	8/1940

'F13' class No. 330 in shops grey with wood insets fitted to the splashers to avoid the lining following in the contours of the splashers.

Courtesy National Railway Museum

THE DRUMMOND 4-6-0s

By the turn of the century the development of the traditional inside cylinder 4—4—0 was rapidly approaching the limit and many mechanical engineers concluded that the increased power and adhesion demanded by the heavier corridor stock and faster schedules could only be provided by 4—6—0s. Generally the current 4—4—0s were admirable engines, whose design was the culmination of some years trial and error, so that their performance was infinitely better than those built earlier. Unfortunately, with the possible exception of Swindon, the same hazardous principle applied to the design of the first express 4—6—0s with the not unexpected consequence that their performance was disappointing and often inferior to that of the smaller, cheaper and more economical 4—4—0s they had superseded. Undoubtedly, with a similar period of gestation, their performance could have been improved, but, with the heavier rolling stock already in service, they were required to maintain schedules at once and not at some unforeseeable date in the future. As a result, many mechanical engineers planning the introduction of 4—6—0s found the risk of failure unacceptable, while others already committed reverted to 4—4—0s.

However, Drummond, with typical Scottish tenacity, decided to disregard criticism and in 1908-12 followed his initial 4—6—0s with three more classes, each progressively better, though seldom eclipsing the 'T9s' and 'L12s'. As a result, when engines were required for the Bournemouth expresses in 1911, he also accepted defeat and ordered ten large 4—4—0s.

'F13' Class

The first 4—6—0s, 'F13' class Nos. 330-4, were ordered from Nine Elms Works for the Salisbury-Exeter expresses in January 1905 and completed at a cost of £3,630 each between September and December 1905. The dimensions were as follows:

Cylinders (4)	16″ x 24″
Bogie wheels	3′ 7″
Coupled wheels	6′ 0″
Wheelbase	6′ 6″ + 6′ 9″ + 6′ 8″ + 6′ 8″ = 26′ 7″
Boiler diameter	5′ 7″
Boiler length	13′ 9″ (Tubeplates 14′ 2″)
Firebox length	9′ 6″
Heating surfaces:	
Tubes (340 x 1¾″)	2,210 sq. ft.
Firebox	160 sq. ft.
Watertubes (112 x 2¾″)	357 sq. ft.
Total	2,727 sq. ft.
Working pressure	175 lb
Grate area	31½ sq. ft.
Weights in working order:	
Bogie	20T 12C
Leading coupled wheels	18T 14C
Centre coupled wheels	18T 17C
Trailing coupled wheels	18T 10C

Engine total	76T 13C
Tender	44T 17C
Engine & Tender	121T 10C

They were massively constructed impressive-looking engines, with high pitched boilers and short mountings, which gave them the appearance of being considerably larger and more powerful than they actually were. Indeed, the dome was too low to accommodate the standard lock-up safety valves and, unusually for Drummond, they had to be positioned over the firebox. Similarly, space could not be found for the Stroudley two-arm regulator and this led to Drummond introducing a single-arm balanced pattern, which gave improved control and became widely adopted in this country and overseas.

The cab contours followed those of the large 4—4—0s, although the roof had to be more steeply arched to suit the large, highly pitched boiler, a modification which proved a constant source of irritation to crews, when the class was relegated to goods service and tender first working became more frequent.

The cylinder layout followed that of the double-singles, with the inside pair being conventionally sited beneath the smokebox and the outside cylinders mounted immediately ahead of the leading coupled wheels. This layout had the advantage of equalising the lengths of the inside and outside connecting rods at 6 ft 6 in, with the former driving the leading and the latter the centre coupled wheels. In regular service the Joy's valve gear of the double-singles had not proved entirely satisfactory, so it was replaced by a combination of inside Stephenson and outside Walschaerts valve gears; the latter having to be inverted to accommodate slide valves below the cylinders. The 90° setting of the inside and outside cranks was unusual, as was the short coupling rod throw, which was obtained by turning the pins 2 in. eccentric from the crank pins. Like the double-singles and 4—4—0s, reversing was by steam and sanding by gravity.

The double bogie tender carried 4,000 gallons of water and 5 tons of coal, and was fitted with sixty-five 1¾ in by 18 ft exhaust steam heating tubes. Boiler feed was by two Duplex pumps and clackboxes at the base of the front tubeplate. To conserve heat, the sides and rear plating was double, this also ensuring that any overheating of the contents would not cause the paint to bubble and peel. No. 330, painted matt shops grey with black bands and fine white lining, was officially photographed outside Nine Elms Works on 29th August 1905, but when shown the full plate prints Drummond objected to the lining following the contours of all three splashers and ordered wood insets to be fitted creating a long splasher on each side similar to current Great Central Railway practice. However, when lined out there was little improvement, so after removing the insets, a third attempt was made in which the lining followed the curvature of the leading and centre splashers before proceeding straight across the firebox water tube casing to the cab sidesheets. This gave a more pleasing appearance and was the style adopted when the green passenger livery was applied.

113

The boiler of 'F13' class 4—6—0 No. 330 being steam tested outside Nine Elms Works on 24th July 1905.   *C. H. Eden*

During a trial run between Salisbury and Exeter with an eight carriage train on 28th September 1905, No. 330 performed reasonably well by completing the 88 miles with stops at Templecombe and Sidmouth Junction in 112 minutes, but on the return journey with nine carriages, 3 minutes were lost to Sidmouth Junction, 2 more to Yeovil Junction and a further 4 to Salisbury, giving a 9 minute late arrival. On a later trial with No. 331 on 31st October 1905, the following results were obtained:

Journey	Total Time	Time Lost	No. of Shops	Load	Coal burnt per Mile	Water consumed per Mile	Ash in Smokebox
Down	114	4	2	8 carriages	46.9 lb	43.2 gallons	188 lb
Up	131	11	3	10 carriages	51.3 lb	46.4 gallons	253 lb
Average coal and water consumption					49.1 lb	44.8 gallons	

This was an unspectacular performance by a specially prepared engine, fired with best quality coal and crewed by experienced Salisbury top link men. Nos. 323/3 are also known to have worked test trains around the same period and to have joined Nos. 330/1 in regular service between Salisbury and Exeter during November 1905, but there was only time for No. 334 to complete its 1,000 mile running-in period before all five were laid aside in store at Nine Elms on 31st December 1905, officially because the light loadings of the West of England services in January to March did not warrant the provision of large engines, but in reality it was to permit various modifications being made to reduce the coal consumption and improve the performance. Unfortu-

nately, the only known reference to these modifications is a series of pencil notes in the Engine Register, details being:-

No.	Mileage	Modifications
330	9,743	4½ in.-5½ in. variable blastpipe, new ashpan, mechanical lubricator.
331	7,459	4¾ in. blastpipe, 1¼ in. lap, 5 lower firetubes removed.
332	4,106	More powerful Duplex pumps (5 in. steam cylinder, 3 7/8 in. by 8¾ in. water cylinder).
333	3,172	4¼ in. blastpipe, 1½ in. lap.
334	1,154	Cylinders lined to 15 in. and the tender base plate angled to feed the coal towards the footplate.

The return to traffic is not recorded, but very probably was in time for Easter 1906.

In part the steaming difficulty was undoubtedly caused by those features differing from established Drummond practice, in particular the provision of a long, flat and shallow grate, instead of the more easily fired short, deep pattern of the 'T9s', 'S11s' and 'L12s'. For such a long firebox the volume was comparatively small and this was further reduced by the two pods of fifty-six 2¾ in. cross water tubes, for which miraculous steaming properties were claimed, but as they also cooled the furnace gases, any gain could only have been marginal. Of equal significance was the lack of depth at the foot of the brick arch and the cramped, poorly ventilated ashpan, both of which impeded combustion, and made the task of keeping the front of the

'F13' class No. 330 being assembled at Nine Elms Works on 23rd August 1905, the boiler and cylinders are mounted, but it is not yet wheeled.

C. H. Eden

'F13' class No. 330 awaiting transfer to the paint shop on 28th August 1905.

C. H. Eden

'F13' class No. 330 at Nine Elms in April 1906 with the wooden splasher insets removed and Drummond's final lining.

grate adequately covered and incandescent difficult, if not virtually impossible. Only a few very able and conscientious top link firemen fully mastered the technique, the others failed dismally and regularly reached Exeter and Salisbury with badly clinkered fires and time booked against their drivers.

The 1906 modifications were well intentioned, but unfortunately proved too minor to influence the steaming, while the tortuous front-end and inadequate bearing surfaces ensured that the steam available could seldom be used to advantage. Possibly the most damning indictment was Urie's assertion that they and No. 335 were the only South Western engines which could not be pushed down banks by the weight of their trains, steam always having to be applied. As a result the return to regular service was no more successful than the previous autumn and in early August 1906 the Locomotive Committee called for a report of their performance on the Salisbury-Exeter services. Details for the month ending 31st July 1906 are:-

Salisbury dep.	Exeter arr.	Booked time	Average time mins	Average time lost mins
12.25 p.m.	2.03 p.m.	98 mins	105	7
12.37 p.m.	2.15 p.m.	98 mins	103½	5½
5.07 p.m.	6.45 p.m.	98 mins	107	9
Exeter	*Salisbury*			
12.00 p.m.	1.39 p.m.	99 mins	106	7
12.22 p.m.	1.56 p.m.	98 mins	104½	6½

All trains were booked non-stop.

After reading and discussing the report, the Locomotive Committee instructed Drummond to remove the class from the best services and to investigate the possibility of employment on less arduous duties, a professional slight which many mechanical engineers would have been unable to overcome, but fortuitously the shed foremen at Exmouth Junction and Salisbury had recently approached Drummond for the provision of more powerful engines to work the West of England fast goods and the Southampton-Eastleigh-Salisbury coal trains. These were services which the '700' classs 0−6−0s were unable to work in bad weather without assistance or a reduction in loads and for which Drummond had considered building a series of 0−8−0s having 'F13' boilers, four 16½ in. by 26 in. cylinders and 4 ft. 10 in. coupled wheels. As a consequence, and very probably more in hope than expectation, Drummond set Nos. 330-4 to work on these services, when to everyone's surprise they proved equal to the task, albeit at the expense of the unfortunate firemen's stamina and a sharp rise in coal consumption. Henceforth, this became their main preoccupation until withdrawal in 1924. As a result the 0−8−0s were cancelled, although their use was reconsidered in October 1912, when five of a modified design were ordered from Eastleigh Works at an estimated cost of £4,200 each. However, before the material was ordered, Drummond died and Urie substituted the 'S15' class 5 ft 7 in. 4−6−0s, a more logical coverage of the main

'F13' class No. 333 standing at Exeter on 3rd July 1906 during the brief period the class was employed on the West of England expresses.
V. Chambers

J. E. Kite Collection

An undated view of 'F13' class No. 334 with a Salisbury-Southampton goods train passing Eastleigh.

line goods requirements for they could also be employed as stand-in passenger engines at busy periods.

In mid-1909 4—6—0s were booked for the following West of England goods:

1.15 a.m. Salisbury-Exeter (arr. 4.06 a.m.). Fast Plymouth goods. Non-stop, maximum load 30 wagons.
Returned on:-
8.25 p.m. Exeter-Salisbury (arr. 1.14 a.m.). Nine Elms goods. Chard Junction 9.41-10.15, Yeovil Junction 10.50-11.07, Templecombe 11.36-12.15, maximum load 50 wagons.
8.35 p.m. Salisbury-Exeter (1.05 a.m.). Nine Elms goods. Templecombe 9.46-9.51, Yeovil Junction 10.20-10.50, Axminster 11.41-11.46, Exmouth Junction 12.56-1.00, 50 wagons to Yeovil Junction, 45 beyond.
Returned on:-
10.25 p.m. Exeter-Salisbury (2.19 a.m.). Market goods. Yeovil Junction 12.15-12.29, maximum load 50 wagons.
8.05 p.m. Exeter-Salisbury (arr. 11.10 p.m.). Market goods. Yeovil Junction 9.45-9.57, 30 wagons to Yeovil Junction, 35 beyond.
Returned on:-
2.10 a.m. Salisbury-Exeter (arr. 5.51 a.m.). Fast Torrington goods. Yeovil Junction 3.42-3.47, Chard Junction 4.26-4.31, maximum load 35 wagons.
10.00 p.m. Exeter-Salisbury (arr. 12.50 a.m.). Market goods non-stop, maximum load 30 wagons.
Returned on:-
4.25 a.m. Salisbury-Exeter (arr. 8.33 a.m.). Yeovil Junction

5.45-6.05, Chard Junction 6.56-7.03, Sidmouth Junction 7.57-8.06, 50 wagons to Yeovil Junction, 45 beyond.
2.00 a.m. Exeter-Salisbury (arr. 6.50 a.m.). 'G14' class. Exmouth Junction 2.05-2.15, Sidmouth Junction 2.40-2.55, Chard Junction 3.45-3.55, Yeovil Junction 4.33-4.43, Templecombe 5.17-5.46.
Returned on:-
11.07 a.m. Salisbury-Exeter (arr. 1.08 p.m.) Passenger. Four members of the class are included in the August 1911 Coal Returns, details being:-

| No. | Mileage | Coal Burnt per Mile | | Oil Consumption per 100 miles | | Duties |
		Allowance lb	Actual lb	Allowance lb	Actual lb	
332	2,948	50.0	46.1	10	13.9	Salisbury-Eastleigh-Southampton coal trains
330	2,142	52.0	62.9	10	14.3	Salisbury-Exeter goods
333	1,946	52.0	63.7	10	14.7	
334	2,367	52.0	64.8	10	15.1	

No. 331 was away at Eastleigh Works.

No. 332 did not require its coal allowance for the Salisbury-Southampton coal trains, but Nos. 330/3/4 substantially exceeded theirs on the more difficult and longer distance West of England goods.

After taking office, Urie replaced the Duplex pumps with hot water injectors, repositioned the clackboxes on the boiler barrel, fitted his own pattern smokebox door and provided new fireboxes without cross water tubes for Nos. 332-4. On these three the lining was adjusted to follow the contours of the coupled wheel splashers in the manner

'F13' class No. 333 in goods service at Yeovil Junction in 1908.   *L & GRP, courtesy David & Charles*

'F13' class No. 331 at Eastleigh on 28th May 1921 in post-World War 1 livery with a Urie smokebox door, boiler barrel clackboxes and the lining following the splasher contours.

H. C. Casserley

rejected by Drummond in 1905. Later, this style also appeared on Nos. 330/1 despite their retention of the cross water tubes.

In early 1917 No. 332 was transferred to Eastleigh for working refrigerated meat, fruit, brassica and potato trains to Oxford (Great Western), the return load being army vehicles, aircraft engines and coal for Southampton Docks.

Superheating was authorised in May 1919, with No. 333 being modified in June 1920, when, in addition to the 269 sq. ft. Eastleigh pattern superheater, it was fitted with an extended smokebox supported by a saddle, a Urie smokebox door, a short stovepipe chimney, an eight-feed Detroit lubricator and a large drag box below the footplate. Officially the weight in working order was 73 tons 18 cwt, but this was adjusted to 77 tons 16 cwt after Grouping. Although looking even more impressive, No. 333's performance was not substantially improved, details being:-

SALISBURY-WOKING GOODS

No.	Total Time of Trip Salisbury to Salisbury	Average No. of Wagons	Coal Burnt per Train Mile
333	10 hrs 09 mins	54	75.2 lb
330	9 hrs 59 mins	57	77.4 lb

SALISBURY-EASTLEIGH-SOUTHAMPTON GOODS

No.	Total Time of Trip Salisbury to Salisbury	Average No. of Wagons	Coal Burnt per Train Mile
333	6 hrs 41 mins	61	66.1 lb
330	6 hrs 34 mins	63	68.3 lb

With such a meagre return for superheating, it is not surprising that Urie decided not to proceed with the remainder of the class.

All five entered Southern Railway stock at Grouping, although only Nos. 330-3 remained serviceable for No. 334 without its boiler had laid derelict in Eastleigh Works yard since 20th December 1921. Only two were given general repairs by the Southern, details being:-

No.	To Works	Ex-Works	Livery
330	15/10/1923	17/11/1923	Urie and lettered LSWR.
332	8/3/1924	24/5/1924	Maunsell, renumbered E332.

No. 331 of Exmouth Junction was condemned on 15th February 1924, but Nos. 330/2/3 remained working the Salisbury-Exmouth Junction and Southampton goods until laid aside in July-August 1924 for rebuilding as 'H15' class mixed traffic 4–6–0s. No. 332 had worked only 92 days since its final general repair.

ENGINE SUMMARY

No.	Date	Order No.	Superheated	Mileage	Withdrawn
330	9/1905	F13	—	438,638	7/1924
331	9/1905	F13	—	443,645	2/1924
332	10/1905	F13	—	409,241	8/1924
333	10/1905	F13	6/1920	394,639	8/1924
334	12/1905	F13	—	361,863	12/1921 (a)

Built at Nine Elms Works and dismantled at Eastleigh Works.

(a) Laid aside unserviceable at this date, withdrawn 10/1924.

Superheated 'F13' No. 333 with extended smokebox, short stove-pipe chimney, Urie smokebox door, boiler barrel clackboxes and no firebox water tubes, at Eastleigh in June 1920.   *A. N. Smart*

No. 333 at Exmouth Junction on 19th July 1924, shortly before withdrawal.   *H. C. Casserley*

Frames of 'E14' class No. 335 in course of erection at Nine Elms Works.

Frames and cylinders assembled.

'E14' class No. 335 on completion at Nine Elms in November 1907.

'E14' Class

Despite the dismal performance of Nos. 330-4, Drummond remained convinced that 4−6−0s were necessary for the Salisbury-Exeter services. Nevertheless, he displayed unusual caution for, although having Locomotive Committee authority to build five, he only ordered one modified 4−6−0 from Nine Elms Works at a cost of £3,800 in January 1907.

Numbered 335 and classified 'E14' when completed in November 1907, it had the same boiler, coupled wheels, cylinder layout and Stephenson-Walschaerts valve gear combination as the 'F13s', but the cylinders were enlarged to 16½ in. by 26 in. and the design of the outside pair revised to accommodate the piston valves above the barrel. This modification raised the height and permitted conventional Walschaerts valve gear to be used. To gain clearance on the 'F13s' it had to be inverted. The wheelbase was 26 ft. 10 in., the additional 3 in. being introduced between the bogie and the leading coupled wheels to provide a more secure means of attaching the outside cylinders. More noticeable was the extension of the splashers to enclose the outside steam chests and the provision of four, two a side, large round openings for inspecting and oiling the valve gear. At first these openings were protected by glass doors, but from 1913 sheet metal was substituted. To assist the steaming, a footplate controlled variable blastpipe with aperture ranges of 4½ to 5½ in. was fitted. The double

bogie 4,000 gallon tender was provided with water pick-up for Drummond envisaged track troughs being laid near Fleet and at Abbey Ford, Templecombe to permit West of England expresses in the busy summer months running non-stop between Waterloo and Exeter. However, when the disappointing performance of the 4−6−0s proved this impractical, the scheme was abandoned and the water pick-up equipment removed. The weights in working order were:-

Bogie	21T 10C
Leading coupled wheels	19T 0C
Centre coupled wheels	19T 0C
Trailing coupled wheels	18T 8C
Engine total	77T 18C
Tender	45T 6C
Engine & Tender	123T 4C

At first the Diagram Book recorded the engine weight as 74 tons 5 cwt, with 52 tons 10 cwt resting on the coupled wheels, but this was revised to 77 tons 18 cwt in January 1909.

No. 335 was run-in on the Waterloo-Salisbury slows until Christmas week 1907 when it was promoted to the Salisbury-Exeter expresses, on which it failed even more dismally than Nos. 330-4. With hindsight this is not surprising for the modifications had left the long, flat grate,

General view of the cramped conditions of the Nine Elms erecting shop, with No. 335 taking shape in the foreground.

Boiler for No. 335 nearing completion.

No. 335 with boiler in position.

No. 335 at the final stages of construction.

cramped ashpan, inadequate coupled wheel boxes and cumbersome front-end. As a result it had to be hastily relegated to the goods services on which the coal consumption was so high that it became known as the *Turkey*, a reputation confirmed by the Western District Coal Returns of August 1909, details being:-

Miles Worked	Coal Burnt per Mile		Oil Consumption per 100 Miles	
	Allowance	Actual	Allowance	Actual
2,399	54 lb	83.2 lb	12.0 lb	15.2 lb

Since it was ex-works following general repairs on 22nd May 1909, this appetite for coal could not be blamed on poor mechanical order. All the trains worked were Exmouth Junction-Salisbury goods.

When asked about this engine in his retirement, Urie recalled drivers complaining that there was barely sufficient coal to reach Exmouth Junction when working a heavy down goods in a westerly gale. On one occasion during the 1909-10 winter, it had to be towed in from Whimple with only a glimmer of a fire remaining. If the tender was fully laden on leaving Salisbury, the coal consumption must have neared 130 lb per mile. The water consumption was equally excessive, therefore the 4,000 gallon tender was exchanged for the 4,500 gallon pattern from 'T7' class double-single No. 720 in January 1908. Fully laden, this tender weighed 48 tons 18 cwt, which increased the total weight to 126 tons 16 cwt.

With such an unenviable performance, one wonders why it was not transferred to the shorter distanced and easier Salisbury-Eastleigh-Southampton coal trains. Possibly this was prevented by violent objections by the Salisbury shed foreman and local crews.

At mileage 122,405 it was stopped for general repairs and on 28th September 1912 was despatched from Exmouth Junction to Eastleigh Works. As a result it was in the yard awaiting attention at Drummond's death, when Urie took the opportunity of delaying entry to the Erecting Shop until confirmed as chief mechanical engineer, when he ordered rebuilding as a two-cylinder 'H15' class mixed

traffic 4—6—0. On returning to traffic at a cost of £4,395 in December 1914, No. 335 was virtually a new engine for little more than the boiler shell, bogie wheels and tender remained of the Drummond 4—6—0.

ENGINE SUMMARY

No.	Date	Built	Order No.	Mileage	Withdrawn
335	11/1907	Nine Elms	E14	122,405	1/1914

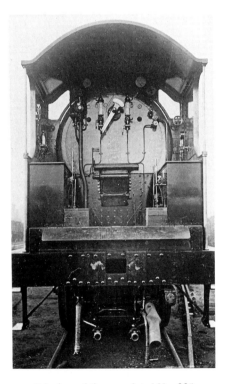

Cab view of the completed No. 335.

'E14' class No. 335, with 4,500 gallon double bogie tender and metal covers to the splasher inspection openings, at Eastleigh Works on 24th April 1911.

W. Beckerlegge

'G14' class 4—6—0s being assembled at Nine Elms Works on 14th March 1908.

J. B. Ashford

'G14' class No. 457 at Nine Elms in September 1908. The headcode of a single white disc on the near side of the smokebox is for Waterloo-Southampton via the main line.

W. Beckerlegge

'G14' and 'P14' Classes

Before No. 335 entered traffic Drummond commenced the design of Nos. 453-7, a class of smaller boilered 4−6−0s for the West of England expresses. Classified 'G14' and costing £3,710 each, they were completed by Nine Elms Works in April-May 1908 and had the following dimensions:

Cylinders (4)	15″ x 26″
Bogie wheels	3′ 7″
Coupled wheels	6′ 0″
Wheelbase	6′ 6″ + 7′ 0″ + 6′ 8″ + 6′ 8″ = 26′ 10″
Boiler diameter	4′ 10¾″
Boiler length	13′ 9″ (Tubeplates 14′ 2 1/8″)
Firebox length	9′ 6″
Heating surfaces:	
Tubes (247 x 1¾″)	1,580 sq. ft.
Firebox	140 sq. ft.
Cross water tubes (84 x 2¾″)	200 sq. ft.
Total	1,920 sq. ft.
Working pressure	175 lb
Grate area	31½ sq. ft.
Weights in working order:	
Bogie	20T 6C
Leading coupled wheels	17T 8C
Centre coupled wheels	17T 5C
Trailing coupled wheels	16T 0C
Engine total	70T 19C
Tender	49T 3C
Engine & Tender	120T 2C

The boiler was of smaller diameter, but otherwise was similar to classes 'F13' and 'E14', although this scaling down was not readily apparent for the pitch remained 9 ft and the mountings were only marginally taller. The two 3 in. lock-up safety valves were sited over the firebox, which incorporated the usual pods of cross water tubes. Other fittings included a variable blast pipe, Duplex feed pumps, exhaust steam feed water heating and a steam drier. The last mentioned was Drummond's variation of the superheater, although, with a heating surface of only 62 sq. ft., it is doubtful whether any useful purpose was served.

The main frames, coupled wheel diameter, cylinder layout, Stephenson-Walschaerts valve gear and wheelbase were similar to 'E14' No. 335, but the cylinder diameter was reduced to 15 in. As with No. 335, the cumbersome splashers were pierced for inspecting and oiling the outside valve gear, the openings being protected by toughened glass doors.

'P14' class No. 455 at Eastleigh running shed in original condition.

W. H. C. Kelland

'P14' class No. 456 again at Eastleigh running shed.

J. E. Kite Collection

The double bogie tenders held 5 tons of coal and 4,500 gallons of water and reputedly incorporated water pick-up scoops. However, the Repair Register fails to record the dates of removal, which it does for the tender originally attached to No. 335, therefore it is doubtful whether the equipment was ever fitted.

All went new to Salisbury and, before 'P14s' Nos. 448-52 entered service in early 1911, were employed almost exclusively on the Exeter expresses, but thereafter also worked some of the Waterloo services. The performance was considerably better than Nos. 330-5, but with the long, flat grate and shallow ashpan inhibiting steaming, the 'T9s' and 'L12s' were seldom excelled, except with semi-fasts in bad weather when the larger boiler and greater adhesion proved advantageous.

The August 1909 Coal Returns (four weeks ending 9th August) give the following details:

No.	Mileage		Coal Burnt per Mile		Oil Consumed per 100 Miles	
	Passenger	Goods	Allowance	Actual	Allowance	Actual
453	2,846	211	42 lb	47.3 lb	12 lb	15.1 lb
454	3,123	293	42 lb	46.8 lb	12 lb	14.7 lb
455	1,019	—	42 lb	44.3 lb	12 lb	13.4 lb
456	3,347	—	42 lb	46.2 lb	12 lb	14.2 lb
457	3,165	189	42 lb	47.6 lb	12 lb	14.6 lb

No. 455 received intermediate repairs in June 1909, and consequently was in better mechanical order than Nos. 453/4/6/7, which had not visited shops since being accepted for revenue earning service.

In August 1909 the timings of the best West of England services were:-

DOWN

Salisbury dep.	Exeter arr.	Mins	Stops
8.13 a.m.	10.09 a.m.	116 (a)	Templecombe, Yeovil Junction
11.07 a.m.	1.08 p.m.	121 (a)	Templecombe, Sherborne, Yeovil Junction
12.21 p.m.	1.57 p.m.	96	Non-stop (Plymouth express)
12.39 p.m.	2.15 p.m.	96 (a)	Non-stop (North Cornwall express)
12.48 p.m.	2.24 p.m.	96 (a)	Non-stop (North Devon express)
1.39 p.m.	3.34 p.m.	115 (a)	Axminster, Seaton Junction, Sidmouth Junction
3.00 p.m.	5.11 p.m.	131	Templecombe, Yeovil Junction, Sidmouth Junction
5.09 p.m.	6.45 p.m.	96	Non-stop
7.56 p.m.	9.53 p.m.	117	Templecombe, Yeovil Junction, Chard Junction

UP

Exeter dep.	Salisbury arr.	Mins	Stops
7.20 a.m.	9.26 a.m.	126	Sidmouth Junction, Axminster, Yeovil Junction, Sherborne, Templecombe
10.17 a.m.	12.10 p.m.	113 (a)	Sidmouth Junction, Templecombe
12.00 n.n.	1.38 p.m.	98 (a)	Non-stop
12.17 p.m.	2.00 p.m.	103	Non-stop
1.00 p.m.	2.54 p.m.	114	Sidmouth Junction, Yeovil Junction
1.57 p.m.	3.35 p.m.	98	Non-stop
2.10 p.m.	4.10 p.m.	120 (a)	Yeovil Junction, Templecombe
4.15 p.m.	6.22 p.m.	127 (a)	Yeovil Junction, Sherborne, Templecombe
6.02 p.m.	8.13 p.m.	131 (a)	Yeovil Junction, Templecombe, Semley

(a) Trains booked for 4—6—0s, which infers that one 'G14' had been transferred to Exmouth Junction to work the 10.17 a.m. up and 1.39 p.m. down.

'P14' class No. 449 at Salisbury in 1911.   *A. G. Ellis*

The great man himself inspects newly completed 'P14' class No. 448 at Eastleigh Works on 5th December 1910.   *Author's collection*

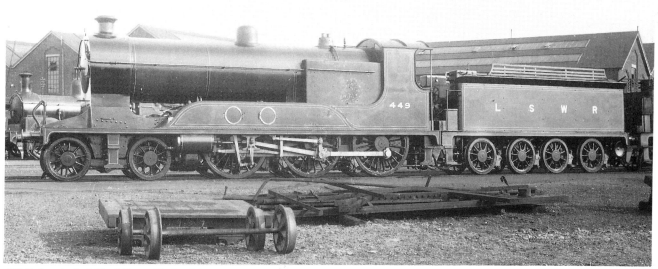

'P14' class 4—6—0 No. 449 outside Eastleigh Works in January 1911.

W. Beckerlegge

Five more 4—6—0s, 'P14' class Nos. 448-52, were ordered from Eastleigh Works at a cost of £3,635 each in January 1910. When completed between December 1910 and March 1911, they were generally similar to the 1908 series, but the inside cylinders were also fitted with 10 in. piston valves. The changed dimensions were:-

Steam drier (72 x 1½" tubes) 114 sq. ft.
Wheelbase   G14   6′ 6″ + 7′ 0″ + 6′ 8″ + 6′ 8″ = 26′ 10″
             P14   6′ 6″ + 7′ 2″ + 7′ 0″ + 7′ 0″ = 27′ 8″
Weights in working order:
      Bogie   20T 14C
      Leading coupled wheels   18T 10C
      Centre coupled wheels   18T 6C
      Trailing coupled wheels   17T 3C
      Engine total   74T 13C
      Tender   49T 3C
      Engine & Tender   123T 16C

The frame length was the same as the 'G14' class, with the 4 in. wider coupled wheel spacing and the additional

2 in. between the bogie and the leading coupled wheels being accommodated by reducing the rear overhang by 10 in. to 5 ft. 2 in. The blast pipe was not variable for experience with the 'G14s' had shown that most drivers employed the smallest (4¾ in.) aperture and this was the size provided. The tender was of the standard 4,500 gallon double bogie pattern with exhaust steam feedwater heating.

All went new to Exmouth Junction for the Exeter-Salisbury expresses, but by March 1912 the allocation of the two classes had become: Nine Elms Nos. 452/5/7; Salisbury Nos. 448/51/3/6; Exmouth Junction Nos. 449/50/4. In regular service west of Salisbury, the 'P14s' proved marginally better than Nos. 453-7, although when tested on the heaviest Waterloo-Bournemouth expresses in mid-1911, neither class was able to maintain time with the standard formation.

The 5th August 1913 Coal Returns give the following details of the mileages worked and the coal and oil consumption for the previous four weeks:

No.	Mileage		Coal Burnt per Mile		Oil Consumption per 100 Miles		Duties
	Passenger	Goods	Allowance	Actual	Allowance	Actual	
			lb	lb	lb	lb	
448	3,163	—	42	46.3	12	14.9	
451	2,988	—	42	46.9	12	14.3	Salisbury-Exeter and
453	2,864	—	42	47.1	12	14.7	Salisbury-Waterloo
456	3,041	—	42	49.9	12	15.4	expresses
450	3,147	496	42	47.8	12	14.3	
454	2,246	2,249	42	55.7	12	15.1	Exeter-Salisbury
455	1,945	2,649	42	54.1	12	15.4	passenger and goods
457	2,867	1,013	42	50.2	12	14.2	

'P14' class No. 449 approaching Tisbury with a West of England restaurant car express circa 1912.

J. B. Ashford

'G14' class No. E455 in Southern livery with a Urie smokebox door, boiler barrel clackboxes and firebox water tubes, at Salisbury on 19th July 1924.   *H. C. Casserley*

Nos. 449/52 were away at Eastleigh Works for general repairs, where they were followed by Nos. 454/5 on 12th August and 23rd September, which probably accounted for their excessively high coal and oil consumption.

After mid-1913 the steam driers were removed, the clack-boxes resited on the boiler barrel, conventional fireboxes provided for Nos. 449/56, Urie smokebox doors fitted and the Duplex pumps replaced by hot water injectors, while superheating at a cost of £480 was authorised on 7th October 1915. However, on 22nd November 1915 this was cancelled and the order transferred to 'S11' class Nos. 395-404. Nevertheless, No. 449 was superheated in July 1923.

By mid-1920 Nos. 448/50/6/7 were stationed at Exmouth Junction, Nos. 449/51-3 at Salisbury and Nos. 454/5 at Eastleigh, the last mentioned being usually employed working meat, potato, brassica, banana and citrus specials from Southampton docks to Nine Elms Yard or the Great Western at Salisbury or Basingstoke. The others were mainly rostered for the West of England semi-fasts and milk trains.

All entered Southern Railway stock at Grouping, with Maunsell confirming the order for reconstruction as 'H15' class mixed traffic 4—6—0s in May 1923. However, because this could not commence before 1925, general repairs were still authorised, details being:-

No.	To Works	Ex-Works	Livery
448	4/4/1923	2/7/1924	Maunsell green, renumbered E448.
449	17/11/1922	21/7/1923	Urie, new firebox, superheated.
450	2/12/1920	8/1/1921	Laid aside unserviceable 6/1/1923.
451	24/2/1923	18/8/1923	Urie, laid aside unserviceable 21/12/1924.
452	4/4/1923	14/8/1924	Maunsell green, renumbered E452.
453	11/2/1924	10/5/1924	Maunsell green, renumbered E453.
454	24/7/1922	4/11/1922	Urie, laid aside unserviceable 2/9/1924.
455	13/8/1923	23/5/1924	Maunsell green, renumbered E455.
456	31/10/1922	1/9/1923	Urie, new firebox.
457	21/7/1922	7/10/1922	Urie, laid aside unserviceable 11/2/1924.

In July 1924 the Traffic Department decided that there was insufficient work for all the mixed traffic 4—6—0s on order for the Western Section and, since gauge restrictions forbade their use on the Eastern and Central Sections, it was decided that rebuilding should be as 'King Arthur' express 4—6—0s.

The official date of withdrawal was January 1925, although Nos. 450/1/4/7 were laid aside unserviceable in 1923-4, while No. 449 was reinstated to become a mobile test bed for the proposed 'Lord Nelson' class. When Nos. 448-57 re-entered traffic at a cost of £6,320 each between February and July 1925, very little except the tenders remained of the Drummond 4—6—0s.

No. 449, THE TRIALS ENGINE

This engine returned to traffic on 21st July 1923 fitted with an Eastleigh superheater, conventional firebox, extended smokebox, short stove pipe chimney and an eight-feed Detroit sight-feed lubricator. The changed dimensions were:-

Heating surfaces:	
Small tubes (128 x 2")	950 sq. ft.
Large tubes (24 x 5¼")	464 sq. ft.
Firebox	157 sq. ft.
Evaporative total	1,571 sq. ft.
Superheater	308 sq. ft.
Total	1,879 sq. ft.
Weights in working order:	
Bogie	20T 15C
Leading coupled wheels	19T 2C
Centre coupled wheels	18T 12C
Trailing coupled wheels	17T 10C
Total	75T 19C

Like the similarly modernised 'F13' class No. 333, there was little improvement in performance, although marginally

'G14' and 'P14' classes Nos. 456, 457, 453, 448 and 455 after withdrawal in 1925 at Eastleigh Works.   *J. E. Kite Collection*

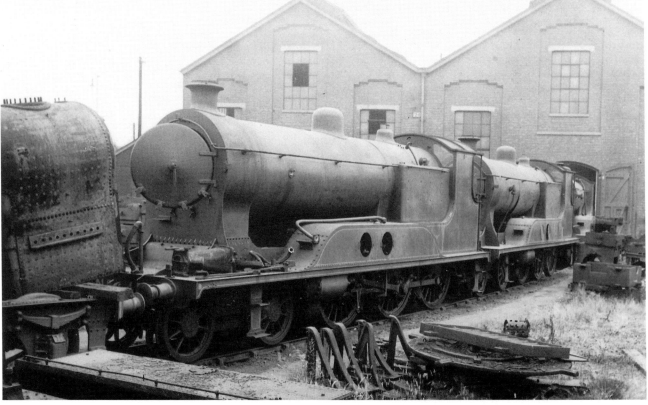

'G14s' Nos. 453/5/6 awaiting breaking up at Eastleigh Works in March 1925.   *Lens of Sutton*

Superheated 'P14' class No. 0449 in Southern livery, with an extended smokebox, short stovepipe, Urie smokebox door, no firebox water tubes and boiler barrel clackboxes, at Salisbury on 26th October 1925.

H. C. Casserley

less coal and water were consumed when working the heavy Salisbury-Southampton coal trains.

By January 1924 Maunsell had decided to modify the Urie 'N15' class for general express passenger service on all three sections, but had not finished the design of a more powerful four-cylinder 4−6−0 for working the heaviest Western Section expresses and the Victoria-Dover Marine Continental services. One of the undecided details was the crank setting for opinion differed at Waterloo and Eastleigh as to whether 90° and four exhaust beats or 135° and eight exhaust beats per revolution was preferable for four-cylinder engines. The latter was favoured by Maunsell, so to prove its superiority he had No. 449 prepared for a series of trial trips on the 5.45 p.m. Salisbury-Basingstoke heavy goods and the 11.05 p.m. return. Details are:-

Date	Total Time of Return Trip* hrs mins	No. of Wagons	Coal Burnt per Engine Mile lb	Water Evaporated per lb of Coal lb
90° CRANK SETTING				
8/4/1924	7 52	66	80.7	8.4
9/4/1924	7 47	62	80.3	7.8
10/4/1924	7 52	67	89.3	7.9
11/4/1924	7 58	66	92.8	8.2
Average	7 52	65.3	85.8	8.1

* Salisbury to Basingstoke and return.

135° CRANK SETTING				
27/5/1924	7 42	65	81.9	8.0
28/5/1924	7 43	66	68.1	7.9
29/5/1924	7 44	64	75.2	8.7
30/5/1924	7 31	58	66.6	8.6
Average	7 40	63.3	73.0	8.3

Apart from a thunderstorm on 30th May, the weather was dry and the winds light.

Coal saving with 135° cranks: 9.5% on ton miles
                                       14.9% on train miles

As a result of these findings fifteen of the sixteen 'Lord Nelsons' had 135° crank settings.

At the completion of the trials No. 449 returned to general service from Salisbury and could usually be found working the:

  2.00 a.m. Salisbury-Eastleigh (arr. 3.10 a.m.)
  6.10 a.m. Bevois Park sidings-Salisbury (arr. 9.44 a.m.)
  11.15 a.m. Salisbury-Eastleigh (arr. 12.34 p.m.)
  3.54 p.m. Eastleigh-Salisbury (arr. 5.05 p.m.)

If unavailable, these duties were delegated to one of the 330 series 'H15s'.

No. 449 was duplicated in June 1925, when 'King Arthur' No. 449 *Sir Torre* entered traffic, while in September 1925 it was painted Maunsell green, renumbered E0449 and coupled to the 4,500 gallon tender previously running with 'E10' class double-single No. 371, its own tender having been transferred to *Sir Torre*, which had been running with the tender belonging to 'N15' class No. 737, while the latter was under repair.

Again No. 0449 returned to Salisbury and worked the Eastleigh goods duties until laid aside on 18th September 1927 and despatched to Eastleigh Works for breaking up on 6th October 1927, 78,159 miles having been run since superheating. The boiler was salvaged and after repair was transferred to 'T14' class No. 462 in August 1930 and scrapped from No. 445 in November 1945.

ENGINE SUMMARY

No.	Order No.	Date	Mileage	Withdrawn
448	P14	12/1910	379,164	1/1925
449	P14	12/1910	403,447 (a)	10/1927
450	P14	1/1911	362,127	1/1925
451	P14	2/1911	392,218	1/1925
452	P14	3/1911	360,035	1/1925
453	G14	4/1908	483,847	1/1925
454	G14	4/1908	464,673	1/1925
455	G14	4/1908	397,689	1/1925
456	G14	5/1908	409,341	1/1925
457	G14	5/1908	447,924	1/1925

'G14s' built at Nine Elms Works, 'P14s' at Eastleigh Works. All broken up at Eastleigh Works.
(a) Final mileage also recorded as 433,147.

Newly completed 'T14' class No. 461, with a 4,500 gallon double bogie tender, outside Eastleigh Works in April 1912.

Author's collection

'T14' Class

All the six-coupled express classes so far described were designed for working the West of England services, but in June 1910 Drummond ordered five 4−6−0s with 6 ft. 7 in. coupled wheels for the Bournemouth and Waterloo-Salisbury expresses. Classified 'T14' and numbered 443-7, they were completed by Eastleigh Works between May and July 1911 at a cost of £3,585 each. The dimensions were as follows:

Cylinders (4)	15″ x 26″
Bogie wheels	3′ 7″
Coupled wheels	6′ 7″
Wheelbase	6′ 6″ + 6′ 9″ + 7′ 2″ + 7′ 2″ = 27′ 7″
Boiler diameter	4′ 10¾″
Boiler length	13′ 9″ (Tubeplates 14′ 2 1/8″)
Firebox length	9′ 6″
Heating surfaces:	
Tubes (247 x 1¾″)	1,636 sq. ft.
Firebox	140 sq. ft.
Cross tubes (84 x 2¾″)	200 sq. ft.
Total	1,976 sq. ft.
Working pressure	200 lb
Grate area	31½ sq. ft.

Weights in working order:

	Drummond	Urie	Southern
Bogie	22T 10C	22T 12C	23T 0C
Leading coupled wheels	18T 0C	18T 0C	18T 5C
Centre coupled wheels	18T 0C	18T 0C	18T 5C
Trailing coupled wheels	16T 0C	17T 3C	17T 8C
Engine total	74T 10C	75T 15C (c)	76T 18C (c)
Tender	49T 0C (a)	60T 8C (b)	60T 8C (b)
Engine & Tender	123T 10C	136T 3C	137T 6C

(a) 4,500 gallons. (b) 5,800 gallons. (c) superheated.

The boiler was similar to that carried by classes 'G14' and 'P14', but the 3½ in. higher pitching and the marginally shorter mountings created the illusion of being larger. The working pressure was higher at 200 lb per sq. in. while No. 447 was fitted with a steam drier having a heating surface of 114 sq. ft.

The cylinders, although being the same size as the 'P14' class, differed in layout for the outside pair were moved forward to bring all four in line below the smokebox, Walschaerts valve gear was provided for the outside

'T14' class 4−6−0 No. 443 under construction at Eastleigh Works in April 1911.   *Author's collection*

'T14' class No. 462, in original condition, alongside Eastleigh coaling stage.

J. E. Kite Collection

cylinders, with rocking levers operating the inside valves. The drive remained divided with the outside cylinders powering the centre pair of coupled wheels and the inside pair the leading drivers. As with the earlier 4—6—0s, the running plate was straight and level with the top of the buffer beam, but the piston valves were above the platform. A very substantial casing joined the cylinders to the smoke-box to create an unusually massive front-end and this gave rise to one of the nicknames, the *Double-breasters*. The other arose from the enormous splashers, which by embracing the coupled wheels and valve gear conjured thoughts of holiday outings by paddle steamers, so not unexpectedly, the class also became known as the *Paddle-boxes*. The splashers were pierced centrally for oiling and inspection, with the circular openings being protected from ash and stone by toughened glass doors. In later years the glass was replaced by metal sheeting.

The double bogie tender was fitted with a tank extension and had a capacity of 4,500 gallons of water and 5 tons of coal. The former proved inadequate when working heavy Bournemouth expresses, therefore during the assembly of 'D15' class 4—4—0s Nos. 463-7 in 1912, five double bogie tenders carrying 5,800 gallons of water and 8 tons of coal were built with them and on completion transferred to the 'T14s'. Details are:-

443 – 7/1912; 444 – 7/1912; 445 – 8/1912; 446 – 9/1912; 447 – 10/1912.

These tenders weighed 60 tons 8 cwt, were the largest used by the South Western and when viewed from rail level appeared truly massive. The discarded 4,500 gallon tenders were transferred to 'D15s' Nos. 463-7.

Five more 'T14s', Nos. 458/60-3, were ordered from Eastleigh Works in May 1911 and delivered at a cost of £3,480 each between December 1911 and July 1912. Before being painted in passenger livery, No. 463 was renumbered 459, this becoming possible by changing the '700' class 0—6—0 of that number to 316. All five engines were equipped with steam driers. Like the earlier series, Nos. 458/60/1 entered service with 4,500 gallon tenders, which were exchanged for the 5,800 gallon pattern in December 1912 and January 1913, but Nos. 459/62 always ran with large tenders. Again the discarded 4,500 gallon tenders were transferred to the 'D15' class.

In regular service the modified front-end and higher working pressure proved advantageous and gave an edge on the 'G14s' and 'P14s', particularly between Waterloo and Basingstoke, although the retention of the long, flat and shallow grate, cramped ashpan and inadequate main bearings demanded highly skilled firing and driving. For firemen the main problem was maintaining the front of the grate well covered for an enormous throw was necessary, with care having to be taken to avoid coal striking the underside of the brick arch and creating a mound. Should this occur, it was virtually impossible to feed the front of the fire and steam pressure fell away unless the crew risked life and limb by employing the 11 ft. fire iron to push the mound forward. Few considered that their terms of employment demanded such conscientiousness, consequently time was lost and when later in the journey drivers attempted recovery

'T14' class No. 446 showing the Drummond steam drier. *Author's collection*

Superheated 'T14' No. 458 in Eastleigh Works yard with an extended smokebox, boiler barrel clackboxes, Urie smokebox door and power classification, conventional firebox and a 5,800 gallon double bogie tender.   *Author's collection*

by thrashing their engines, hot boxes developed. As a result, the class seldom eclipsed well-crewed 'T9s' and 'L12s', while for the Bournemouth expresses the 'D15s' proved better engines. Nevertheless, the availability was reasonably good and the mileages worked to the first general repairs were excellent. Details are:-

443	4/1915	118,643	458	10/1913	79,349
444	12/1913	69,068	459	8/1914	73,012
445	8/1915	113,517	460	5/1914	80,437
446	3/1915	101,903	461	2/1914	73,419
447	5/1914	96,618	462	6/1914	81,864

Like the earlier 4—6—0s, the boiler was fed by two Duplex pumps, but these did not prove entirely satisfactory when working hard and as early as October 1913 were being replaced by hot water injectors. Other early modifications included the fitting of sheet metal splasher inspection doors, the removal of the steam driers and repositioning the clackboxes on the boiler barrel.

When new Nos. 443-7/58/9 were stationed at Nine Elms for the Bournemouth and Salisbury expresses, while Bournemouth had Nos. 460-2 for the Waterloo expresses until all ten 'D15s' were in service, when they were transferred to Salisbury.

In July 1912 the fastest Bournemouth expresses were booked 120 minutes for the 108 mile journey non-stop at an average speed of 54 mph, timings which many Nine Elms crews found impossible to achieve with the original 4,500 gallon tenders, for 5 or 6 minutes were either lost taking water at Southampton West or by uninspired driving to conserve the available supply and avoid the unscheduled stops. In contrast, 'T9s' and 'L12s' with their 4,000 gallon

tenders had no difficulty completing the journey in either direction non-stop. With the 5,800 gallon tender, the problem disappeared and 'T14' timing on these services became exemplary.

At this period the best West of England express, the 11.00 a.m. Waterloo-Salisbury, was allowed 91 minutes non-stop for the 83¾ miles, but this was increased to 94 minutes, also non-stop, for the 11.10 a.m., 12.00 p.m. and 3.30 p.m. services. The fastest up expresses, the 7.20 a.m., 10.17 a.m. and 12.00 p.m. from Exeter, were booked 92 minutes non-stop into Waterloo from Salisbury, while for those stopping at Andover Junction and Basingstoke this was increased to 104 minutes. Generally these services proved easier to work than the fast Bournemouths for although two or three minutes were frequently dropped to Worting Junction with down trains, they were usually regained by Salisbury.

The Coal Returns for the four weeks ending 5th May 1913 give the following details for those stationed at Nine Elms:

No.	Mileage Worked	Coal Burnt per Mile		Oil Consumed per 100 Miles	
		Allowance lb	Actual lb	Allowance lb	Actual lb
443	2,984	40	46.4	12	15.1
444	3,099	40	47.8	12	14.8
445	1,847	40	45.9	12	14.2
446	2,796	40	48.3	12	14.6
447	3,148	40	47.8	12	14.7
458	1,746	40	46.1	12	13.9
459	2,654	40	47.6	12	14.4

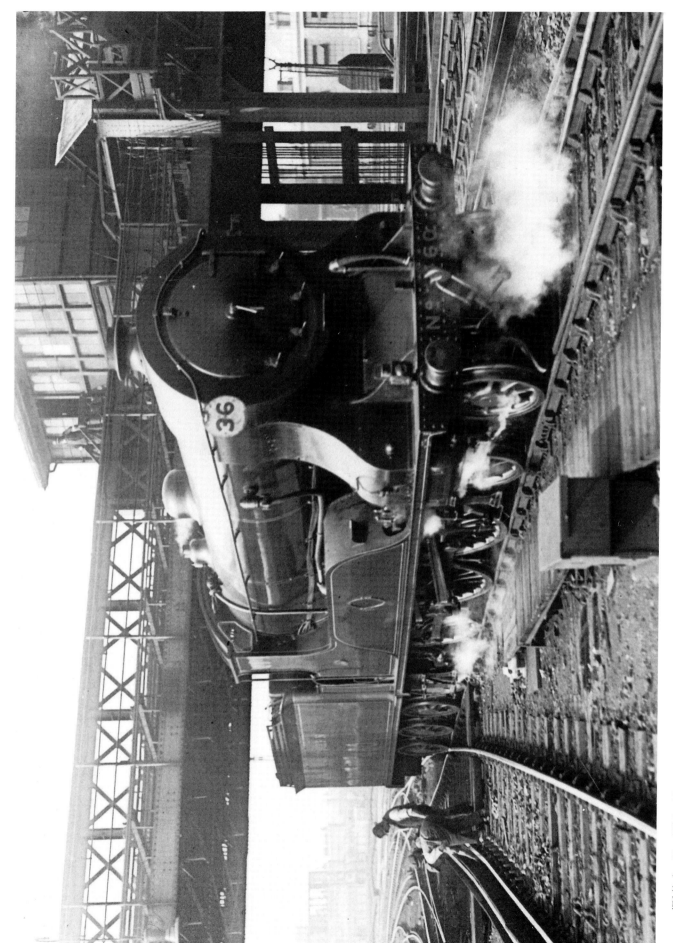

H. G. W. Household

'T14' class No. 460 backing out of Waterloo station on 6th August 1927.

'T14' class No. E443 in Southern livery, with a Maunsell superheater and smokebox snifting valves, heading a Salisbury semi-fast in April 1930.
Photomatic

After consulting this return and those for the rest of the year, Urie concluded that superheating was the only means of reducing the operating costs and on 24th April 1914 ordered the necessary material for Nos. 443/5/6/58. The work was undertaken by Eastleigh at a cost of £384 each in August-December 1915, when in addition to the superheater, a conventional firebox, an extended smokebox and saddle, a Urie smokebox door, two Detroit sight-feed lubricators, a heavy dragbox below the footplate and a shorter chimney were fitted, the dragbox to compensate for the weight of the superheater.

No. 458, the first modified, ran a series of test runs on the Waterloo-Salisbury expresses in September 1915 and probably on the Salisbury-Exeter services also, for it was observed at Queen Street on 2nd October 1915. Although not proving capable of 'H15' performance, it nevertheless displayed a marked improvement as well as burning considerably less coal. Details of the Waterloo-Salisbury trials are:-

Coal Burnt per Mile		Oil Consumed per 100 Miles		Loads
Allowance	Actual	Allowance	Actual	
35 lb	39.4 lb	12 lb	14.6 lb	8 bogies and a van

With such encouraging results, Urie had no hesitation in authorising similar treatment for Nos. 444/7/59-62 on 7th October 1915.

The changed dimensions were:-

Heating surfaces:

Small tubes (118 x 2″)	873 sq. ft.
Large tubes (21 x 5¼″)	407 sq. ft.
Firebox	158 sq. ft.
Total evaporative	1,438 sq. ft.
Superheater	269 sq. ft.
Total	1,707 sq. ft.
Working pressure	175 lb

Weights in working order:

	LSWR	Southern (1928)
Bogie	22T 12C	23T 0C
Leading coupled wheels	18T 0C	18T 5C
Centre coupled wheels	18T 0C	18T 5C
Trailing coupled wheels	17T 3C	17T 8C
Engine total	75T 15C	76T 18C

Dates of superheating are:-

443	11/1915	447	2/1917	460	9/1916
444	7/1917	448	8/1915	461	2/1918
445	12/1915	459	5/1917	462	10/1917
446	11/1915				

In this form the class appeared considerably larger and more impressive for the extended smokebox gave a more balanced look to the hitherto rather cumbersome front end.

During the war regular appearances were made on the heavier Waterloo-Salisbury services, troop specials, van trains and Nine Elms-Southampton docks goods. Hitherto

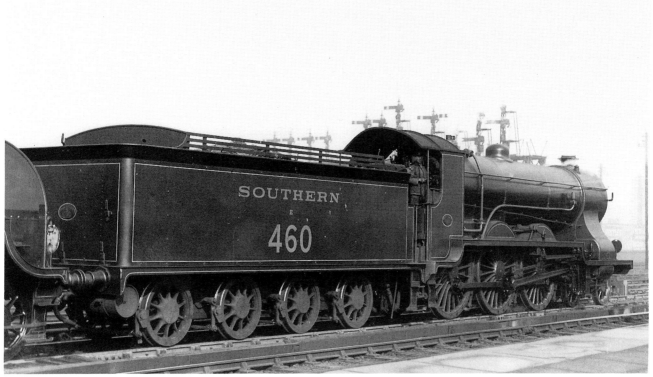

'T14' class No. E460 after the 1930 Maunsell modifications at Clapham Junction, on 24th February 1931.　　　*H. C. Casserley*

hot boxes had not proved a problem, but either because of superheating, inferior maintenance or poorer quality lubricating oil, there was a dramatic increase and by mid-1919 the average mileage between occurrence was only 8,300. As a result the class was replaced on the best services, first by the 'H15s' and later by the new Urie express 4–6–0s.

At Grouping all entered Southern Railway stock to be painted Maunsell green and receive the E-prefix. Details are:-

443	3/1924	447	1/1924	460	11/1924
444	10/1925	458	4/1924	461	12/1925
445	3/1924	459	5/1924	462	5/1924
446	1/1925				

The class remained at Nine Elms working a variety of secondary passenger duties, including the Salisbury and Southampton via Alton semi-fasts, van trains, seaside excursions and ocean liner specials, until mid-1924 when Nos. 444/58/60/1 were transferred to Salisbury as replacements for 'F13' class Nos. 330-4 on the Eastleigh and Southampton docks coal and goods trains. However, this was only a temporary measure for when Maunsell 'S15s' Nos. 828-32 became available in mid-1927, they were returned to Nine Elms.

On summer Saturdays, despite the availability of thirty 'King Arthurs' and the post-Grouping 'H15s', it remained necessary to roster the class for Bournemouth reliefs, therefore in January 1930 Maunsell decided to improve their performance by fitting mechanical lubricators, removing the cumbersome splashers and raising the running plate to expose the coupled wheel boxes to the cooling effect of the atmosphere. These dates and those for the

fitting of Maunsell superheaters and the removal of the E-prefix are:-

No.	Maunsell Superheater	Modified	E-prefix Discarded
443	11/1928 (a)	7/1931	7/1931
444	3/1931	3/1931	5/1933
445	1/1929 (a)	2/1931	12/1932
446	10/1929 (a)	8/1931	8/1931
447	9/1930	9/1930	2/1932
458	11/1930	11/1930	9/1932
459	1/1931	1/1931	9/1932
460	4/1930	4/1930	11/1931
461	6/1931	6/1931	6/1931
462	8/1930	8/1930 (b)	4/1932

(a) Maunsell superheaters and smokebox snifting valves fitted before modification (superheater heating surface 295 sq. ft.).

(b) No. 462 carried the boiler removed from the 'Lord Nelson' class trials engine No. 0449.

Despite the removal of the splashers the Diagram Book only records a small weight reduction:-

Bogie	21T 5C
Leading coupled wheels	18T 18C
Centre coupled wheels	18T 11C
Trailing coupled wheels	17T 16C
Total	76T 10C

In regular service from Nine Elms, the modifications proved most beneficial and in April 1932 Maunsell reported that the availability and fuel consumption was similar to the Urie 'H15s'.

'T14' class No. 459 passing Vauxhall on 2nd June 1934. *G. K. J. Kerley*

No major duty changes occurred, although on summer Saturdays greater use was made of the class on the Bournemouth reliefs and Waterloo-Lymington services. Probably the best indication of the rejuvenation was their use on the Saturday up 'Bournemouth Belle' during the summer months of 1934-5. The down train was rostered for a 'King Arthur', but the poorly patronised late afternoon return working could be safely entrusted to lesser engines, while the 'King Arthur' returned earlier to Waterloo with a heavy holiday express. Nos. 445/59/61/2 were recorded in 1934 and Nos. 444/60/2 in 1935. Also used were 'N15s' and Maunsell 'H15s', with occasional appearances by the Urie 'H15s'. Nevertheless, after 'Schools' Nos. 924-33 were released by the Portsmouth electrification, Bulleid found the class expendable and forbade the manufacture of further major parts. Fortunately two spare fireboxes and a set of cylinders had recently been provided for stock and therefore were available when Nos. 458/61 with serious defects arrived at Eastleigh Works later in the year, but No. 443 with faulty cylinders was condemned on 5th January 1938. However, because of the deteriorating political situation, Bulleid rescinded his instructions and No. 443 was returned to traffic in March 1938. In view of the extensive use made of the class during the final peacetime summer and later throughout World War 2, this was probably as well. Details for August Bank Holiday Saturday 1939 are:-

No.	Duties
462	9.17 a.m. to Bournemouth Central, 2.57 p.m. return.
446	9.22 a.m. to Bournemouth West, stopper to Eastleigh, 6.40 p.m. goods to Salisbury and milk tanks to Vauxhall.
459	9.27 a.m. to Bournemouth West, 1.11 p.m. return.
444	10.47 a.m. to Bournemouth Central, 3.20 p.m. return.
461	11.22 a.m. to Bournemouth Central, 3.40 p.m. return.
443	12.22 p.m. to Bournemouth Central, 5.05 p.m. return.

Of the others, No. 445 worked the 1.04 p.m. Waterloo-Salisbury, No. 447 was stopped at Nine Elms, No. 458 worked empty carriage stock to Southampton docks and No. 460 had charge of a Clapham Junction-Bulford Camp troop special.

Apart from these relief workings, there were only two booked Nine Elms duties, these being: Tuesdays and Wednesdays only: 10.42 a.m. Waterloo-Weymouth, returning at 7.32 p.m. (excursion). Daily: 3.08 a.m. Clapham Junction-Salisbury milk train, 6.57 a.m. Salisbury-Waterloo semi-fast, carriage piloting at Clapham Junction and empty carriage stock to and from Waterloo, 2.54 p.m. Waterloo-Salisbury and 7.54 p.m. return. (This duty was often shared by two members of the class.)

After the outbreak of war, evacuee specials were worked from the London area and Southampton to Brockenhurst, Christchurch, Bournemouth, Poole and Dorchester, but following the introduction of the emergency timetable, Nos. 444/6/60 were placed in store and Nos. 459/61 relegated to carriage heating at Clapham Junction. All returned to traffic for the extra Christmas services.

The Bulleid livery changes first affected the class in mid-1940, details being:

Maunsell green, unlined, cabside numerals, Bulleid lettering: Nos. 444 (July 1940), 447 (October 1940).
Malachite green, unlined, cabside numerals, Bulleid lettering: No. 459 (November 1940).

All later repaints, commencing with No. 446 in August 1941, were plain black. Because of wartime shortages, it was June 1945 before the green finally disappeared with the repainting of No. 459.

When No. 447 required a replacement chimney in October 1940, Eastleigh was unable to supply a spare from stock, so a short stovepipe of similar pattern to those currently carried by the large Urie tanks was fabricated and fitted. In course of time all, except No. 458, were similarly fitted, dates being:-

443	8/1942	446	8/1941	460	12/1945
444	2/1946	447	10/1940	461	1/1946
445	11/1945	459	11/1940	462	8/1942

As often occurs when circumstances force a modification, the new chimney materially improved the steaming.

The loan of 4−6−0s to the Great Western and LNER in 1941-2 left the Western Section short of some twenty modern engines, which was made good numerically by returning the 'T14s' to main line duty and borrowing Atlantics, 4−6−2 tanks and 4−4−0s from the Central and Eastern Sections. Consequently, for the remainder of hostilities, the class was fully employed working the Waterloo-Basingstoke-Salisbury semi-fasts, Yeovil milk tankers, troop and petroleum tanker specials, van trains and heavy goods. The latter included those from Nine Elms yard and Feltham to Reading, Willesden and Neasden for which Nos. 443/5/7/60 were shedded at Feltham in 1943-4. No. 444, newly painted black, was noted heading an up goods at Seaton Junction on 27th October 1943, while No. 462 was standing on Exmouth Junction shed on 17th November 1944. By this date all were filthy dirty and often in such poor mechanical order that the front-end was continually shrouded in steam and the exhaust beat so irregular that instead of four equal beats per revolution there was a roar, two feeble grunts and a gasp. That most duties were completed could only be credited to the massively strong construction.

No. 458 had the misfortune to be standing on Nine Elms shed when a number of high explosive bombs fell in the area. One struck its firebox casing and on exploding caused such extensive damage that breaking up was ordered on 2nd October 1940. The remainder of the class survived hostilities and in 1945-6 received badly needed heavy repairs, the dates being:-

443	11/1945	446	9/1945	460	12/1945
444	2/1946	447	11/1946	461	1/1946
445	11/1945	459	6/1945	462	7/1946

All were painted plain black, but Nos. 443/4/60 received new fireboxes and Nos. 446/60/1 had their cylinders replaced. Despite the presence of Merchant Navy and West Country Pacifics, Nos. 443/6/7/60-2 appeared regularly on the summer Saturday reliefs in 1946-7 and, although often losing time, nevertheless reached their destinations, which was more than many of their modern replacements achieved.

'T14' class No. 445 in wartime black livery and fitted with a short stove-pipe chimney, at Eastleigh shed awaiting breaking up on 5th November 1948.

Author

'T14' class No. 30461 in British Railways plain black livery with lettered tender, buffer beam numerals and the snifting valves removed, being coaled at Eastleigh on 19th August 1950.　　　　　　　　　　　　　　　　　　　　　　　　　　　　　　*W. Gilburt*

All nine entered British Railways stock at Nationalisation, although only three were renumbered, their details being:-

30446　8/1948　plain black, buffer beam numerals and tender lettered British Railways
30461　4/1948　ditto
30447　12/1949　not repainted

All three had the snifting valves removed, as they were from No. 447 in November 1947.

The 1948 summer again saw the class heading Bournemouth reliefs, the Waterloo-Basingstoke-Salisbury semi-fasts, empty carriage stock trains, the occasional troop special and the Yeovil milk tankers. The most consistent performers were Nos. 444/60, 30461 and 462. However, with more light Pacifics entering traffic and taking over duties hitherto worked by 'King Arthurs', the end was in sight, with Nos. 445/9/60 being condemned in October and November 1948. The next casualty came in May 1949, when No. 443 fractured its motionplate, while No. 30447, after receiving light repairs in November 1949 and being despatched to Eastleigh shed on 2nd December 1949, failed five days later with serious frame fractures and was condemned.

The four survivors, Nos. 444, 30446/61 and 462, remained working van, fish and empty carriage stock trains until February 1950, when Nos. 444/62 were laid aside, leaving the more recently repaired Nos. 30446/61 available for a final summer season. Few anticipated a major role being played, but poor Bulleid Pacific availability led to No. 30461 appearing regularly on the ten carriage 1.24

p.m. Waterloo-Salisbury and No. 30446 on the 3.54 p.m. Waterloo-Basingstoke or the Yeovil milk tankers. No. 30446 made its final main line appearance on 23rd December 1950 with a Waterloo-Poole parcels train, thereafter odd local goods and van duties were undertaken until withdrawn in April 1951. Appropriately haulage to Eastleigh for breaking up was performed by No. 30461, which on this occasion escaped a similar fate, only to succumb six weeks later with a fractured steam pipe.

ENGINE SUMMARY

No.	Date	Order No.	Large Tender	Superheated	Modified	Withdrawn
443	5/1911	T14	7/1912	11/1915 (b)	7/1931	5/1949
444	5/1911	T14	7/1912	7/1917	3/1931	2/1950
445	6/1911	T14	8/1912	12/1915 (b)	2/1931	10/1948
446	6/1911	T14	9/1912	11/1915 (b)	8/1931	4/1951
447	7/1911	T14	10/1912	2/1917	9/1930	12/1949
458	12/1911	B15	12/1912	8/1915	11/1930	10/1940
459 (a)	7/1912	B15	7/1912	5/1917	12/1930	11/1948
460	2/1912	B15	12/1912	9/1916	4/1930	11/1948
461	4/1912	B15	1/1913	2/1918	6/1931	5/1951
462	5/1912	B15	5/1912	10/1917	8/1930	2/1950

All built at Eastleigh Works. Disposal: Nos. 443/4/6/7/61/2 broken up at Eastleigh Works, No. 458 at Nine Elms shed and Nos. 445/59/60 at Dinton.
(a) No. 459 was built as No. 463, but renumbered before entering traffic.
(b) Nos. 443/5/6 were fitted with Maunsell superheaters in 11/1928, 1/1929 and 10/1929, the remainder when modified. Mileages: Nos. 443 – 1,014,996; 447 – 1,103,419; 458 – 846,752; 459 – 1,044,200; 461 – 1,054,621.

GENERAL CLASSES

'700' class 0—6—0 No. 691 at Nine Elms in April 1897, with Drummond's smokebox spark arrester, conical smokebox door, train organ pipe whistles, numberplates, SWR lettered 13 ft wheelbase six-wheeled tender and additional boiler barrel lining. *V. Chambers*

'700' Class Six-Coupled Goods

Adams was unable to attend the February 1895 Locomotive Committee meeting because of illness and was represented by W. F. Pettigrew, the Nine Elms Works manager, who on behalf of his chief, sought authority to order 25 or 30 18 in. goods engines from outside contractors at an estimated cost of £95,000. Agreeing in principle, the Committee saw no reason why approved manufacturers should not be approached for tenders and delivery dates, but wished to examine and discuss the drawings with Adams before recommending an order to the Court of Directors. Unfortunately, before this could occur, rapidly deteriorating health forced Adams to offer his resignation, which was accepted with genuine regret on 13th June 1895. A new locomotive superintendent was immediately sought and until his advice became available the order was held in abeyance. Consequently, Drummond, on taking office, was able to substitute drawings of his own and when tenders had been received from seven manufacturers, belatedly notified the Locomotive Committee. Rightly they expressed annoyance at not being kept informed of the negotiations, but nevertheless agreed to consider the offers on 8th July 1896, when that by Dübs & Co. at £2,700 was accepted for delivery by 30th June 1897. Details of the other tenders are: Beyer Peacock & Co. £2,990; Kitson & Co. £2,800; Vulcan Foundry £2,800; Neilson & Co. £2,785; Sharp

Stewart & Co. £2,695; Robert Stephenson & Co. £2,675. The last mentioned offer was rejected because delivery could not be promised before January 1898, while on becoming aware of the slightly lower tender, Dübs agreed to reduce their price to match it.

Known as the '700' class and numbered 687-716 when delivered between March and August 1897, they were similar in appearance and power to engines built some years earlier by Drummond for the Caledonian Railway. Many parts, including the boiler, firebox, cylinders and motion were standard with the 'C8' class 4—4—0s and 'M7' class 0—4—4 tanks and, apart from the firebox cross water tubes, also with the 'K10' class mixed traffic 4—4—0s. The dimensions were as follows:

Cylinders	18½″ x 26″
Coupled wheels	5′ 1″
Wheelbase	7′ 6″ + 9′ 0″ = 16′ 6″
Boiler diameter	4′ 5″
Boiler length	10′ 6″ (Tubeplates 10′ 9 3/8″)
Firebox length	6′ 4″
Heating surfaces:	
Tubes (216 x 1¾″)	1,068 sq. ft.
Firebox	124 sq. ft.
Total	1,192 sq. ft.
Working pressure	175 lb
Grate area	20.4 sq. ft.

Weights in working order:

Leading coupled wheels	13T 12C
Centre coupled wheels	16T 6C
Trailing coupled wheels	12T 17C
Engine total	42T 15C
Tender	37T 14C
Engine & Tender	80T 9C

The class conformed to Drummond's early South Western style by having cabside numberplates, organ pipe whistles, lever reversing, boiler barrel clackboxes, injectors, unbalanced crank axles, spark arresters, conical smokebox doors and gravity sanding. The neat six-wheel 13 ft equally divided wheelbase tender was lettered SWR and had a capacity of 4 tons of coal and 3,500 gallons of water. The Diagram Book and 31st December 1922 Engine List record the fully laden weight as 36 tons 14 cwt, but Dübs' order book gives the following details:

Empty weight	19T 5C
Coal	4T 0C
Water	15T 12½C
Sand	1C
Tools	0½C
Total (fully laden)	38T 19C

In 1928 the Southern Railway recorded 37T 14C for all '700' class tenders, regardless of whether the wheelbase was 13 or 14 ft.

Most new engines suffer teething-troubles during their first thousand miles, but the '700s' developed more problems than most, for the regulators had an unpleasant tendency of jamming open, the crank axles of Nos. 687-91 developed serious flaws, the boilers steamed badly, several tyres worked loose and lineside residents objected to the organ pipe whistles.

On inspection, the regulator assembly was found to deviate from the drawings and had to be rectified by Nine Elms works at Dübs' expense, although not before No. 688 fell into the Bournemouth turntable pit and No. 690 crashed into the six carriage 6.40 a.m. Yeovil Junction-Town train on 10th July 1897. For a time the organ pipe complaints were ignored by Waterloo, no doubt in the assumption that lineside residents would become accustomed to their sound, but they did not and after the cause was taken up by several local and two national newspapers, the Locomotive Committee on 4th August 1897 instructed Drummond to replace them forthwith by standard whistles. This instruction was reported as having been complied with on 24th

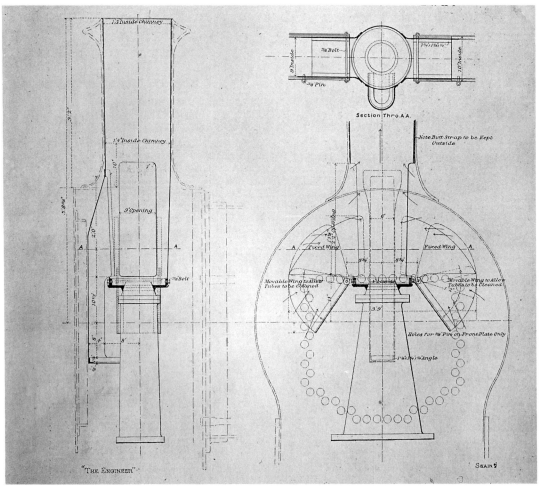

The Drummond spark arrester.   *Engineer*

A close look at the '700' class front end when delivered by Dübs showing the separate smokebox hand railing and three securing wheels. No. 689 at Salisbury with a West of England goods in 1897.

J. B. N. Ashford

December 1897, but a photograph exists of No. 693 with an Adams smokebox door and the tender lettered LSWR, yet still carrying an organ pipe. The axles of Nos. 687-91 and the tyres of Nos. 698-701 were replaced at Dübs' expense in September-October 1897, but Drummond's attempt to blame the erratic steaming on poor workmanship and deviation from specification proved abortive, when Dübs' representative found that it was caused by the hoods and baffle plates of the spark arresters. As a result, the apparatus was hastily discarded, although it was 1902-4 before the conical smokebox doors were replaced by Adams' pattern. Once these early teething-problems were overcome, the class gave sound, trouble-free service until superseded on the heaviest main line goods by the Urie 'S15s' in 1920-1.

Unlike many railways, the South Western seldom confused and irritated historians with apparent needless re-numberings, but the '700s' proved an exception for in 1898 Nos. 702-16 were altered to 306/8/9/15/7/25-7/39/46/50/2/5/68, 459 to make way for the Dübs built 'T9' class 4-4-0s. A further complication became necessary in June 1912, when No. 459 (ex-No. 716) had to be renumbered

316 to make way for the new Drummond 'T14' class 4-6-0s.

As soon as run-in, the class replaced the Adams '395s' and 'Jubilees' on the West of England, Southampton, Portsmouth, Bournemouth and Dorchester goods. However, most of the other services remained with the Adams classes, for the '700s' were rostered regularly for secondary passenger duties, excursions and troop specials, including those of the Boer war when on one day no less than nineteen trains were worked to Southampton docks. Nos. 308/15/7/25/6/52, 457, 687-9/95/7/8 went new to Nine Elms and formed the subject of a Locomotive Committee report in June 1901. Details are:-

Average yearly mileage	27,194
Average mileage to general repair	67,908
Average availability	79%
Coal consumption: Heavy goods	50.8 lb per mile
Local goods	44.6 lb per mile
Excursions & specials	36.7 lb per mile

At this period the remainder of the class were stationed at: Strawberry Hill Nos. 309/27/46, 693; Fratton Nos. 691/9; Northam Nos. 306/50/5, 692; Salisbury Nos. 690/4,

'700' class No. 459 (ex-No. 716) passing St. Cross with the 10.20 a.m. Nine Elms-Southampton goods on 19th August 1901.   *C. H. Eden*

701; Bournemouth No. 699; Exmouth Junction Nos. 339/68, 691/6. The small West of England allocation was because the Plymouth, North Devon and North Cornwall goods remained with the Adams '380' 4—4—0s, '395' 0—6—0s and 'Jubilee' 0—4—2s. However, by March 1904 Nos. 691/3/4 were also stationed at Exmouth Junction and mainly employed on the stone ballast trains.

The frequent use on troop trains, excursions and horse-box specials led to Nos. 687 (November 1912) and 700 (June 1912) being equipped with the Westinghouse air brake. The fittings were obtained from 'Jubilees' Nos. 529/54 and like the dual-braked members of that class, the air pump was attached to the right-hand side of the firebox, where the cab lookout was not impeded. Before Grouping No. 687 was usually stationed at Fratton and No. 700 at Nine Elms or Strawberry Hill. The fittings were removed from the former in October 1935 and the latter in January 1936.

Before superheating, the boiler was interchangeable with classes 'C8', 'M7' and 'K10' (after Urie removed the firebox cross water tubes) but no interchange occurred before 1905-7, when five spare boilers were provided and fitted to:- 459 — 7/1907; 691 — 9/1907; 694 — 8/1907; 'M7s' 36 — 10/1905; 37 — 11/1905. The object of standardisation was to work the services with the minimum number of different boilers and major components, thereby reducing the construction and operating costs, a most laudable

practice, but unfortunately, having built a series of standard classes, many locomotive superintendents were loathe to authorise deviations. Consequently, boilers well suited to passenger operation frequently reappeared on goods classes where a larger pattern would have proved advantageous. This was a failing which beset the '700s', for the boiler and firebox giving excellent service on the 'M7' 0—4—4 tanks, proved wanting in bad weather on the West of England and Southampton market goods. The class badly needed the larger 'T9' boiler.

As a result of this failing, Drummond decided in 1906 to construct five four-cylinder 0—8—0s having the same boiler tender and other details as the 'F13' class 4—6—0s. However, before the drawings had been prepared and authorisation sought from the Locomotive Committee, the failure of these 4—6—0s in express service had left them available for working the Exmouth Junction-Salisbury goods and removed the need of new construction. Nevertheless, it would probably have been wiser to have cancelled the final 'L11' class mixed traffic 4—4—0 orders and substituted a similar number of '700s' with the wheelbase lengthened between the centre and trailing coupled wheels to accommodate the larger and better steaming 'T9' boiler.

During the war the volume of goods increased so rapidly that by mid-1915 the Drummond 4—6—0s and Urie 'H15s' were unable to cover all the main line duties and the '700s' had to bear the brunt of the additional services, especially those routed via Alton to reduce occupation of the Woking-Basingstoke line. To Drummond's credit, they withstood the many demands, double manning and scanty maintenance exceptionally well, with those in the London District averaging 83,000 miles between heavy repairs and on occasions working deep into 'foreign' territory, with Nos. 688/9 being recorded at Oxford in March 1915, No. 327 at Gloucester in June 1917, No. 696 at Bedford in October 1917 and Nos. 368, 699, 701 at Peterborough in February 1918. In March 1917 Nos. 309/46, 700 were fitted with tablet exchange apparatus at Highbridge Works for service on the Somerset & Dorset Joint line.

After the Armistice Urie decided that even more useful and economic work was possible by superheating and on 9th October 1919 ordered No. 316 (ex-Nos. 716 and 459) to be fitted with 18 in. frame extensions, 19 in. cylinders, a Detroit four-feed lubricator and an Eastleigh superheater. The saturated boiler was retubed, fitted with new tubeplates and firebox, an extended smokebox supported by a saddle, a Urie smokebox door and a capuchon-topped stove pipe chimney. Other changes included a 9 in. higher boiler pitch and a heavy drag-box below the footplate to compensate for the weight of the superheater — a most judicious reconstruction, which for a modest outlay of £772, transformed a modest Victorian goods engine into a modern 0-6-0 capable of working all but the heaviest main line goods. The changed dimensions were as follows:-

Cylinders	19" x 26"
Heating surfaces:	
Tubes, small (120 x 1¾")	593 sq. ft.
large (18 x 5¼")	266 sq. ft.
Firebox	117 sq. ft.
Total evaporative	976 sq. ft.
Superheater	167 sq. ft.
Total	1,143 sq. ft.
Working pressure	180 lb
Weights in working order:	
Leading coupled wheels	15T 9C
Centre coupled wheels	17T 0C
Trailing coupled wheels	14T 5C
Engine total	46T 14C

No. 316 returned to traffic on 23rd December 1920 and early in the New Year ran a series of trials on the Southampton-Nine Elms Yard and Eastleigh-Salisbury goods to compare the performance and coal consumption with the saturated members of the class. In June 1921 Urie reported a saving of 6.8 lb of coal per train mile and on the strength of this was authorised by the Locomotive Committee to superheat ten more. Details are:-

308	9/1922	350	3/1922	689	12/1922
326	6/1923	368	11/1922	694	2/1922
339	5/1924	687	6/1923	700	1/1923
346	11/1923				

'700' class No. 326 (ex-No. 708) at Nine Elms on 26th February 1908 with the spark arrester removed, conventional smokebox door substituted for the conical pattern, continuous boiler handrailing, standard whistle, transfer numerals, footsteps between the leading and centre coupled wheels and LSWR lettered tender.

J. B. Ashford

Superheated '700' class No. 700 at Nine Elms on 17th April 1923 with an extended smokebox, Urie pattern smokebox door and power classification, tall capuchon topped stove-pipe chimney and the Westinghouse brake.

H. C. Casserley

After Grouping Maunsell extended modernisation to the remainder of the class using his own pattern superheater, which had a slightly larger heating surface (182 sq. ft.) and was distinguishable by two smokebox top snifting valves. When those fitted with Eastleigh superheaters required heavy repairs, the Maunsell pattern was substituted.

The dates when this pattern superheater was fitted and those for receiving Southern Railway livery and losing the E-prefix, are as follows:-

No.	Southern Livery	Maunsell Superheater	E-prefix Removed
306	10/1925 (a, c)	4/1929	2/1932
308	10/1925	11/1931	11/1931
309	1/1925	1/1925	8/1934
315	10/1925	10/1925	4/1932
316	5/1925	3/1931	9/1933
317	4/1925	4/1925	8/1933
325	9/1925	9/1925	7/1933
326	3/1926	6/1931	6/1931
327	2/1926	2/1926	8/1931
339	5/1924	2/1931	7/1933
346	10/1926	11/1933	10/1933
350	7/1926	7/1929	2/1933
352	10/1924 (c)	5/1927	12/1933
355	10/1924 (c)	7/1929	9/1932
368	3/1925	3/1930	6/1932
687	2/1926	1/1932	1/1932
688	2/1924 (c)	8/1927	10/1933
689	12/1925	10/1931	10/1931
690	2/1926	2/1926	4/1932
691	11/1926	11/1926	7/1932
692	12/1926	12/1926	12/1932
693	4/1926 (d)	4/1926	4/1932
694	5/1925	4/1931	2/1934
695	1/1926 (d)	1/1926	4/1932
696	12/1923 (b, c, d)	9/1926	10/1931
647	9/1925	9/1925	12/1933
698	10/1925	10/1925	9/1931
699	2/1924 (c)	3/1927	3/1932
700	11/1926	5/1929	8/1932
701	6/1924 (c)	3/1927	7/1932

(a) No. 306 ran in LSWR livery attached to a Southern painted tender from January to July 1925, when works were entered for a general repair.
(b) No E-prefix when despatched from shops, added by Eastleigh shed.
(c) Southern livery before superheated.
(d) New boiler when superheated.

In 1925-6 the class was involved in a complicated series of tender exchanges to provide 'T9s' Nos. 300/1/4/7/10-4/36 and 'D15s' Nos. 463-72 with six-wheel 13 ft. wheelbase 3,500 gallon tenders for service on the Eastern Section and the Portsmouth-Waterloo line. The '700s' concerned were Nos. 306/8/9/15/7/25/7/50/2/5/68, 689-93/5-8, which in return received similar capacity, but 14 ft. wheelbase six-wheel tenders from classes 'K10' and 'L11'. Full details of these exchanges will be found under classes 'T9' and 'D15'.

After the Maunsell 'S15s' entered traffic, most of the main line goods duties were lost, but fortunately the rapid withdrawal of the early Adams 'Jubilees' left ample scope and in mid-1931 the class was well scattered throughout the Western Section for working transfer and local goods, van trains and Sunday excursions to the Central Section seaside resorts. The allocation was:- Nine Elms Nos. 697, 700; Feltham Nos. 308/9/15/46/68, 687/8/98/9, 701; Guildford Nos. 350/2, 690/2/4; Eastleigh Nos. 316/25/7/39, 689/95; Salisbury Nos. 317, 691/6; Bournemouth No. 355; Exmouth Junction Nos. 306/26, 693.

The maximum chimney height was greater on the Western Section than elsewhere; consequently when chimney renewal was necessary, the replacement stove pipes were without capuchons. Other minor changes around the same period, included the omission of the E-prefix, the

Saturated '700' class No. E699 in Southern Railway lined goods livery at Feltham circa 1925.   *G. E. Mitchell*

'700' class No. E695 with a Maunsell superheater and smokebox snifting valves, October 1926.   *W. Beckerlegge*

'700' class No. 698 with Maunsell superheater and smokebox snifting valves.   *R. C. Riley Collection*

use of 15 in. instead of 18 in. tender numerals and, commencing with No. 691 in August 1935, the omission of the lining.

The classification was changed to C, the same as the Urie power rating, in December 1936, but, since this caused confusion with the Eastern Section ex-SE & CR Wainwright 0—6—0s, it was returned to the original terminology from October 1937.

For some years the stretch of line between the south end of Sevenoaks tunnel and Hildenborough had suffered badly from water-logged ballast and earth slips. Various minor remedial measures had failed to overcome the problem, so in March 1938 the Engineer's Department commenced excavating the clay sub-soil and replacing it with stone ballast from Meldon Quarry. These stone trains were worked from Salisbury by '700s' Nos. 317, 346/68 (on loan from Feltham), 691/6 via Woking, Guildford, Redhill and Tonbridge, with engines often being absent from Salisbury for several days. As soon as this task was completed the same engines commenced appearing at Rochester, Chatham and Gillingham, where the track was being re-ballasted and renewed in preparation for electrification the following year. On Sunday, 2nd October 1938 nos. 315/7/46, 696 were noted on Gillingham shed and No. 700 at Redhill.

Twenty modern and relatively powerful six-coupled goods of Maunsell design, 'Q' class Nos. 530-49, were constructed by Eastleigh Works at a cost of £7,000 each (without tenders) between January 1938 and September 1939, but, because they were intended as replacements for withdrawn Adams 'Jubilees', their arrival on the Western Section did not materially affect the '700s', whose allocation and duties were:-

Shed	Allocation	Duties
Nine Elms	339, 701	One duty, a goods to Leatherhead and Bookham. At weekends both were usually employed ballasting.
Feltham	308/9/25-7/46/52/68, 687-9/93/5-7/, 700	There were eleven booked duties: Goods to Wokingham and Reading; Brent (two duties); Teddington and Brent; Neasden and Farnham; Weybridge, Guildford and Hither Green; Shepperton and Windsor; Richmond and Barnes; Staines and Willesden; Neasden and Brent; Micheldever (constructing and equipping an Army depot).
Guildford	692/4/8/9	Three booked duties: Local goods and shunting in Aldershot area; Guildford-Petersfield (S.O. worked Midhurst passenger services); Farnham and Petersfield goods (S.X. worked Midhurst passenger services).
Salisbury	315/7/55, 690/1	Five booked duties: Goods to Andover Junction and Basingstoke; goods to Andover Junction, 1.06 p.m. passenger to Basingstoke and return to Salisbury with milk vans (S.O. 2.38 p.m. passenger Basingstoke-Reading and 6.15 p.m. return) 12.20 a.m. milk train to Salisbury; goods to Wimborne and Hamworthy Junction; Ballast trains Salisbury-Woking-Guildford and beyond as required (two duties).

Eastleigh 306/16/50 One booked duty, 7.15 a.m. goods Eastleigh-Petersfield, shunting, Petersfield-Woking, shunting, light engine to Guildford shed, 5.28 a.m. (next day) Woking-Rowlands Castle and Petersfield-Eastleigh (two day duty). The spare engines often worked the Eastleigh-Alton goods in place of the 'Jubilees'.

Summer Sundays and Bank Holidays

Feltham: Excursions from Wimbledon, Feltham, Windsor and Reading to Bognor Regis, Brighton, Littlehampton, Eastbourne and Hastings.

Guildford: Excursions from Surbiton and Reading to Bognor Regis and Littlehampton.

Most were routed via Christ's Hospital, where engines were changed, and the '700s' worked light to Horsham shed to spend the day gently simmering alongside local 'C3s' and 'D1s'.

The Bulleid livery changes of the immediate pre-war years did not affect the class and plain black with tender numerals and Maunsell lettering remained standard until November 1939, when No. 327 left Eastleigh Works with cabside numerals and Bulleid lettering. Because of the war there were fewer repaints; consequently it was not until August 1943 with No. 326 that the Maunsell livery was finally superseded.

During the first year of hostilities few duty changes occurred, but, following the French capitulation, attacks on coastal shipping caused such severe losses that it became necessary to transfer much of the north-south freight to the railways. As most of these routes crossed London and were vulnerable to air attack, a safer if devious route avoiding the Metropolis was created between the LMS, LNER and all three sections of the Southern Railway, but particularly the Western and Eastern Sections, which involved the provision of spurs at Staines Moor Junction, Sandy, Bletchley and Calvert. When completed in mid-September 1940, the route from the LNER (GE Section) was via Cambridge, Bletchley, Claydon, Calvert, High Wycombe, Northolt, Greenford and West Drayton to Staines Moor Junction, with traffic from the LNER (GNR Section) feeding in at Sandy, the LMS (Midland Division) at Bedford, the LMS (Western Division) at Bletchley and the LNER (GC Section) at Calvert. The motive power arrangement was for the Southern to work as far as Greenford or Northolt, although at the height of the bombing this was not strictly adhered to and Southern engines frequently worked through to Bletchley or Bedford and occasionally Cambridge. As the Staines West line was restricted to Great Western 'yellow' classes, the use of 'S15s', 'H15s' and 'N15s' was precluded, consequently '700s' became the standard motive power, occasionally assisted by Adams '0395s' Nos. 3400/40/2/96 and ex-SE & CR 'C' class 0-6-0s on loan from the Eastern Section. To cover these extra duties, the Nine Elms '700' allocation was increased to twenty, Nos. 308/9/25-7/39/46/52/68, 687-9/92-7 and 700/1, until mid-1943 when the reduced bombing permitted greater use of the direct routes.

All survived hostilities and at Nationalisation entered British Railways stock to be renumbered into the 30,000 series and painted goods black. Two, No. S316 from 6th March to 27th November 1948, and No. S326 from 14th February 1948 to 1st July 1949, carried the temporary

S-prefix. Around the same period the smokebox top snifting valves were removed and these dates, together with those of renumbering and receiving British Railways livery, are as follows:

No.	BR No.	BR Livery	Snifting Valves Removed
306	3/1949	3/1949	3/1951
308	1/1951	1/1951	2/1948
309	11/1949	11/1949	11/1949
315	10/1948	11/1951	10/1948
316	11/1948	3/1948 (a)	3/1948
317	8/1948	10/1950	10/1950
325	12/1950	12/1950	12/1950
326	7/1949	2/1948 (a)	2/1948
327	9/1948	11/1951	9/1948
339	9/1948	9/1948	9/1948
346	12/1949	12/1949	12/1949
350	5/1948	5/1948	5/1948
352	4/1950	5/1952	4/1950
355	10/1950	10/1950	10/1950
368	10/1949	10/1949	10/1949
687	8/1948	8/1948	8/1948
688	7/1948	7/1948	7/1948
689	10/1948	10/1948	10/1948
690	7/1950	7/1950	7/1950
691	12/1951	12/1951	1/1948
692	7/1948	9/1951	7/1948
693	10/1951	10/1951	11/1947
694	9/1948	9/1948	9/1948
695	9/1949	9/1952	9/1949
696	6/1948	6/1948	6/1948
697	11/1950	11/1950	11/1950
698	4/1951	4/1951	4/1951
699	10/1950	10/1950	10/1950
700	5/1948	5/1948	5/1948
701	2/1950	2/1950	2/1950

(a) S-prefix and BR black goods livery.

After working a train of loaded ballast hoppers to Redhill on 31st July 1948, Salisbury's No. 690 was commandeered by Brighton shed for the 8.04 a.m. all stations passenger to Tunbridge Wells West and the 12.10 p.m. return, while even more unexpectedly on 2nd August Three Bridges Duty 691 was worked. This covered the 7.08 a.m. to Forest Row, then light engine to Tunbridge Wells West for the 10.52 a.m. to London Bridge, returning with the 4.44 p.m. East Croydon-Tunbridge Wells West-Tonbridge and the 7.44 p.m. Tonbridge-Redhill. On the following day it was noted passing through Guildford with ballast empties for Woking.

In mid-1949 the allocation was: Nine Elms Nos. 30339, 30692/4, 699, 701; Feltham Nos. 309/46/52, 30687-9, 697/8; Guildford Nos. 308/25, S326, 30327; Basingstoke Nos. 368, 693; Eastleigh Nos. 30306/16/50; Bournemouth Nos. 695, 30696, 30700; Salisbury Nos. 30315/7, 355, 690/1. By this date employment was almost exclusively on light goods and shunting duties, but on summer Saturdays several were rostered by Nine Elms and Feltham for ECS workings, while Bournemouth's Nos. 695, 30696 and 30700 shared two passenger turns, one spending all day on

'700' class No. 30700 at Southampton in British Railways black livery with shaded lettering, **BR** number on the buffer beam and no smokebox numberplate.

R. H. Tunstall

the Lymington branch before working the 6.57 p.m. Brockenhurst-Bournemouth Central, while the other covered ECS to Hamworthy Junction and thence via Wimborne to Brockenhurst. Although not booked to do so, the third engine usually spent the day on the Swanage branch substituting for an 'M7'.

Withdrawal commenced in September 1957 with No. 30688, the engine involved in the head-on collision with an electric train at Staines Central the previous month. Nos. 30352 and 30687 followed in 1959-60 and the remainder of the class in succeeding years as diesels became available for the secondary goods services, with the last, Nos. 30309/15/6/25/46/68, 30689/90/5/7, 30700, being laid aside in November and December 1962. However, since most remained serviceable, a number were hastily recalled to duty for snow clearance, when arctic weather swept across

'700' class No. 30629 at Eastleigh in British Railways black livery with smokebox numberplate and Gill Sans lettering.　　　　　　*W. Gilburt*

'700' class No. 30694 at Eastleigh on 2nd May 1953 in British Railways black livery with the snifting valves removed, a plain stove-pipe chimney, smokebox number and shed plates, small tender totems and the Urie power classification below the cab numerals. *Author*

Southern England over the Christmas period and extended well into the New Year. Guildford only employed No. 30325 until mid-January, but it was early February 1963 before Eastleigh could dispense with No. 30316, which wandered as far afield as Basingstoke, Newbury, Alton, Brockenhurst and Guildford. Nos. 30689/97, 30700 were similarly employed by Exmouth Junction until relieved by 'Q' class Nos. 30530/1 in mid-January 1963. Apparently, there was no urgency for despatch to Eastleigh Works and breaking up for they rusticated on the shed until 31st December 1963, when No. 30700 was steamed to tow 'S15' class No. 30842 to Eastleigh Works for repair, while No. 30689 departed behind 'Z' class No. 30951 on New Years day and No. 30697 in charge of Bulleid Pacific No. 34065 *Hurricane* on 11th January 1964.

ENGINE SUMMARY

No.	Date	Superheated Eastleigh	Superheated Maunsell	Withdrawn
687	3/1897	6/1923	1/1932	10/1960
688	3/1897	—	8/1927	9/1957
689	3/1897	12/1922	10/1931	11/1962
690	3/1897	—	2/1926	12/1962
691	3/1897	—	11/1926	7/1961
692	3/1897	—	12/1926	2/1962
693	3/1897	—	4/1926	7/1961
694	3/1897	2/1922	4/1931	6/1961
695	3/1897	—	1/1926	12/1962
696	3/1897	—	9/1926	8/1961

No.	Date	Superheated Eastleigh	Superheated Maunsell	Withdrawn
697	4/1897	—	9/1925	11/1962
698	4/1897	—	10/1925	5/1962
699	5/1897	—	3/1927	7/1961
700	5/1897	1/1923	5/1929	11/1962
701	5/1897	—	3/1927	7/1961
702/306	5/1897	—	5/1929	4/1962
703/308	5/1897	9/1922	11/1931	9/1961
704/309	5/1897	—	1/1925	12/1962
705/315	5/1897	—	10/1925	12/1962
706/317	5/1897	—	4/1925	7/1961
707/325	6/1897	—	9/1925	12/1962
708/326	6/1897	6/1923	6/1931	2/1962
709/327	6/1897	—	2/1926	5/1961
710/339	6/1897	5/1924	2/1931	5/1962
711/346	8/1897	10/1923	11/1933	11/1962
712/350	8/1897	3/1922	7/1929	3/1962
713/352	8/1897	—	5/1927	7/1959
714/355	8/1897	—	7/1929	2/1961
715/368	8/1897	11/1922	3/1930	12/1962
716/459/316	8/1897	12/1920	3/1931	12/1962

All built by Dübs & Co. (Works Nos. 3510-39). Renumbering: 6/1898 Nos. 706/7 to 317/25; 7/1898 Nos. 702/4/5/8/9 to 306/9/15/26/7; 8/1898 Nos. 703/10-6 to 308/39/46/50/2/5/68, 459; 6/1912 No. 459 (originally 716) to 316. Disposal: Nos. 326/39, 698 broken up at Ashford Works, the remainder at Eastleigh Works. Mileages: Nos. 316 — 1,561,992; 368 — 1,504,031; 688 — 1,599,717; 698 — 1,712,572; 699 — 1,698,795; 700 — 1,663,763.

'M7' class (1897 series) No. 245 at Nine Elms in May 1897, of the same series as No. 242, but without the spark arresting equipment or conical smokebox door, no footsteps between coupled wheels and lettered SWR without stops.

J. B. Ashford

'M7' class (1897 series) No. 242 at Portsmouth in April 1898, with short frames, combined leading splashers and sandboxes, spark arrester, conical smokebox door, boiler barrel clackboxes, injectors, two-organ pipe whistles, broken handrailing, numberplates and lettered S.W.R.

V. Chambers

'M7' Class Bogie Tanks

When Drummond took office, twenty 'T1' class 0–4–4 tanks, Nos. 358-77, were on order from Nine Elms Works with boilers for the first ten being constructed and the frames, cylinders and driving wheels on order from Beyer Peacock & Co. They were completed with minor modifications in mid-1896, but Nos. 368-77 were cancelled on 27th May 1896, when Drummond was authorised by the Locomotive Committee to seek tenders for the supply of twenty large passenger bogie tanks of his own design at an estimated cost of £1,600 each. This computation proved hopelessly optimistic for when tenders were considered on 8th July 1896, the lowest offer exceeded this figure by £790. Details are: Robert Stephenson & Co. £2,390; Kitson & Co. £2,580; Dübs & Co. £2,460; Neilson & Co. £2,545; Beyer Peacock & Co. £2,425; Vulcan Foundry £2,500; Sharp Stewart & Co. £2,425. All were considered excessively high and, after conferring with Drummond, the Locomotive Committee decided that the order should be increased to twenty-five and transferred to Nine Elms Works for delivery on or before 31st December 1897. Other orders followed until, when the last entered service in December 1911, the class totalled 105. Details are:

Order No.	Engine Nos.	Total	Cost	Delivery
M7	242-56, 667-76	25	£1,580	Feb.-Dec. 1897

Short front platform, lever reversing, combined leading splashers and sandboxes, injectors, clack boxes on the boiler barrel and numberplates. Nos. 242-56 were fitted with two organ pipe hooters, Nos. 667-76 with single standard whistles, Nos. 242-4 with spark arresters and conical smokebox doors and Nos. 667-76, according to the Engine Register, but not confirmed by photographs, steam sanding. Lettering: No. 242 S.W.R., Nos. 243-56 SWR, Nos. 667-76 LSW.

Order No.	Engine Nos.	Total	Cost	Delivery
V7	31-40	10	£1,500	Mar.-June 1898
E9	22-6, 41-4, 241	10	£1,400	Jan.-May 1899

As Nos. 667-76, except for having clackboxes at the base of the front tubeplate, gravity sanding and the side tanks lettered LSWR.

Order No.	Engine Nos.	Total	Cost	Delivery
B10	112, 318-21	5	£1,650	July-Sept. 1900
C10	322-4/56/7	5	£1,650	Sept.-Nov. 1900

As Orders V7 and E9, except for having the front sandboxes inside the smokebox with no external openings for replenishment.

Order No.	Engine Nos.	Total	Cost	Delivery
G11	123/4/30/2/3	5	£1,520	Mar.-April 1903
H11	374-8	5	£1,520	May-June 1903

Long front platform, multiple steam pipes, standard whistle, steam reversing, injectors, front tubeplate clackboxes, numberplates, and smokebox sandboxes with external replenishment openings.

Order No.	Engine Nos.	Total	Cost	Delivery
B12	21/7-30	5	£1,620	Jan.-March 1904
C12	108-11, 379	5	£1,620	March-May 1904
X12	45, 104-7	5	£1,550	April-May 1905

Long front platform, standard whistle, steam reversing, front tubeplate clackboxes, feed water heating, single-ram feed pumps, balanced crank axles, standard gravity sanding and transfer numerals.

Order No.	Engine Nos.	Total	Cost	Delivery
B13	51-5	5	£1,550	Nov.-Dec. 1905
D13	56-60	5	£1,550	Feb.-March 1905
X14	125-9	5	£1,605	Aug.-Oct. 1911
A15	131, 328, 479-81	5	£1,605	Oct.-Dec. 1911

As Orders B12, C12, X12 and Y12, except for Duplex feed pumps and Krupp steel axles and coupled wheel tyres.

All were built by the South Western, Nos. 125-9/31, 328, 479-81 at Eastleigh Works, the remainder at Nine Elms Works.

The dimensions were as follows:

Cylinders	18½" x 26"
Coupled wheels	5' 7"
Bogie wheels	3' 7"
Wheelbase	7' 6" + 9' 7" + 6' 6" = 23' 7"
Boiler diameter	4' 5"
Boiler length	10' 6" (Tubeplates 10' 9 3/8")
Firebox length	6' 4"

Heating surfaces:

Tubes (216 x 1¾")	1,068 sq. ft.
Firebox	124 sq. ft.
Total	1,192 sq. ft.
Working pressure	175 lbs (reduced to 150 lb)
Grate area	20.4 sq. ft.
Tank capacity	1,300 gallons
Bunker capacity	3 tons
Length overall: Short frame:	35' 0¼"
Long frame:	36' 3¼"

Weights in working order:

	Short frame	Long frame
Leading coupled wheels	16T 10C	17T 8C
Trailing coupled wheels	17T 16C	18T 0C
Bogie	24T 10C	24T 16C
Total	58T 16C	60T 4C

The LSWR diagram book and engine lists record 54 tons 13 cwt (16T 0C + 18 T 0C + 20T 13C) for both the long and short frame series, weights which also appear in the Board of Trade report of the Tavistock derailment, despite the inspecting officer suspecting that No. 252 was heavier than Drummond admitted.

Compared with the Adams 'T1s', the boiler was larger in diameter, but 6½ inches shorter, while the firebox was 4 inches longer with an inclined grate. The 'T1' firebox was deeper with a horizontal grate and was more difficult to fire. Like all Drummond main line classes, the drive was left hand, whereas Adams and Beattie engines were right hand.

No. 242-4 entered traffic fitted with a conical smokebox door, a complicated system of baffle plates and a semi-circular hood covering the top rows of tubes, the intention being to stop all red hot char and sparks reaching the blast pipe by deflecting them downwards to the base of the smokebox. There was an almost total cessation of fire throwing, but only at the expense of poor steaming for the apparatus severely disrupted the gas flow and clogged the tubes. The '700' class 0-6-0s, 'T1' class No. 364 and '135' class No. 136 were similarly afflicted and, like them, Nos. 242-4 had the equipment removed at the first general repair, although it was not until 1904-5 that standard smokebox doors were fitted.

The sound of the deep-toned Caledonian pattern organ pipe whistles carried by Nos. 242-56, double single No. 720 and the thirty '700' goods was not appreciated by lineside residents, particularly those living at Surbiton and Twickenham. Therefore after numerous letters and several complaining newspaper articles, the Locomotive Committee ordered their replacement by the standard pattern in August 1897. Drummond reported that this had been completed by the end of the year, but the Repair Register records Nos. 242/55 carrying organ pipes until May and September 1900.

The boiler was similar to that carried by the 'C8' class 4-4-0s and '700' goods, and also, apart from the firebox cross water tubes, to the 'K10' class mixed traffic 4-6-0s. After five spare boilers were provided in 1905-7 and fitted to '700s' Nos. 459, 691/4 and 'M7s' Nos. 36 (October 1905), 37 (September 1905), there were regular exchanges between classes 'M7', 'C8' and '700', but not with the 'K10s' until Urie removed the firebox cross water tubes. Like these three classes, the 'M7' working pressure was 175 lb per sq. in., but commencing with No. 112 this was lowered to 150 lb to reduce boiler maintenance. After Grouping, the higher pressure was returned.

Those built under Orders B10, C10, G11 and H11 in 1900-3 had the leading sandboxes sited within the smokebox; this kept the sand dry and free-flowing, but replenishment proved time-consuming and difficult, especially the B10 and C10 series. So by mid-1907 most had their sand containers repositioned below the platform.

Those built in 1904-11 were equipped with feed water heating, with each side tank containing a grid of twenty 2 inch copper tubes having a length of 11 ft. 3 in. and a heating surface of 117 sq. ft. These engines were readily identifiable by the brass pipes conveying the exhaust steam from the cylinders through the sides of the smokebox to the leading end of the side tanks. At the base of each tank there was a vent for depositing the condensed steam on the track. Boiler feed was either by two single-ram or Duplex pumps until Urie took office, when he had hot water injectors substituted. At the same time the clackboxes were repositioned on the side of the boiler barrel, this necessitating the exhaust steam pipes being raised to enter the top of the side tanks. These modifications had no sooner been completed than Urie decided to abandon feed water heating and from May 1922 commenced removing the equipment

'M7' class (1897 series) No. 670 at Nine Elms in June 1898, of the same series as No. 245, but fitted with steam sanding, continuous hand-railing, a standard whistle and lettered LSW.   *F. Burtt, courtesy National Railway Museum*

and fitting standard pattern injectors, a change of policy undoubtedly influenced by the findings of the two year maintenance comparison trials with hot and cold water boiler feed members of the class. The former averaged 1.2 lb of coal less per train mile, but required five more shed days per annum and additional maintenance costing the equivalent of 0.4 lb of coal per train mile.

On taking office, Drummond found the London suburban services being operated successfully by the '415' class 4-4-2 tanks and 0-4-4 tanks of classes 'T1' and 'O2'. Consequently only Nos. 244/5/9/50, 667-70 of the original series went new to Nine Elms for use on the Guildford, Windsor and Reading services. Of the others Nos. 242/3, 671/5 were stationed at Fratton, Nos. 252/3/5, 676 at Exmouth Junction, Nos. 254/6, 672 at Guildford, Nos. 673/4 at Bournemouth, Nos. 246/7 at Salisbury and Nos. 248/51 at Northam for secondary main line passenger duties. These included the Portsmouth-Waterloo, Salisbury-Southampton-Portsmouth, Bournemouth-Weymouth and Exeter-Plymouth semi-fasts. It was while so engaged on 6th March 1898 that No. 252, running chimney first, left the track two miles north of Tavistock and ran along the ballast for 210 yards before coming to rest parted from its train, the seven-carriage 5.30 p.m. Exeter-Plymouth. By good fortune the stock remained upright and no one was seriously injured. At the Board of Trade inquiry, the driver stated that his speed was 35 to 40 mph, but in view of the 1 in 82 falling gradient, easy curvature and clear signals, the inspec-

ting officer found this difficult to accept and suggested that the train was probably travelling at 50 to 55 mph when derailment occurred. This speed he considered excessively high for a heavy front-coupled tank engine running over 82 lb per yard rails and sleepers removed from the Salisbury-Templecombe line. As a result, the class was restricted to suburban and other services not demanding periods of high speed. Consequently the March 1906 allocation was: Nine Elms Nos. 21/5/6/8, 30/5/6/9, 52/9, 111/30, 242/3/5-8/50, 357/74/6/8/9, 671-5; Strawberry Hill Nos. 32/3/8, 45, 50/1/4/5/7, 104-8/24, 241/52/3/6, 321/2/4/56, 668/9; Woking No. 27; Windsor Nos. 23, 60; Leatherhead No. 46; Kingston No. 112, 377; Twickenham Nos. 133, 375; Guildford Nos. 24, 40-2/7-9, 109/10, 251/4, 318/9/23; Salisbury Nos. 43, 58; Fratton Nos. 29, 56; Eastleigh Works (for repair) Nos. 22, 31/4/7, 53, 123/32, 244/9/55, 320, 667/70/6. The stationing of so many in the London District led to numerous '0415s' and some 'T1s' being transferred to the provinces, while more 'O2s' were relegated to empty stock workings and carriage piloting at Clapham Junction.

Ten more, Nos. 125-9/31, 328, 479-81, were built by Eastleigh Works in 1911, with all being sent to Nine Elms, except No. 481 which was fitted experimentally with Drummond's electric advanced warning system and used for a series of trials on the up slow line between Woking and Weybridge. At each distant signal an electrically insulated bar was positioned longitudinally between the rails and connected by rodding to the operating wire. If

'M7' class (B10 series) No. 318 at Nine Elms in August 1900, with short frames, smokebox sand containers (no external replenishment openings), footsteps between coupled wheels, tubeplate clackboxes, standard whistle, numberplates and lettered LSWR.

J. B. Ashford

'M7' class (B13 series) No. 54 at Nine Elms on 13th February 1908. Similar to the X12 series, except for the Duplex feed pumps.

'M7' class (X12 series) No. 107 with long frames, leading splasher sandboxes, front tubeplate clackboxes, single ram pumps, feed water heating, balanced crank axles, standard whistle, continuous handrailing, transfer numerals and lettered LSWR. *J. B. Ashford*

'M7' class (X14 series) No. 126 at Eastleigh Works on 6th September 1911.   *Author's collection*

'M7' class No. 481 at Eastleigh on 21st August 1912 fitted with Drummond cable and pulley motor-train equipment.   *Author's collection*

the signal was off, the bar was deflected sideways and could not make contact with an arm suspended from No. 481, but should the signal be on then contact was made, and this activated a warning whistle in the cab and partially applied the vacuum brake. The intention was to bring the train smoothly to a halt at the home signal, therefore the positioning of the contact bar was determined by the speed trains normally approached each distant signal and not by the length of the block. For additional safety, a bell rang continuously in the signal box to ensure that the signalman did not forget the train's presence, this ceasing only when the home signal was released. Unfortunately, the system did not prove entirely satisfactory as rain and damp seriously affected the insulation, the batteries frequently failed and the engine contact arm was damaged by tools and other permanent way equipment left between the rails by gangers. On one occasion when No. 481 was travelling at 50 mph, this arm was dislodged by a faulty line bar and thrust into the motion, bringing the trials to an abrupt halt. As a result, the equipment was dismantled and the trials abandoned.

No. 481 remained on loan to Eastleigh and in June 1912, with 'Terrier' No. 735, was fitted with cable and pulley motor-train gear for a series of test runs with suitably equipped sets of one, two and three bogie carriages between Clapham Junction and Kingston. Later the trials were extended to the Bournemouth West-New Milton, Wareham-Swanage, Lymington branch and Guildford-Effingham Junction-Leatherhead services with equal success. Both engines were equipped with cables for operating the duplicate controls in the motor-train driving compartment while running chimney or bunker first, but drivers found that the cables running forward via pulleys on the dome and chimney sides seriously impeded signal sighting, so later motor-train engines were only fitted with cables leading across the cab roof and bunker to the trailer cars. Before Nos. 481 and 735 entered regular service the forward running motor-train gear was removed.

At the conclusion of the trials, Nos. 21, 109 and 667, together with a number of 'O2s', 'T1s' and 'O415s' were similarly equipped for motor-train operation and superseded the railcars and small motor-tanks on most of these services. The 'M7s' were transferred to Bournemouth for the New Milton trains. After electrification was extended to Claygate on 20th November 1916, steam motor trains were provided thence to Guildford worked by 'O415' class 4-4-2 tanks Nos. 052, 0106, 520/4 and two carriage sets, but at busy periods all intending passengers could not be accommodated and they were replaced by 'M7s' Nos. 36, 242/8, 672 and three carriage motor-trains. This avoided passengers having to be left behind, although many had to stand. This would probably have become standard practice if the extra suburban traffic generated by electrification had not inundated the facilities. More stock was necessary, but, since additional electric sets could not be provided until hostilities with Germany ceased, the only solution was a reduction of electric mileage and not unexpectedly the choice fell on the Waterloo-Claygate services, which reverted to steam on 1st May 1917. As a result, Nos. 36, 242/8, 672 were transferred to the Bentley-Bordon and Guildford-Aldershot-Farnham services, while the Waterloo-

Claygate-Guildford trains were shared by Nos. 24, 44, 53, 319/20, 673/5.

The Waterloo-East Putney electrification of 25th October 1915 did not radically affect the London area steam allocation, but when extended to Shepperton, Strawberry Hill, the Hounslow loop, Hampton Court and Claygate the following year, fifty-six fewer tank engines were required by the London District sheds. As a result seven 'M7s', eight 'O2s', five 'T1s' and thirty-six 'O415s' were transferred away to Bournemouth, Fratton, Eastleigh, Salisbury, Exmouth Junction and Weymouth, many of the 'O415s' to complete their mileage before being laid aside at Eastleigh Works.

No more 'M7s' were motor-train equipped until hostilities ceased, when the number was increased, partly to replace withdrawn 'O415s', but mainly to provide additional engines to cover routine maintenance and visits to works. Consequently, no less than forty-five, Nos. 21/5/9, 32/6/9, 46/9, 52/4/5/7/9, 104-11/25/8-31, 241-5/7-52/5/6, 375/7, 481 and 667/70/2, are recorded by the Engine Register, of which Nos. 49 and 670 were equipped as late as mid-1927. However, at any one period less than half were actually engaged working motor-train services.

The successful modernisation of the large Drummond 4-4-0s and '700' goods No. 316 decided Urie to superheat one 'M7'. The engine chosen, No. 126, entered Eastleigh Works in February 1921, when in addition to the superheater, it was fitted with 19 in. cylinders, an extended smokebox supported by a saddle, a stovepipe chimney with a capuchon, a taller spectacle plate, a more rounded cab roof and a four-feed Detroit lubricator. The drawings show a new Urie pattern boiler, but in fact it was the Drummond pattern transferred from No. 106 fitted with new tubes, tubeplates and firebox, pitched 9 in. higher to accommodate the saddle and having the working pressure raised to 175 lb.

The changed dimensions were:-
Heating surfaces:

Small tubes (120 x 1¾")	593 sq. ft.	
Large tubes (18 x 5¼")	266 sq. ft.	
Firebox	117 sq. ft.	
Total evaporative	976 sq. ft.	
Superheater	167 sq. ft.	
Total	1,143 sq. ft.	
Working pressure	175 lb	

Weights in working order:

	LSWR	Southern (1928)
Leading coupled wheels	19T 8C	19T 13C
Trailing coupled wheels	19T 10C	20T 0C
Bogie	24T 0C	24T 19C
Total	62T 18C	64T 12C

After being run-in on the Eastleigh-Bournemouth slows in late July 1921, No. 126 spent several months working the Bournemouth-Weymouth semi-fasts before returning to Nine Elms for suburban service. In April 1922 Urie reported that it burnt 18 per cent less coal and used 13 per cent less water than the saturated members of the class when working the Waterloo-Guildford services. Unfortunately, it proved too heavy for regular use between Malden and Strawberry Hill, including the Fulwell curve, or over the Ascot, Frimley, North Camp and Aldershot line. Consequently, it was heartily disliked by shed foremen and the

Superheated 'M7' No. 126 with extended smokebox, Urie smokebox door, stove-pipe chimney, valance power classification and raised cab roof.

Collection R. C. Riley

Traffic Department, which probably accounts for no others being modified.

A new Drummond pattern boiler with a Maunsell superheater and snifting valves was fitted in October 1928 and a stovepipe chimney with a shorter capuchon in May 1932, but otherwise there were no modifications before withdrawal with a mileage of 781,263 in May 1937. Latterly employment had been mainly on the Reading vans and empty carriage stock duties. After breaking up, the frames were transferred to No. 254 in August 1937, thereby converting it to the long frame series.

At Grouping the entire class entered the Southern Railway to be painted Maunsell green and receive the E-prefix. Details are:-

No.	Southern Livery	E-prefix Removed	No.	Southern Livery	E-prefix Removed
21	9/1924	4/1932	43	8/1927	1/1932
22	11/1923	5/1933	44	3/1924	4/1932
23	7/1925	11/1933	45	9/1924	6/1932
24	12/1924	7/1931	46	9/1924	8/1931
25	11/1924	10/1931	47	2/1926	7/1932
26	10/1925	10/1931	48	2/1924	8/1931
27	2/1924	3/1932	49	10/1924	11/1931
28	5/1924	7/1932	50	7/1924	3/1932
29	1/1924	3/1933	51	1/1925	10/1931
30	7/1924	10/1931	52	8/1925	6/1933
31	8/1924	10/1931	53	11/1923	6/1932
32	4/1925	10/1931	54	6/1926	3/1932
33	7/1925	5/1933	55	11/1923	10/1931
34	5/1926	6/1933	56	3/1926	1/1934
35	4/1924	5/1934	57	2/1924	1/1932
36	8/1925	8/1934	58	2/1925	3/1933
37	1/1926	2/1932	59	3/1925	1/1933
38	7/1925	4/1932	60	7/1924	8/1932
39	1/1925	3/1932	104	2/1925	9/1933
40	4/1925	10/1933	105	11/1924	5/1932
41	5/1924	3/1932	106	5/1927	5/1933
42	6/1924	6/1934	107	1/1925	1/1933

No.	Southern Livery	E-prefix Removed	No.	Southern Livery	E-prefix Removed
108	3/1924	8/1933	256	7/1925	1/1935
109	1/1926	3/1934	318	11/1924	10/1931
110	4/1924	2/1933	319	9/1924	8/1932
111	3/1925	4/1932	320	9/1924	11/1933
112	7/1924	8/1931	321	9/1927	7/1933
123	10/1925	4/1934	322	4/1924	1/1934
124	9/1925	9/1936	323	12/1923	2/1934
125	11/1924	12/1931	324	9/1924	2/1932
126	9/1925	6/1932	328	12/1924	4/1934
127	3/1926	9/1931	356	11/1924	6/1932
128	9/1926	11/1931	357	6/1925	10/1934
129	8/1924	4/1933	374	3/1926	6/1933
130	9/1924	1/1932	375	8/1925	6/1932
131	8/1926	7/1932	376	3/1925	6/1934
132	11/1925	12/1932	377	7/1924	1/1935
133	1/1926	10/1931	378	7/1925	5/1932
241	9/1926	10/1931	379	8/1924	11/1932
242	6/1925	11/1934	479	2/1924	10/1931
243	10/1924	7/1931	480	6/1926	8/1931
244	7/1924	10/1931	481	10/1924	3/1934
245	10/1925	12/1931	667	1/1926	5/1933
246	10/1924	8/1931	668	6/1924	1/1934
247	7/1926	1/1932	669	3/1927	9/1933
248	12/1923	3/1935	670	3/1926	11/1931
249	5/1925	12/1931	671	9/1926	3/1932
250	12/1926	3/1934	672	3/1926	10/1933
251	4/1925	4/1934	673	3/1924	12/1934
252	3/1924	9/1931	674	2/1925	2/1934
253	8/1926	4/1932	675	7/1924	4/1933
254	5/1925	7/1931	676	1/1925	9/1934
255	3/1925	11/1932			

There were no major duty changes until April 1924, when motor-fitted Nos. 108/10, 251/5/6 were transferred to Feltham, three to be sub-shedded at Chertsey for the Weybridge-Virginia Water services, while in December 1924

'M7' class No. 669 in Urie livery at Wimbledon Park Electric Power station sidings on 29th April 1925. *H. C. Casserley*

Nos. 125/8, 245 took over the Wimbledon-Ludgate Hill trains.

Despite the availability of the more efficient compressed air motor-train control system on the Eastern and Central Sections, there was no attempt to introduce it on Western Section services and in all probability the mechanical system would have remained in use for some considerable time if several potentially dangerous malfunctions had not occurred on the Bournemouth West-Wimborne-Brockenhurst services in mid-1929. On becoming aware of these incidents, the Board instructed Maunsell to cease employing this means of motor-train control and allotted funds for the immediate conversion of thirty-one 'M7s' and four 'O2s' to the compressed air system. The air pumps and piping was to be obtained from stocks held at Brighton Works off withdrawn LB & SCR engines. Until the 'M7s' and 'O2s' became available, a number of Central Section 'D1' class 0—4—2 tanks and motor-train sets were transferred to the Western Section. Dates of conversion are:-

21	7/1930	50	7/1930	59	8/1930	110	6/1930
27	8/1930	51	8/1930	60	7/1930	111	10/1930
28	6/1930	53	7/1930	104	2/1931	125	8/1930
29	11/1930	54	8/1930	105	7/1930	128	9/1930
45	9/1930	55	10/1931	106	6/1930	129	11/1930
46	8/1930	56	9/1930	107	7/1930	131	12/1930
47	7/1930	57	7/1930	108	6/1930	481	12/1930
49	8/1930	58	6/1930	109	9/1930		

All belonged to the long frame series for there was insufficient space ahead of the cylinders to fit the air reservoir on the short frame engines. The air pump was attached to the right hand side of the smokebox and the operating cylinder to the leading end of the right side tank, while the additional front and rear buffer beam hose connections were lettered 'BACK PRESSURE', 'MAIN STORAGE' and 'REGULATOR CONTROL'. The allocation was: Bournemouth Nos. 21/7, 45/7/9, 50/1/6/9, 105/11 for the Brockenhurst (via Wimborne), Christchurch-Ringwood and

Wareham-Swanage services; Eastleigh Nos. 57, 60 for the Lymington branch; Feltham Nos. 104/6/8/9/25/8, 481 for the Weybridge-Chertsey services; Guildford Nos. 28/9, 46, 53/4/5/8, 107/10/29/31 for the Bordon branch, Petersfield-Midhurst, Aldershot-Ascot and Farnham-Tongham-Guildford services. This over-generous allocation allowed Bournemouth to roster several for piloting at the West station and working local goods, while those at Feltham worked some of the Kensington shuttle services, van trains and empty coaching stock from outlying sidings to Waterloo. This surplus led to No. 55 being loaned to Maidstone West from August to October for the Strood-Tonbridge motor trains, while 'R1s' Nos. A700/4 were away at Ashford Works for repair. In October 1932 No. 45 was transferred to Exmouth Junction for the Seaton branch, while in January 1934 responsibility for the Lymington branch was changed from Eastleigh to Bournemouth and Guildford 'M7s' replaced Reading 'R' class 0-4-4 tanks on the Ash-Aldershot services. Later the same year, Nos. 131 and 481 were

loaned to Stewarts Lane for the Swanley, Sevenoaks and Gravesend West motor-trains. On several occasions No. 481 also appeared on the Westerham branch, while from November 1934 until electrification, both worked the Sevenoaks-Orpington services.

Returning to the non-motor-fitted members of the class, the allocation in January 1931 was: Nine Elms Nos. 30/2/3, 40/1/3/48, 127/30/2, 241/5/6/51/2/4, 319/21/3/56/7/75/6, 479/80, 671/2/3/5; Feltham Nos. 23/5, 31/4/7, 124/6, 379, 670/4; Guildford Nos. 22/4/6, 38/9, 112, 243/4/89, 318/22/4/78, 667/76; Salisbury No. 133; Exmouth Junction Nos. 35, 42, 253, 320/8/74, 669; Barnstaple Nos. 36, 242/50/6, 377, 668; Bournemouth Nos. 52, 123, 247/55. By this date, with most of the inner suburban lines electrified, those at Nine Elms and Feltham were employed working the Woking, Guildford, Haslemere, Alton and very early morning Waterloo-Twickenham-Kingston services, the Brookwood Necropolis specials, vans to Woking and Guildford, local goods and empty carriage stock. Superheater

'M7' class No. E480 inside Nine Elms shed on 26th March 1927, in Southern Railway livery with rear buffer beam numerals, bunker back-plate numberplate, protected look-out windows and additional coal rails.
H. C. Casserley

Non-motor train equipped short frame 'M7' class No. 357 in post-1931 Maunsell livery.

A. B. MacLeod

No. 126 often worked the Reading services. Therefore, despite electrification, much hard work remained as the Alton and Haslemere commuter trains were heavily loaded and smartly timed, while some of the main line carriage sets were berthed as far afield as Hampton Court, Wimbledon Park and Oatlands Sidings, Walton. In contrast, the solitary Salisbury representative could usually be found propelling the odd carriage around the West End Yard. In the West Country 'M7s' were in the process of taking over the Exmouth branch services from the 'O2' class, while those at Barnstaple banked at Mortehoe and worked the Ilfracombe and Torrington services.

In October 1931 No. 672 and 'King Arthur' class No. 774 *Sir Gaheris* were fitted with Strowger-Hudd automatic train control equipment. This was an intermittent induction system incorporated in the existing manual block signalling, which entailed the provision of two inductors on the track at distant signals, one some 20 yards ahead of the other. The first was a permanent magnet and the second an electromagnet only energised when the distant signal was clear. The cabs of both engines were equipped with electric hooters, which gave a single blast to indicate clear and a continuous note for caution which persisted until silenced by the driver pressing an acknowledgement button. This warning was supplemented by a visual reminder, which changed to an arresting pattern of black and white stripes when a distant signal was passed at danger and remained

displayed at eye level even after the driver had acknowledged the warning, cancelled the automatic brake application and resumed control of the train. The trials proved entirely successful, but the Southern could not afford the cost of adoption and in November 1931 the equipment was dismantled. Later this train control system gave reliable service on the Tilbury Section of the LMS and following Nationalisation in a modified form was extended to the British Railways network.

After the 1898 Tavistock derailment, the class was not again involved in a major accident until 25th March 1933, when No. 107 left the track at 45 mph some 400 yards east of Raynes Park signal box while heading the five carriage 3.10 p.m. Waterloo-Alton semi-fast. At the time 'U' class 2—6—0 No. 1621 was approaching on an adjacent line with the 12.11 p.m. Southampton Terminus-Waterloo at about 50 mph and, before the driver was able to stop, it crashed into the wreckage, killing five passengers and injuring a further thirty-four. At the Board of Trade inquiry, the inspecting officer found that the accident was the result of a permanent way gang attempting to lift the track and pack the sleepers between trains, when the correct and safe procedure should have been the imposition of a 10 mph speed restriction or taking full line possession. No blame could be placed on No. 107 or the rolling stock and there was no objection to the class being employed on semi-fast main line services providing schedules did not demand

Superheated 'M7' No. 126 at Waterloo on 6th June 1956 in post-1931 Maunsell livery with 15 in. numerals, Maunsell superheater and a short capuchoned stove-pipe chimney.
Author

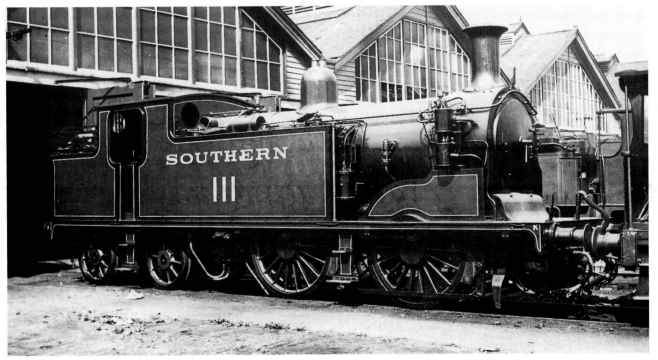

Long frame 'M7' No. 111 at Eastleigh on 7th August 1937, in post-1931 Maunsell livery with 15 in. numerals and compressed air motor-train equipment.
J. G. Sturt

speeds exceeding 50 mph. Nevertheless, the Running Department requested that as far as possible 2—6—0s or 4—4—0s should be rostered for the Alton services and if an 'M7' had to be employed, then the driver should be warned of the speed restriction and the guard instructed to accurately record passing times in his journal.

Apart from further transfers to Exmouth Junction, there were few duty changes before 3rd January 1937, when the Weybridge-Virginia Water electrification left motor-fitted Nos. 45/9, 105-7 redundant at Feltham. Nos. 45, 105 were immediately transferred to Eastleigh, but the others remained in store until mid-year, when the Alton electrification caused the introduction of motor-train services to Southampton and over the Meon Valley line. To cater for these additional duties five more 'M7s' were motor-fitted, raising the total to 36. Details are:-

48 7/1937   52 7/1937   328 7/1937   379 6/1938   480 6/1937

In mid-1937 the allocation and duties worked were:-

Shed	Allocation	Duties
Guildford	56/8, 108/10/1/28, 328/79, 481	Two duties: Bentley-Bordon and Petersfield-Midhurst-Pulborough. Spare engines acted as Guildford South End and Woking East End pilots and worked the Cranleigh and Reading services.
Eastleigh	29, 48, 52/9, 125	Three duties: Southampton Terminus-Winchester-Alton (two engines), Lymington branch. One of the spare engines often carriage piloted at Eastleigh.
Fratton	45/9, 54, 60, 105/9/29, 480	Two duties: Gosport-Alton (two engines). Spare engines worked local trips to Eastleigh, Romsey and Southampton (not motor-trains).
Bournemouth	21/8, 47, 50/1/3/7, 104/6/7/31	Four duties: Bournemouth-Wimborne-Brockenhurst (three engines); Wareham-Swanage. Spare engines usually shunted at Bournemouth West and Branksome or worked local trips to Wareham and Hamworthy.
Exmouth Junction	27, 46, 55	One duty: Seaton Junction-Seaton, with an evening return trip to Axminster. Spare engines worked the Exeter-Exmouth services or replaced one of the bankers.

The 68 non-motor-fitted members of the class were stationed and employed as follows:-

Nine Elms	32/3/8, 40, 112/30/2, 241/9, 319/22, 479, 667/73	Ten duties: 5.30 a.m. vans Waterloo-Guildford, return as ordered; Clapham Junction-Kensington shuttle 6.05 a.m.-9.16 p.m.; Vans and ECS Waterloo-Clapham Junction-Epsom-Kensington; Early morning passenger to Kingston and return, then Waterloo ECS (4 engines); 11.44 a.m. Waterloo-Brookwood, 2.13 p.m. return and Waterloo ECS; 1.10 a.m. vans Waterloo-Kingston, 1.49 a.m. return and shunting at Wimbledon Park 11.00 a.m.-4.30 p.m.; Waterloo-Clapham Junction ECS.
Feltham	23/5, 30/1, 244/8/51, 674	Feltham station pilot and transfer trips to the yard; 3.47 a.m. Feltham-Waterloo, 5.27 a.m. ECS to Clapham Junction, 7.03 a.m. to Kensington, returning at 7.20 a.m. and local goods/shunting at Twickenham and Hampton Court.
Guildford	22/6, 43, 127, 246, 324/78, 672/6	Eight duties: Freight shunting at Alton, then 6.34 p.m. Guildford and 7.48 p.m. return; 8.13 a.m. Guildford-Reading, shunting at Reading until 6.10 p.m. Reading-Ash, returning at 7.46 p.m. and 11.05 p.m. Reading-Guildford; Woking East End pilot; Guildford South End pilot; 8.52 a.m. Guildford-Bramleigh, 9.20 a.m. return and 6.15 p.m. Guildford-Reading and 8.22 p.m. return; ECS Walton/Waterloo/Clapham Junction/Surbiton (SO); 9.31 a.m. Woking-Waterloo, then ECS workings (SO).
Eastleigh	242, 357	7.52 a.m. Eastleigh-Gosport, 8.47 a.m. to Fareham, 11.08 a.m. to Southampton Central, 12.10 p.m. to Portsmouth, then shunting at Cosham and Fareham.
Fratton	No non-motor-fitted M7s	Three duties worked by motor-fitted Nos. 45/9, 54, 60, 105/9/29, 480 not employing this equipment. 6.00 a.m. Portsmouth-Southampton and 8.02 a.m. return, then local trips Portsmouth, Eastleigh, Romsey etc; Shunting at Cosham and Gosport, then local trips to Eastleigh and Southampton; Shunting at Fratton/Havant, then 5.18 p.m. goods Havant-Chichester and 8.11 p.m. return goods to Fratton.

Bournemouth	243/5/54/5, 318	Eight duties, so assistance necessary from the shed's motor-fitted M7s. Shunting at Bournemouth West/Branksome, then 4.47 p.m. Bournemouth West-Salisbury and 8.14 p.m. return; Local passenger trips Bournemouth/Wareham/Swanage (two engines); 7.00 a.m. Bournemouth West-Brockenhurst, 7.57 a.m. return and shunting at Poole; Local trips Wareham-Swanage-Hamworthy; Bournemouth Central pilot, then 3.56 p.m. Central-Eastleigh, 8.57 p.m. to Winchester and 10.33 p.m. back to Bournemouth Central; 7.59 a.m. Wimborne-Brockenhurst, then workmen's special to Blandford, as required; Local trips Bournemouth-Swanage.
Salisbury	41, 675	West yard pilot. Spare engine occasionally took over Bournemouth locals from T1 class No. 10.
Exmouth Junction	24, 34/7/9, 44, 123/4/33, 256, 321/3/56/74/5/6/7, 669/71	Thirteen duties: Exeter-Exmouth (2 engines), Exeter-Exmouth-Sidmouth (5 engines), Exeter-Sidmouth-Honiton-Axminster (2 engines, 1 SO); Exeter-Exmouth-Sidmouth Junction (2 engines); Seaton branch (SO); Sidmouth-Sidmouth Junction (SO).
Bude	252, 320, 668	Two duties, engines sub-shedded by Exmouth Junction, both branch trips Bude-Halwill.
Barnstaple	36, 42, 247/50/3	Four duties: Barnstaple-Ilfracombe trips and SO banking Mortehoe; Torrington line passenger and goods and SO banking at Mortehoe; SO Barnstaple-Ilfracombe trips and banking at Mortehoe (2 engines).
Ilfracombe	670	Sub-shedded from Barnstaple, Ilfracombe-Barnstaple trips and shunting at Ilfracombe. On Saturdays a second M7 was usually obtained from Barnstaple for carriage piloting, with the E1R class taking over its Torrington line duties.
Plymouth	35	Tavistock and Brent locals.

When built all were fitted with smokebox wingplates, which on most engines served the dual role of being decorative and forming the end plates of the leading sandboxes. However, the sand containers of Nos. 112/23/4/30/2/3, 318-24/56/7/75-8 were positioned below the platform and therefore on these engines the wingplates served no useful purpose. Consequently, commencing with No. 323 in April 1939, they were discarded when the smokebox was renewed. As was to be expected, this proved a lengthy process and it was March 1946 before the last, No. 376, was divested.

The Bulleid livery changes first affected the class in May 1939, when Nos. 41/9 were painted Maunsell green with tankside numerals and green and yellow lining. These were followed by:-

Maunsell green, black and yellow lining, tankside numerals:
Nos. 357, 676 (June 1939); 105/11, 375 (July 1939); 23, 33, 123, 356 (August 1939).

Maunsell green, unlined, Bulleid lettering, numerals on bunker sides:
Nos. 398, 479 (September 1939); 53, 249, 377 (October 1939); 128/3, 256 (November 1939); 57 (January 1940); 126, 673 (March 1940); 131, 668/9 (April 1940); 22, 480, 667/75 (May 1940); 671 (June 1940); 27, 106, 253 (July 1940); 376 (August 1940); 107 (September 1940); 44 (October 1940); 125, 374 (January 1941); 50/1, 324 (February 1941).

Malachite green, unlined, Bulleid lettering, numerals on bunker sides:
Nos. 56, 104 (October 1940); 127, 242 (December 1940); 54 (January 1941).

Such was the confused state of painting at this period that No. 125 was released to traffic with Maunsell green boiler, cab and bunker, but malachite green coupled and bogie wheels. All later repaints until December 1948, commencing with Nos. 59 and 379 in March 1941, were plain black with Bulleid lettering and bunker numerals.

Shortly after the outbreak of war Nos. 22/6/9, 32/8, 40/7, 58, 108/29, 250/3, 319/22/56 and 481 were placed in store, but by Christmas 1939 all had been returned to traffic, with Nos. 58 and 129 being transferred to Yeovil as replacements for 'O2s' Nos. 187 and 207 on the Town-Junction and Pen Mill services. From 30th May to 4th June 1940 all public passenger trains between Redhill and Reading were suspended to allow unhindered passage for the numerous troop specials transporting the British Expeditionary Force from Dunkirk. A wide selection of Southern engines were employed, including 'M7s' Nos. 246 and 324 which station piloted at Redhill for much of the period as well as working empty stock to Tonbridge on several occasions.

To permit the transfer of LMS engines to more important duties in September 1941, the Southern accepted responsibility for the Somerset & Dorset line and immediately transferred 'S11s' Nos. 395-404 and 'T1s' Nos. 1-6. The last mentioned were replaced at the provincial sheds by the transfer of 'M7s' Nos. 22/8, 40, 241 and 319 from Nine Elms where their place was taken by the loan of 'H' class 0-4-4 tanks Nos. 1263/5, 1319 and 1552/3 from the Eastern Section.

In February and March 1942, following bomb damage, the Waterloo-Alton services had to be replaced by 'M7s' and five carriage sets running to EMU schedules. Time was usually kept in daylight, but after dark, station and other delays accumulated and late arrivals were common. The engines concerned were Nos. 26, 33, 43, 123/8, 249 and 667/72/3/6. Approaching Alton in the black-out, the driver of No. 667 lost his cap and while walking back along the track to retrieve it, he had the misfortune to be apprehended by the Home Guard and escorted back to the station. There his release was negotiated by the station master, but only after explaining to higher Army authority that the suspected enemy agent could only be conveyed to Aldershot for further interrogation if he was allowed to drive the train. Unfortunately, we shall never know what happened at Aldershot or whether the cap was retrieved.

Normally the class was repaired at Eastleigh, but in 1942-5 assistance had to be sought from Ashford and Brighton, with the former attending to Nos. 43/4, 106/32, 256, 374, 481 and the latter Nos. 22/9, 51, 104/7, 375, 672. Running-in was on local passenger services, so the use of No. 256 on an Ashford-Tonbridge goods on 2nd April 1942 was unusual.

Several had lucky escapes during the war, but none more so than No. 48 on 19th August 1942, while heading the 2.10 p.m. Alton-Eastleigh motor-train between Ropley and Alresford. Suddenly, without warning by the air raid sirens, it was shot-up by a single FW190 fighter. The crew and passengers escaped injury and, after inspecting the damage, the driver decided to take the train on as the two-carriage set had been entirely missed, while the 20mm cannon shells had only indented the side tanks, boiler and coupled wheels. As soon as hostilities in Europe ceased, there was a concerted attempt by all Southern Railway departments to return to the standards appertaining pre-war. For the engine stock this principally involved improved maintenance, more

frequent cleaning and the reappearance of malachite green on the express classes. Secondary passenger engines remained black until December 1946, when it was decided to paint malachite green a number of 'M7s' regularly employed station piloting or working empty carriage stock to and from Waterloo, details being:-

| No. | Stationed | Malachite Green | | BR Lined |
		Southern	BR	
242	Eastleigh	12/1946	—	4/1950
243	Salisbury	8/1947	7/1948	8/1952
676	Nine Elms	12/1947	—	3/1952
30038	Nine Elms	—	8/1948	2/1953
30241	Nine Elms	—	7/1948	3/1953
30244	Nine Elms	—	9/1948	12/1951

The regular appearance of well-groomed malachite green empty stock engines in the vicinity of the principal stations gave rise to much favourable comment and for a relatively modest outlay did more to promote rail travel than most other forms of advertising. No. 243 received a second application of malachite green when renumbered into the 30,000 series in July 1948, but Nos. 242 and 676 retained Southern livery until painted lined black in 1950-2. Malachite green finally disappeared from the class with No. 30241 in March 1953.

Despite the upheaval of World War 2 and the passage of six years, the January 1946 allocation was surprisingly similar to mid-1939. The main difference was found at Nine Elms and Feltham, where the loss of ten 'M7s' to the provincial sheds was in part made good by the loan of 'H' class Nos. 1544/51/2/3 and 'R1s' Nos. 1696/8 from the Eastern Section. Yeovil retained Nos. 58 and 129 for the Town-Junction and Pen Mill shuttle services, while Salisbury's allocation had increased to four, Nos. 41, 60, 243 and 675, which were employed as the West Yard pilot and working the Idmiston Halt and Bulford services, together with a Sunday afternoon return trip to Wimborne. A new location was Basingstoke where a shortage of 'G6s' led to Nos. 244/8 shunting the East and West yards, duties for which they were not well suited, so as soon as possible they were transferred to Nine Elms and replaced by 'G6' No. 265 and 'E4' No. 2490.

Except for withdrawn No. 126, the entire class entered British Railways stock at Nationalisation, although No. 672 had the misfortune to fall down the Waterloo & City line lift shaft and was broken up on 9th June 1948. The remaining 103 were renumbered into the 30,000 series and painted lined black. Nine also carried the temporary S-prefix, details being: S27 24/1/1948-28/10/1949; S34 20/3/1948-4/4/1952; S58 13/3/1948-15/12/1950; S255 31/1/1948-8/6/1951; S256 28/2/1948-3/2/1951; S318 13/3/1948-4/8/1950; S379 14/2/1948-7/7/1950; S668 17/1/1948-25/11/1949.

All were plain black with British Railways lettered side tanks, as were the first ten 30,000 series repaints:

30036 9/1948; 30056 7/1948; 30059 7/1948; 30104 7/1948; 30105 6/1948; 30107 4/1948; 30132 6/1948; 30254 7/1948; 30320 4/1948; 30377 8/1948.

Short frame 'M7' No. 676 at Nine Elms in March 1948, resplendent in Bulleid malachite green livery for working empty carriage stock to and from Waterloo.

C. H. S. Owen

All later repaints were lined black and these dates, together with those of renumbering are:

No.	BR No.	Lined Black Livery	No.	BR No.	Lined Black Livery	No.	BR No.	Lined Black Livery	No.	BR No.	Lined Black Livery
						108	8/1950	8/1950	250	6/1951	6/1951
						109	5/1949	2/1951	251	3/1951	3/1951
21	6/1949	3/1951	43	10/1949	10/1949	110	10/1949	10/1949	252	1/1950	1/1950
22	8/1949	8/1949	44	10/1950	10/1950	111	9/1950	9/1950	253	11/1951	11/1951
23	12/1949	4/1952	45	5/1949	5/1949	112	12/1949	12/1949	254	7/1948	10/1952
24	9/1950	9/1950	46	6/1949	6/1949	123	2/1949	2/1949	255	6/1951	6/1951
25	12/1949	12/1949	47	8/1950	8/1950	124	5/1949	2/1952	256	2/1951	2/1951
26	5/1949	4/1950	48	9/1949	10/1950	125	7/1949	7/1949	318	8/1950	6/1952
27	10/1949	8/1950	49	4/1951	4/1951	127	2/1951	6/1952	319	10/1949	10/1949
28	3/1949	3/1949	50	12/1950	12/1950	128	3/1949	1/1951	320	4/1948	2/1951
29	10/1948	8/1950	51	5/1949	5/1949	129	11/1949	11/1951	321	6/1949	6/1949
30	4/1949	4/1949	52	9/1949	9/1949	130	8/1949	8/1949	322	11/1949	11/1949
31	1/1949	1/1949	53	11/1949	11/1949	131	6/1950	6/1950	323	9/1949	9/1949
32	4/1949	4/1949	54	4/1950	4/1950	132	6/1948	1/1952	324	4/1950	4/1950
33	1/1950	1/1950	55	12/1948	12/1948	133	3/1950	3/1950	328	3/1950	3/1950
34	7/1951	7/1951	56	7/1948	5/1953	241	7/1948	3/1953	356	5/1951	5/1951
35	12/1948	12/1948	57	9/1949	9/1949	242	4/1950	4/1950	357	12/1948	12/1948
36	9/1948	3/1951	58	12/1950	12/1950	243	7/1948	8/1952	374	12/1948	12/1948
37	2/1949	2/1949	59	7/1948	10/1951	244	9/1948	1/1952	375	12/1948	12/1948
38	8/1948	2/1953	60	10/1948	10/1948	245	8/1949	9/1951	376	6/1949	6/1949
39	9/1948	9/1948	104	7/1948	11/1949	246	8/1951	8/1951	377	8/1948	2/1951
40	3/1950	3/1950	105	6/1948	6/1951	247	11/1949	11/1949	378	7/1949	7/1949
41	8/1949	8/1949	106	11/1948	1/1951	248	11/1948	11/1951	379	7/1950	7/1950
42	4/1952	4/1952	107	4/1948	9/1951	249	7/1950	7/1950	479	4/1949	4/1949

Short frame 'M7' No. 30038 in early British Railways malachite green livery at Eastleigh on 4th September 1948. *W. Gilburt*

Long frame 'M7' No. 30376 at Eastleigh on 21st June 1949 in early British Railways lined black livery, with smokebox numberplate, plain side tanks, Urie power classification below the numerals, backed coal rails, smokebox wingplates removed and below-platform sand containers. *Author*

No.	BR No.	Lined Black Livery	No.	BR No.	Lined Black Livery
480	12/1948	12/1948	671	8/1949	8/1949
481	9/1950	9/1950	673	1/1949	1/1949
667	9/1950	9/1950	674	2/1949	2/1950
668	11/1949	11/1949	675	8/1949	8/1949
669	2/1950	2/1950	676	2/1952	2/1952
670	3/1951	3/1951			

All were painted lined black at Eastleigh Works, except Nos. 30038 and 30106 which were dealt with at Brighton Works. Since most 'M7s' remained in service until 1960-4, several BR general repairs and repaints were received, again mostly at Eastleigh, but Brighton dealt with Nos. 30027/36/43/6/7/9, 30109 in 1953, Nos. 30021/8/54, 30105, 30324 in 1954, Nos. 30048/56, 30110, 30248, 30357, 30669 in 1955, Nos. 30055, 30107, 30246/7, 30667 in 1956 and Nos. 30023/49/53, 30320 in 1957. One, No. 30055, received light attention at Ashford Works in April 1960. The last to receive a heavy repair and repaint was No. 30053 in May 1962.

In February 1949 motor-fitted Nos. 21/7, 47 and 50 were transferred to Horsham as replacements for withdrawn ex-LB & SCR 'D3' class 0—4—4 tanks Nos. 2366/73/87, 32389 on the Midhurst, Guildford and Brighton services. Nos. 21, 47 and 50 came from Bournemouth, where their carriage piloting duties at the Central and West stations were taken over by 'O2s' Nos. 204/12. Other transfers at this period took Nos. 30037, 30107, 356, 30375 to Plymouth for the Turnchapel, Tavistock and Brentnor services, while the number stationed at Exmouth Junction was increased to twenty-five, giving the class monopoly of the local passenger services as well as providing several for carriage piloting, local goods and banking.

No other significant changes occurred until mid-1951, when a series of inter-shed transfers commenced with the intention of grouping engines as far as practical in numerical sequence, details being: Nine Elms Nos. 30123/4, 30241-4/8/9, 30319/22; Feltham Nos. 30038/43, 30254; Guildford Nos. 30022/6-8, 30108/10/25/7, 30246, 30324/8, 39479/80; Bournemouth Nos. 30055-60, 30104-7/11/2/28, 30318; Eastleigh Nos. 30029/31-3, 30109/30/2, 30378/9, 30481; Fratton Nos. 30051-4; Salisbury Nos. 30673-5; Yeovil Nos. 30129/31; Exmouth Junction Nos. 30021/3-5/30/40-2/4-6, 30133, 30320/1/3/56/7/74-7, 30667-71/6; Plymouth Nos. 30034-7/9; Barnstaple Nos. 30245/7/50-3/5/6; Horsham Nos. 30047-50.

Unfortunately, these transfers had no sooner been completed when LMR Class 2 2—6—2 tanks Nos. 41313-5 and BR Class 3 2—6—2 tanks Nos. 82010-3 were delivered to the Southern Region and allocated to Exmouth Junction for the Exmouth, Sidmouth Junction-Sidmouth, Honiton, Axminster and Crediton services. On 23rd July 1952 No. 41314 ran a series of trials between Exeter and Exmouth with the maximum 'M7' loading of seven carriages, but although time-keeping was exemplary, it did not prove noticeably better than that class. However, Class 3 No. 82011 gave a much superior performance and by October 1952 Nos. 82010-3/7-9 were monopolising these services, with occasional help from No. 41314 and 'M7s' Nos. 30023/5/45, 30667/9. As a result, Nos. 30320/1, 30676

were transferred to Nine Elms, No. 30040 to Plymouth, Nos. 30356/7 to Fratton and Nos. 30376/7 to Eastleigh.

The disastrous Kent Coast flooding between Herne Bay and Birchington on Sunday, 3rd February 1953, so severely damaged the track and sea defences that all main line services had to be terminated at Faversham and shuttle trains introduced to Herne Bay. During the morning and evening rush hours these were formed of two motor-train sets with the engine sandwiched between. At first the motive power was provided by 'R' class Nos. 31660/71 and 'H' class No. 31161, but on 14th March 'M7s' Nos. 30052/3 arrived from Fratton and No. 30129 from Yeovil. They remained working from Faversham until the line reopened on 21st May 1953, when all three were transferred to Brighton as replacements for withdrawn 'D3' class 0—4—4 tanks Nos. 32368/72/85 on the Horsham services.

For much of 1948 the class regularly worked the 8.45 a.m. Redhill-Reading, but thereafter only very occasional appearances were made until early December 1953, when repairs to the Reading turntable necessitated all eleven trains in each direction being worked by tank engines. Apart from one double Redhill duty rostered for an LMR class '4' 2—6—4 tank, these workings were covered entirely by 'M7s', for which Nos. 30123, 30245, 30377 were transferred to Redhill and Nos. 30022, 30104, 30374, 30667 to Reading. Nos. 30109/10, 30376 of Guildford also made regular appearances, with the last mentioned keeping time with six well-filled corridors on 15th December 1953. At this period the only other comparable services worked by 0—4—4 tanks were those between West Hartlepool, Middlesbrough and Whitby on the North Eastern Region.

The introduction of regular interval services on the Oxted line was scheduled to commence with the 1955 summer timetable and in anticipation of the greater demand for motor-train engines, ten 'M7s' were assigned to the Central Section. However, their arrival and the commencement of the timetable was delayed by a footplatemen's strike and it was 15th June before the new services operated and only then by employing borrowed engines, including 'R' class No. 1666 and 'D3' class No. 32390. By 17th June Nos. 30028/52 and 30379 (later replaced by No. 30328) had reached Three Bridges for that shed's two motor-train duties, while Nos. 30054-9 began arriving at Tunbridge Wells West for Duties 668/9/71/2 a few days later. Three Bridges had not housed motor-train engines for many years, so for a time crews insisted in running round trains at the end of each journey, with subsequent delays in the East Grinstead area, while Tunbridge Wells West crews compared 'M7' performance unfavourably with the ex-SE & CR 'H' class. However, with experience and the reduced loadings of the winter timetable, most services were worked to time and passengers benefited greatly by the more frequent and standard timed services. Nevertheless, the class remained unpopular and in June 1956 Tunbridge Wells West received 'H' class Nos. 31278, 31310/27/9, 31544 and Three Bridges Nos. 31521/30 as replacements, with Nos. 30052/4-6 being transferred to Brighton, Nos. 30057-9 to Bournemouth and Nos. 30028, 30328 to Eastleigh. For some reason No. 30054's departure was delayed, when, in view of the men's dislike of the class, its restriction to the least onerous duties might have been anticipated, but instead it was rostered for Duty 669, which on Mondays

Long frame 'M7' No. 30480 in motor-train service at Medstead & Four Marks on 7th May 1955.

R. C. Riley

Motor-train fitted 'M7' No. 30051 at Godalming Old Station, on 5th October 1957, with a special train.
R. C. Riley

to Fridays included the four-carriage 6.36 p.m. East Croydon-Tunbridge Wells West, the rear portion of the 6.10 p.m. commuter train from Victoria. Time-keeping was excellent, suggesting that much of the unpopularity was in the mind and not fact.

No such reservations were held on the Western Section, where in an emergency crews were expected to obtain main line performance from the class. An instance on 15th November 1955 saw No. 30256 summoned from van piloting at Woking to take over the ten carriage 6.45 a.m. Salisbury-Waterloo semi-fast from ailing Bulleid Light Pacific No. 34052 *Lord Dowding*. After the expected slow start, speed was gradually increased to 45 mph and, after overcoming two minor signal delays, No. 30246 came to rest at Waterloo in 43 minutes. Later in the morning it returned to Woking with vans, apparently unscathed by the experience.

General withdrawal commenced in June 1957 with No. 30042, but despite the dieselisation of many Hampshire local services on 4th November 1957, only three others, Nos. 30041, 30244/50, were laid aside before the end of the year. No. 30110 and Ironclad set No. 384 worked the Bordon branch during the final week of operation, 10-14th September 1957, while Nos. 30028/9, 30125 and 30479 had charge of the Southampton Terminus-Alton motor-train services for the final weeks of steam traction. For a time minor failures and stock shortages beset the diesel units, but these only occasionally affected the 'M7s' before May 1958, when for several months bogie and coupling modifications made it necessary to reduce the diesel mileage by terminating alternate Portsmouth-Andover Junction services at Eastleigh and providing steam motor-trains for the remainder of the journeys. At first Nos. 30028/9, 30379 were in charge, but later they were joined by No. 30125, while on several occasions in June 1958 No. 30479 substituted for failed diesels on the Alton line.

In February 1958 responsibility for the twenty engines stationed at Plymouth, four diesel shunters, three 'B4s',

one 'G6', four 'O2s', four Ivatt class '2s' and 'M7s' Nos. 30034-7, was transferred to the Western Region. No. 30037 was almost immediately withdrawn, while No. 30035 was replaced by Ivatt class '2' No. 41310 in February 1960, but Nos. 30034/6 remained active until virtually the end of steam in the area. Latterly, they only had charge of the 4.14 p.m. to Brentor and the 5.30 p.m. return, all other local passenger duties being in the charge of LMR class '2s'. Both were transferred to the Southern Region in August 1962 and on 'paper' replaced by Nos. 30321/75, but the latter remained at Nine Elms and Eastleigh until condemned the following month.

Further withdrawals in 1958-9 saw Nos. 30022/6/7/30/7/8/46/54, 30123/30, 30242/3/52/6, 30318/22-4/56/74/6, 30481 and 30671/5 being despatched to Eastleigh Works for breaking up. Most were of the short frame non-motor-fitted series, the duties of which had been largely usurped by diesel sets, LMR class '2s' and BR class '3s', but the loss of motor-fitted Nos. 30047/58, 30106 during the following year made it necessary to augment the stock of these engines. Details are:-

No.	Date						
30031	1/1961	Long frames & motor-train gear from No. 30106					
30133	4/1960	"	"	"	"	"	No. 30047
30378	2/1962	"	"	"	"	"	No. 30050
30667	3/1961	"	"	"	"	"	No. 30128

Nos. 30133 and 30378 were built with long frames, but Nos. 30031 and 30667 were of the short frame series. The total mileages were adjusted to accord with the transplanted frames, cylinders, wheels etc.

In July 1960 a return was made to the Oxted services, when Nos. 30328/79 were transferred to Tonbridge, where local crews found them heavy on coal and water. Nevertheless, the performance was adequate and on the 3½ mile climb to High Brooms they usually bettered the 'H' class. On leaving Tonbridge the Hastings line curves sharply away at 1 in 53 from the London-Dover main line, steepens to

'M7' class No. 30031 at Eastleigh on 4th February 1961, a late conversion to motortrain service using the long frames and equipment removed from No. 30128. In final British Railways lined black livery with 2nd totem and 3P classification above the numerals.   *E. W. Fry*

1 in 47 and then varies between 1 in 72 and 1 in 30 until High Brooms; therefore even with only two carriage motorsets, much hard work was necessary. Recordings of 53 journeys gave the 'M7s' a 23 second advantage over the 'H' class, although running down the bank the latter proved considerably faster. In July 1960 Nos. 30328/79 were replaced by 'Hs' Nos. 31543/51 and transferred to Brighton.

The remaining Southern Region West Country sheds were transferred to the Western Region in December 1963, although by this date only eight 'M7s' remained, Nos. 30025/48, 30667 at Exmouth Junction, Nos. 30052, 30129 at Yeovil and Nos. 30251/4, 30670 at Barnstaple. No. 30125, withdrawn by the Southern Region in December 1962, was stored at Exmouth Junction awaiting despatch to Eastleigh for breaking up and, although never entering Western Region stock, it was moved to Exeter St. David's and rusticated there until called to Eastleigh in January 1964. Nos. 30025, 30251/4 were returned to the Southern Region in January 1963 and replaced by Nos. 30039, 30112, 30320, but the latter were condemned on arrival, as was Barnstaple's No. 30670 in March 1963. There was a repeat performance in April-May 1963, when Nos. 30048/52, 30129, 30667 were transferred to Bournemouth in exchange for Nos. 30031, 30105/10, the latter being condemned shortly after reaching Exmouth Junction.

On 2nd May 1963 a commendably clean No. 30048 and a three-carriage Southern Region motor-set worked the Seaton branch for the last time, the relief being Western Region pannier tank No. 6400 and two trailer cars. These transfers and the withdrawals gave the following allocation of the survivors: Bournemouth Nos. 30025/36/48/52/6/7, 30107/8/11/27/9, 30254, 30480, 30667 (several unserviceable); Feltham Nos. 30032, 30251; Salisbury Nos. 30021, 30241/9; Tunbridge Wells West Nos. 30029/53/5, 30133, 30379.

On 19th July 1963 Nos. 30056, 30667 were working the Swanage branch, Nos. 30048/52 the Bournemouth West-Wimborne-Brockenhurst motor-trains, No. 30480 the Lymington branch and No. 30108 station piloting at Bournemouth Central, while at Salisbury Nos. 30241/9 were sharing the unadvertised early morning and late afternoon Porton and Idmiston Halt Ministry of Works personnel trains and No. 30021 was carriage piloting. Nos. 30029/53/5, 30133, and 30379 had been sent to Tunbridge Wells West in January 1963 for the Oxted motor-trains and when that shed closed on 9th September 1963, they were transferred to Three Bridges, although one stabled overnight at the West for the first up morning service. None remained at Nine Elms, the Waterloo ECS workings having been taken over by BR class '3' 2-6-2 tanks in November 1962, although Nos. 30032/5 and 30251 lingered on until midFebruary 1963.

With the commencement of the winter timetable, the Oxted line motor-trains were discontinued and all traffic between South Croydon and East Grinstead and from Hurst Green to Ashurst Junction via Edenbridge Town became diesel operated. However, at peak hours steam workings remained between Three Bridges and East Grinstead, with one through trip to Tunbridge Wells West, duties which were shared by Nos. 30029/53. On 8th December 1963 No. 30053 was sent to Tunbridge Wells West to act as station pilot during the Christmas period and to work as required vans to Tonbridge and Sevenoaks. This proved to be the final Central Section fling for on 4th January 1964 all regular steam workings ceased and Three Bridges shed closed. Two days earlier No. 30053 towed 'H' class No. 31543 to Eastleigh Works for breaking up and then proceeded to Bournemouth, where later it was joined by Nos. 30029 and 30133.

At this period withdrawn Southern Region engines were being sold to scrap merchants for breaking up and it was while *en route* to T. W. Ward Ltd. of Briton Ferry that No. 30111 was reprieved by Nine Elms and employed for much of February 1964 shed piloting. The same month saw Nos. 30025, 30254 carriage piloting at Salisbury, Nos. 30029/52/3, 30107 appearing on the Swanage and Lymington branches and Nos. 30053, 30108, 30480, 30667 working the Bournemouth-Wimborne-Brockenhurst services.

By now all except No. 30053 were badly run down and with a gradual reduction in duties it came as no surprise when all the survivors were withdrawn in May 1964. No. 30053 was steamed again on 27th June and on the following day ran up to Nine Elms where it was cleaned in preparation for working an enthusiasts special on 5th July

1964. Later it was sold for preservation at Steamtown, Vermont, USA.

After fifteen years in store in various locations, No. 245 was returned to London & South Western livery by apprentices at Litchurch Lane Carriage Works, Derby in 1982.

ENGINE SUMMARY

No.	Date	Order No.	Air P & P	Withdrawn
21	1/1904	B12	7/1930	3/1964
22	1/1899	E9	—	5/1958
23	"	"	—	10/1961
24	"	"	—	3/1963
25	2/1899	"	—	5/1964
26	"	"	—	5/1959
27	1/1904	B12	8/1930	11/1959
28	"	"	6/1930	9/1962
29	2/1904	"	11/1930	5/1964
30	3/1904	"	—	10/1959
31	3/1898	V7	1/1961	5/1963
32	"	"	—	7/1963
33	4/1898	"	—	12/1962
34	"	"	—	2/1963
35	"	"	—	2/1963
36	5/1898	"	—	1/1964
37	"	"	—	5/1958
38	"	"	—	3/1958
39	"	"	—	3/1963
40	6/1898	"	—	6/1961
41	3/1899	E9	—	8/1957
42	"	"	—	6/1957
43	"	"	—	6/1961
44	"	"	—	9/1961
45	5/1905	X12	9/1930	12/1962
46	"	Y12	8/1930	2/1959
47	"	"	7/1930	2/1960
48	6/1905	"	7/1937	1/1964
49	"	"	7/1930	6/1962
50	"	"	7/1930	1/1962
51	11/1905	B13	8/1930	9/1962
52	12/1905	"	7/1937	5/1964
53	"	"	7/1930	5/1964
54	"	"	8/1930	1/1959
55	"	"	10/1931	9/1963
56	1/1906	D13	9/1930	12/1963
57	"	"	7/1930	6/1963
58	3/1906	"	6/1930	9/1960
59	"	"	8/1930	2/1961
60	"	"	7/1930	7/1961
104	4/1905	X12	2/1931	5/1961
105	"	"	7/1930	6/1963
106	"	"	6/1930	11/1960
107	5/1905	"	7/1930	3/1964
108	3/1904	C12	6/1930	5/1964
109	"	"	9/1930	7/1961
110	"	"	4/1930	5/1963
111	4/1904	"	10/1930	1/1964
112	7/1900	B10	—	2/1963
123	2/1903	G11	—	7/1959
124	"	"	—	5/1961
125	8/1911	X14	8/1930	12/1962
126	9/1911	"	—	5/1937
127	"	"	—	11/1963
128	"	"	9/1930	1/1961
129	10/1911	"	11/1930	11/1963
130	2/1903	G11	—	12/1959
131	10/1911	A15	12/1930	12/1962
132	3/1903	G11	—	10/1962
133	"	"	4/1960	3/1964
241	5/1899	E9	—	7/1963
242	2/1897	M7	—	7/1958
243	3/1897	"	—	9/1958
244	"	"	—	10/1957
245	4/1897	"	—	11/1962
246	"	"	—	10/1961
247	"	"	—	10/1961
248	5/1897	"	—	7/1961
249	"	"	—	7/1963
250	"	"	—	7/1957
251	6/1897	"	—	7/1963
252	"	"	—	2/1959
253	"	"	—	10/1961
254	8/1897	"	—	5/1964
255	"	"	—	9/1960
256	"	"	—	5/1959
318	8/1900	B10	—	12/1959
319	"	"	—	1/1960
320	9/1900	"	—	3/1963
321	"	"	—	9/1962
322	"	C10	—	11/1958
323	10/1900	"	—	12/1959
324	"	"	—	9/1959
328	11/1911	A15	7/1937	3/1963
356	10/1900	C10	—	12/1958
357	"	"	—	4/1961
374	4/1903	H11	—	10/1959
375	5/1903	"	—	9/1962
376	"	"	—	1/1959
377	"	"	—	8/1962
378	6/1903	"	2/1962	12/1962
379	5/1904	C12	6/1937	10/1963
479	11/1911	A15	—	4/1961
480	"	"	6/1937	5/1964
481	12/1911	"	12/1930	6/1959
667	8/1897	M7	3/1961	5/1964
668	9/1897	"	—	9/1961
669	"	"	—	7/1961
670	10/1897	"	—	3/1963
671	"	"	—	7/1959
672	"	"	—	5/1948
673	11/1897	"	—	8/1960
674	"	"	—	8/1961
675	12/1897	"	—	3/1958
676	"	"	—	7/1961

Nos. 125-9/31, 328, 479-81 were built at Eastleigh Works and the remainder at Nine Elms Works. Disposal: All broken up at Eastleigh Works except Nos. 53, 245 preserved, Nos. 21/5/9, 36, 48, 52, 107/8/11, 254, 480, 667 sold to T. W. Ward, Briton Ferry, No. 104 to R. S. Hayes, Bridgend, Nos. 32/5, 249, 320 R. S. Hayes, Queenborough and No. 133 to J. Cashmore, Newport. Mileages: Nos. 25 — 1,613,964; 51 — 1,876,636; 108 — 1,544,694; 126 — 781,263; 242 — 1,689,457; 245 — 1,603,998; 676 — 1,572,497.

C. H. Eden

Joint railcar No. 1 at Eastleigh Carriage Works on 13th April 1903.

THE JOINT COMMITTEE
AND SOUTH WESTERN RAILCARS

Steam powered carriages for local and branch line duties were introduced in this country by William Bridges Adams on the Bristol & Exeter and Eastern Counties Railways in 1848-9. However, in this early and primitive form they failed to gain acceptance and by the turn of the century had almost been forgotten, when a combination of rising operating costs and competition by electric tramways revived interest and led to further trials by most major railways.

The first of these later-day steam railcars were designed and built by Drummond for the short Fratton-East Southsea branch, which was operated jointly with the LB & SCR and whose existence was threatened by an electric tramway.

In service these initial railcars did not prove entirely satisfactory, but nevertheless they were sufficiently promising for fifteen others of a more powerful design to be built to South Western account. By 1906 they had charge of a variety of local and branch line services around Eastleigh, Andover, Bournemouth, Guildford, Exeter, Plymouth and Wadebridge. The envisaged savings and extra traffic were realised, but unfortunately these attributes caused their downfall for in most instances the additional passengers could only be accommodated by substituting conventional trains. As a result, railcars fell into disrepute and by World War 1 had largely been replaced by motor-train equipped 0—4—4 or 4—4—2 tanks and trailer cars.

'K11' Class (Joint Committee)

Two steam railcars costing £1,280 each were ordered by the LSWR and LB & SCR Joint Committee for the 1¼ mile Fratton-East Southsea branch in November 1902, with the engines' framing and trailing bogies being constructed by Nine Elms Works and the coachwork by Eastleigh Carriage Works. Numbered 1 and 2 in a separate Joint Committee list, both engines were painted Drummond green, but the carriage of No. 1 was finished in LB & SCR chocolate and cream while No. 2 was LSWR salmon and dark brown. The dimensions were as follows:

Cylinders (outside)	7″ x 10″
Wheel diameter	2′ 9″
Bogie wheelbase	8′ 0″
Total wheelbase	47′ 11″
Boiler diameter	3′ 0″
Boiler length	3′ 3″
Firebox length	2′ 8″
Heating surfaces:	
Tubes	97 sq. ft.
Firebox	32 sq. ft.
Total	129 sq. ft.
Working pressure	150 lb
Grate area	5 sq. ft.
Water capacity	170 gallons
Coal capacity	6 cwt

Weights in working order:

Engine bogie	14T 2C
Trailing bogie	10T 6C
Total	24T 8C

The diminutive vertical boiler, coal bunker and water tank were mounted on an adapted carriage underframe, which was supported at the leading end by the engine unit and at the rear end by an inside-framed bogie. The power bogie cylinders were mounted outside the frames to the front of the trailing axle and drove the leading pair of wheels by Walschaerts valve gear, the first instance of its use by Nine Elms Works. A conventional pattern cab was

The vertical boiler of Joint railcar No. 1 being steam tested at Nine Elms Works on 11th March 1903.　　　　*C. H. Eden*

Joint railcar No. 1 being assembled at Nine Elms Works on 17th March 1903.   *C. H. Eden*

The power bogie of Joint railcar No. 1 at Nine Elms Works on 3rd March 1903.   *C. H. Eden*

A rear view of Joint railcar No. 1 showing the poorly protected secondary driving position. Later this was remedied by fitting a full height weatherboard with round look-out windows.

C. H. Eden

positioned between the boiler and the carriage, which was partitioned into luggage, 3rd class and 1st class compartments served by two open platforms protected by flexible metal gratings. The trailing platform was equipped with duplicate driving controls, but only protected from the elements by a low weatherboard. Despite strong objections by the Board of Trade, lighting was by oil and braking by hand. There was spartan accommodation for thirty-two 3rd class and fourteen 1st class passengers.

No. 1 was officially photographed on 13th April 1903 at both Eastleigh Carriage Works and Fratton station before running several trial journeys over the East Southsea branch. A return was then made to the Carriage Works before being despatched overnight to Waterloo for inspection by officials of the two companies. Unfortunately, a demonstration run to Woking and back had to be abandoned near Hersham, when the trailing bogie overheated.

In early May 1903 No. 1 was borrowed by the Great Western Railway for a series of trial runs between Chalford and Stonehouse, when some measure of success must have been achieved as by 1908 Swindon had no less than 112 engine units and 99 trailer cars in service. However, the former were considerably larger and more powerful, requirements also apparent to Drummond, for during construction he had the boiler barrel of No. 2 extended to increase the steam capacity by 35 per cent. Further trials were then held with both railcars between Cosham and Havant, when it was claimed that No. 2 accelerated from stationary to 25 mph in 55 seconds.

Shortly after the Chalford trials, Drummond received a letter from T. Hurry Riches, locomotive superintendent of the Taff Vale Railway, requesting the supply of drawings and patterns, so that a similar but marginally more powerful railcar could be constructed at Cardiff (West Yard) Works. This was agreed by the Locomotive Committee on 16th June 1903 and on 25 August Drummond visited Cardiff to offer advice and inspect the progress. On his recommendation the working pressure was increased by 20 lb. per sq. in. and modifications made to the springing of the trailing bogie. The completed car was noted in the works yard on 22nd October 1903, with trials commencing in the Cardiff district on 29th October and regular service entered between Cardiff (Clarence Road) and Penarth on 21st December 1903. It differed from the Joint design by having two short boiler barrels arranged transversely, one on each side of the firebox, while the carriage was articulated from the engine. As a result, it proved more flexible and consequently reasonably successful.

Three more railcars of generally similar design to the Joint pair were built in 1904-5, two at £1,585 each by the Glasgow Railway & Engineering Company of Govan, a firm associated with Drummond, for the Alexandra (Newport & South Wales) Docks & Railway Company for service between Caerphilly and Pontypridd. One was converted to a conventional carriage in April 1911, but the other remained in service until mid-1917. The third railcar was built at Inchicore Works by R. Coey for the Goulds Cross-Cashel services of the Great Southern & Western Railway.

The Joint cars commenced working the East Southsea branch services 2nd June 1903, there being three trains an hour from 8.00 a.m. to 7.30 p.m. on weekdays, but no service on Sundays. In regular traffic it quickly became

Joint railcar No. 2 with the enlarged vertical boiler at Fratton in June 1903.

V. Chambers

Joint railcar No. 2 with a locomotive type boiler and full height rear weatherboard in September 1913.

F. Burtt, courtesy NRM

Joint railcar No. 1 with the horizontal boiler fitted in 1903, at Fratton working the East Southsea branch services.   *J. E. Kite Collection*

apparent that when fully laden even No. 2 with the enlarged boiler was incapable of maintaining time and it became standard practice to pilot the heavily patronised early morning and evening services with 'O2s' or 'Terriers'. As a result No. 1 was returned to Nine Elms Works in mid-September 1903 to have the vertical boiler replaced by one of larger dimensions, positioned horizontally with the smokebox overhanging the leading end. At the same time the cylinder diameter was increased to 7¾ inches and the springing of the trailing bogie modified to improve the riding when driven from that end. The changed dimensions were:-

Cylinders (outside)	7¾" x 10"
Boiler diameter	3' 1"
Boiler length	3' 10"
Firebox length	2' 4"
Heating surfaces:	
Tubes	94 sq. ft.
Firebox	76 sq. ft.
Cross water tubes	119 sq. ft.
Total	289 sq. ft.
Working pressure	150 lb.
Grate area	6¾ sq. ft.
Weights in working order:	
Engine bogie	16T 1C
Trailing bogie	10T 6C
Total	26T 7C

On returning to traffic in October 1903, No. 1 proved steadier running and capable of working all the branch services unaided, so No. 2 was similarly modified in June 1904. The discarded boilers saw further employment with the steam cranes at Fratton coal stage and Redbridge permanent way depot. At a later date, probably the 1908-9 winter, better protection was given to the auxiliary driving position by extending the weatherboarding to the roof and providing round look-out windows.

Overcrowding was frequently the bane of railcar operation, but on this branch it only applied to one or two early morning and evening trains for at other times local residents found the competing electric trams more convenient, cheaper and cleaner. As a result, by 1912 the Joint Committee was losing about £820 annually. Nevertheless, the provision of new fireboxes and improved seating in the 1912-3 winter suggests that the service would have lingered on for some years if the outbreak of World War 1 had not presented an excellent excuse to cease operation on 4th August 1914. Both cars were stored at the rear of Eastleigh Works until September 1919, when the carriage from No. 2 was modified for LSWR motor-train service and car No. 1 despatched to Brighton Works for breaking up.

ENGINE SUMMARY

No.	Date	Order No.	Laid Aside	Withdrawn
1	4/1903	K11	8/1914	9/1919
2	5/1903	K11	8/1914	9/1919

The engine units were built by Nine Elms Works and the coachwork by Eastleigh Carriage Works.

'H12' Class

The first South Western railcars were ordered at a cost of £1,380 each on 13th December 1903 for working the Basingstoke & Alton Light Railway, a delightful 14¼ mile rural line, which was promoted and opened by the South Western on 1st June 1901 with the sole purpose of ensuring that the Great Western never gained direct access from Paddington to Portsmouth. This was achieved, but only at the cost of constructing and operating a line which ran at a loss from opening to closure. As a result, economic working was essential and this Drummond attempted to gain by introducing railcars.

Nine Elms Works assembled the engine units, framing and rear bogies, with Eastleigh Carriage Works adding the coachwork and seating. Advantage was taken of experience with the Joint cars to increase the power, mount the horizontal boiler facing the carriage and enclose the engine unit in a slab-sided casing. Numbered 1 and 2 in a separate railcar list, they entered traffic in May and June 1904. The dimensions were as follows:

Cylinders (outside)	9" x 14"
Wheel diameter	3' 0"
Bogie wheelbase	8' 0"
Total wheelbase	41' 1"

Length over buffers	51' 2½"
Boiler diameter	3' 1"
Boiler length	2' 2"
Firebox length	3' 10"
Heating surfaces:	
Tubes	152 sq. ft.
Firebox	76 sq. ft.
Water tubes	119 sq. ft.
Total	347 sq. ft.
Working pressure	150 lb.
Grate area	6¾ sq. ft.
Water capacity	530 gallons
Coal capacity	1 ton
Weights in working order:	
Leading bogie	22T 5C
Trailing bogie	9T 7C
Total	31T 12C

The provision of two passenger entrances and the siting of the luggage compartment next to the engine on the Joint cars had not proved entirely satisfactory, therefore the 1st class saloon was transferred to the leading end and a single entrance provided between it and the larger 3rd class saloon, which in turn was divided from the auxiliary driving position by the luggage compartment. There was seating for eight

'H12' class railcar No. 2 with auxiliary driving end leading at Cliddesden in July 1904, while working the Basingstoke-Alton services.

L & GRP, courtesy David & Charles

'H12' class railcar No. 2 at Plymouth in October 1904 for the Friary-Turnchapel services. *Author's collection*

1st class and thirty-two 3rd class passengers. Braking was by hand only and lighting by oil until September 1904, when the vacuum system was fitted and electricity substituted following strong representation by the Board of Trade. The ungainly engine casing, cylinders and wheels were painted royal green and the carriage salmon and dark brown.

To the casual observer the easy timing and sparse traffic of the Basingstoke-Alton line appeared well suited to railcar operation, but unfortunately practice proved otherwise for the sharp curvature and steep gradients near Cliddesden frequently brought the service to a halt until assistance could be summoned from Basingstoke shed. As a result, the line was only worked by the two railcars from 1st July until 12th August 1904, when both were replaced by 'O2s' and transferred away for trials on local services at Bournemouth and Plymouth before being returned to Nine Elms Works for attention to the blast pipes, braking and lighting. On returning to traffic No. 1 was stationed at Eastleigh and took over the Bishops Waltham branch services on 1st October 1904, the same date that No. 2 commenced working between Plymouth Friary and Turnchapel.

In May 1906 No. 1 ran a series of trials with fifty fully-equipped soldiers between Aldershot and Alton to evaluate the use of railcars in the event of mobilisation. Later similar trial runs were made between Winchester Chesil and Southampton docks. In August 1906 the same railcar was loaned to the Somerset & Dorset Joint Railway for service between Highbridge and Burnham, but the ventilation proved inadequate in hot weather, while at busy periods not all

intending passengers could be accommodated. Consequently, after a brief stay, a return was made to the Bishops Waltham branch.

No. 2 remained working at Plymouth until February 1910, when it was transferred to Strawberry Hill for the Gunnersbury-Hounslow-Twickenham services (extended to Kingston on Sundays), After a brief spell in charge of the Royal Pier-Southampton Town tramway in the closing weeks of 1912, No. 1 was also transferred to Strawberry Hill for these services.

No. 1 was laid aside with a mileage of 117,592 in October 1914, but No. 2 remained working the Gunnersbury services until they ceased in February 1915, when it was employed conveying parcels and staff between Waterloo, Clapham Junction and suburban stations until condemned with a mileage of 137,779 in November 1916. Both were dismantled in mid-1917 and the engine units sold for £485 each to the War Department for stationary duty at Kinmel Camp, North Wales. The carriages were converted for motor-train service about March 1919.

ENGINE SUMMARY

No.	Date	Order No.	Carriage No.	Withdrawn
1	5/1904	H12	4201	11/1916
2	6/1904	H12	4202	11/1916

The engine units were built by Nine Elms Works and the coachwork by Eastleigh Carriage Works.

'H13' class railcar No. 5 at Eastleigh circa 1910.

'H13' Class

At the Locomotive Committee meeting of 5th November 1904, Drummond requested authority for the construction of seven more railcars of a modified and improved design costing £1,475 each for working the Whitchurch-Fullerton (2), Poole-Bournemouth-Christchurch (2), Wadebridge-Bodmin and Padstow (2) and Plymouth-Turnchapel (1) services. However, because of the Basingstoke-Alton line failure, sanction was withheld pending the report of the performance of the 'H12s' on the Bishops Waltham branch and at Plymouth. Fortunately, this was favourable and on 3rd May 1905 all seven railcars were authorised, with the proviso that they were vacuum braked and had sufficient reserve power to haul a 15 ton trailer car on the level at 25 mph.

As Nos. 3 to 9 in the railcar list and classified 'H13', they were completed by Nine Elms and Eastleigh Carriage Works between October 1905 and February 1906. The changed dimensions were:-

Cylinders (outside)	10" x 14"
Working pressure	165 lb.
Length over buffers	52' 7"
Water capacity	485 gallons
Coal capacity	18 cwt.
Weights in working order:	
Engine bogie	21T 14C
Trailing bogie	10T 12C
Total	32T 6C

They differed from the 'H12' series by having the engine unit totally enclosed by the coachwork, and the 1st class saloon at the trailing end. Only the wheels, cylinders and power bogie were painted green, the remainder being salmon pink and dark brown with gold lining. Unlike most 20th century South Western bogie stock, all the vertical body corners, except at the extreme top and bottom, were rounded. Their appearance was neat and a great improvement on the 'H12' series.

After being run-in on the Bishops Waltham branch, the allocation became: Bournemouth Nos. 3, 4; Exmouth Junction Nos. 5, 6; Plymouth No. 7; Guildford Nos. 8, 9. At Bournemouth Nos. 3 and 4 commenced working the Poole-Christchurch services on 5th November 1905, with these being extended to New Milton and Ringwood (via Hurn) on 1st March 1906. Those stationed at Exmouth Junction took over the Exeter-Whimple-Sidmouth Junction-Honiton services on 26th January 1906 and from Exeter to Topsham on 31st May 1908, after the line had been doubled and additional halts provided. At Plymouth Nos. 7 and 8 (transferred from Guildford in mid-1906) joined No. 2 on the Friary-Turnchapel services and some of those to St. Budeaux from 26th September 1906, while Guildford employed No. 9 on the Bentley-Bordon branch from 7th March 1906.

Not all these duties and allocations accorded with the Locomotive Committee minutes, but this was remedied when six more basically similar railcars, Nos. 10-15, were ordered in three batches on 31st May, 18th October and 29th November 1905. Because of servicing difficulties with the earlier series, Nos. 12-15 were fitted with two large doors and a removable floor section, so that the engine could be separated from the carriage without having to lift the boiler off the power bogie.

No. 10 replaced No. 8 on the Bordon branch, while Andover Junction received Nos. 11/2, Wadebridge Nos. 13/4 and Bournemouth No. 15. Those at Andover took over the Whitchurch-Hurstbourne-Fullerton services on 1st June 1906 and proved so popular that one journey each day was extended to Basingstoke, the up journey being via Fullerton, Longparish and Whitchurch, while the return was routed over the main line to Andover Junction, where a reversal was necessary to reach the Town station. At night the spare car conveyed signalmen, permanent way gangs, staff coal and churned drinking water to outlying signal boxes, track works and level crossing keepers' cottages. On 1st June 1906 Nos. 13/4 commenced working the Wadebridge-Bodmin and Wadebridge-Padstow services, while No. 15 ran a series of trial runs over the PD & SWJR Bere Alston-Callington branch but, being without sanding, proved incapable of overcoming the Dartmoor fret. In October 1906 the Bodmin vicar petitioned the Locomotive Committee to have No. 13 renumbered, but this was politely refused.

Three more railcars of greater carrying capacity and having 40 per cent more power, steam-sanding gear, variable blast pipes, feedwater heating and Stone's patent electric lighting, were ordered for the Plymouth-Tavistock services at a cost of £2,080 each on 7th March 1906. The trailing ends were to be fitted with vestibule connections for use with a similar number of 3rd class 32 seat trailer cars having matching connections at one end and driving compartments at the other. They were allotted Nos. 26-8, not 16-8 as might have been expected. However, before the end of the month, Drummond received a report from one of his inspectors describing a series of trials he had witnessed on the Great Western with an elderly 0-4-2 tank and three motor-train equipped bogie carriages. At once Drummond sought Locomotive Committee authority to cancel the railcars and replace them with an order for small single-driver motor-tanks and trailer cars at approximately the same cost. This was agreed and the 'C14' class was conceived.

Despite the cancellation, vestibules did make an appearance on railcars Nos. 10 and 11, although apparently to no useful purpose for there is no evidence that they ever worked with similarly equipped trailer cars.

On local and branch line service, railcars proved considerably cheaper to operate than conventional trains, but their use also created problems for, like all steam locomotives, regular shed visits were necessary to clean fires, remove ashes, replenish the coal supply and carry out routine maintenance. With conventional motive power, this posed no difficulty, but the indivisibility of railcars made it necessary for the carriage units to trail the engines through the murky depths of running sheds, where the soot, ash and sulphurous fumes inherent with coal-burning played havoc with the windows, door handles, entrance gangways, hand-rails and seating. As a result, it became standard practice to stable railcars away from the sheds in bay platforms, cattle docks, carriage sidings or goods yards. Even so, before traffic commenced daily, all the surfaces likely to soil passengers' clothing and hands had to be inspected and if necessary cleaned. Fortunately, this proved more of a staff irritant than an operational failing for the effect on passengers was minimal, although this did not apply to peak period overcrowding for, like present day electrification, railcars invariably increased traffic, but, unlike EMUs, their carrying capacity could not be readily expanded. Indeed, this proved the main cause of their replacement, first by small motor-tanks with trailer cars and later by motor train equipped 'M7s', 'T1s', 'O2s' and '0415s' heading one, two or three carriage sets.

Most regular travellers disliked the railcars, particularly after bogie stock, carriage heating and toilets gravitated to the local services, although probably these feelings were mollified by the frequent service, conveniently sited halts and competitive fares. The last mentioned was possible because of the moderate running costs, details being:-

| Service | Coal Consumption per Train Mile | | |
| | Railcars | Motor-tanks | O2 class |
	lb	lb	lb
Guildford-Farnham	16.3	20.1	30.6
Bishops Waltham branch	11.1	16.9	28.9
Bournemouth-New Milton	12.1	21.2	29.7
Gunnersbury-Twickenham	17.3	–	31.8
Friary-St. Budeaux/Turnchapel	11.2	19.2	31.4
Bordon branch	13.2	18.6	26.8
Average	13.5	19.2	29.9

| | Running Costs per Mile | | |
	d	d	d
Guildford-Farnham	3.7	6.3	10.6
Bishops Waltham branch	3.1	5.8	9.4
Bournemouth-New Milton	3.4	5.6	11.5
Gunnersbury-Twickenham	3.9	–	10.8
Friary-St. Budeaux/Turnchapel	3.9	6.1	10.3
Bordon branch	3.4	5.7	11.1
Average	3.6	5.9	10.6

By early 1907 the availability of motor-tanks and trailer cars at Exeter, Plymouth and Bournemouth not only relieved the pressure on the railcars, but also permitted a number of transfers to other lightly patronised services. Thus No. 7 joined Nos. 9 and 10 at Guildford to share the Bordon branch and from 1st January 1907 the Guildford-Aldershot-Farnham services, while No. 4 was sent to Fratton for the Cosham-Havant shuttle services on 1st March 1907. These trains provided cross-country travellers with a convenient connecting link, via the Farlington spur, between the South Western and London, Brighton & South Coast systems. However, being patronised by family parties travelling with copious baggage, these services were not well served by a railcar and No. 4 was quickly replaced by a motor-tank.

For some years the Portland branch, worked jointly with the Great Western, had lost money, therefore in April 1908 it was agreed that the latter should build two high capacity railcars at a cost of £2,350 each and the South Western provide a new station at Melcombe Regis to avoid the time and expense of reversal at Portland Junction to reach Weymouth terminus. The Melcombe Regis project was completed by mid-1909, but for some reason the Swindon-built railcars failed to materialise, leaving the South Western to commence railcar operation with one of its own on 1st September 1909. This was usually No. 12, but No. 4 was in charge on Christmas Eve 1909. Again success was not achieved, primarily because of early morning and evening overcrowding, so from 1st January 1910 the services became a 'C14' responsibility.

The Lee-on-the-Solent Light Railway, which left the Fareham-Gosport line at Fort Brockhurst, was worked

'H13' class railcar No. 10, with trailing end corridor connection, at Bentley circa 1907.   *J. Gough collection*

'H13' class railcar No. 12 with modified front-end window layout at Hurstbourne circa 1908, while working the Whitchurch-Fullerton services.

Lens of Sutton

under contract by the South Western until 1st August 1909 when it was absorbed, although exactly how this would prove advantageous is difficult to imagine for the 1908 working costs and interest exceeded expenditure by £408 11s 2d. Consequently economic operation was essential and with this intent railcars were introduced, at first employing No. 10, but later No. 9 was usually in charge of the services.

Other changes occurred in 1910, when motor-tanks and trailer cars displaced the railcars entirely at Plymouth and on the Guildford-Aldershot-Farnham services. However, no redundancy occurred as sheds still operating railcars were allowed to retain spare cars to avoid the provision of conventional trains to cover routine maintenance or failures, while on 1st January 1910 new railcar services were introduced between Gunnersbury, Hounslow and Twickenham (extended to Kingston on Sundays) and from 9th December 1909 on the Southampton Royal Pier tramway. For the Gunnersbury services Nos. 2, 8 and 14 were transferred to Strawberry Hill, while the Royal Pier services, together with occasional visits to Southampton West and Winchester, were shared by Nos. 1 and 11. Around this period, probably commencing with No. 6 in May 1913, the numerals were transferred from the buffer beams to above the look-out windows, the engine end being denoted by a small 'D' after the numerals and the trailing end by a small 'P'.

In mid-1912 'M7' No. 481 and 'Terrier' No. 735 were equipped for motor-train operation and ran successful trials in the London area and around Bournemouth with one, two and three carriage sets. As a result other 'M7s', as well as 'O2s', 'T1s' and '0415s', were similarly modified in 1913-4 leading to more railcar redundancies until by July 1914 only the Bishops Waltham branch, Royal Pier, Wadebridge-Padstow/Bodmin and Gunnersbury services were being regularly worked, mainly by the recently repaired Nos. 3, 4, 7, 9, 10/1/3.

After the outbreak of World War 1, further reductions occurred, when the Bishops Waltham branch reverted to 'O2' operation, the Royal Pier line closed to passengers and the Gunnersbury services terminated, leaving only Nos. 3, 4 and 10 active at Wadebridge. In November 1916 Nos. 5-9, 11-15 were condemned, with the carriages of Nos. 11/4/5 being converted into motor-train trailers. The others were stored at Micheldever until similarly modified between March and October 1919. Officially the engine units were broken up in January 1921 but prior to this most of the boilers had been sold to market gardeners.

Nos. 3, 4 and 10 received general repairs in March-June 1916 and remained working from Wadebridge, latterly only on the Bodmin services, until replaced by motor-train 'O2s' in March 1918, when they were laid aside with mileages of 188,462, 196,329 and 192,996. The carriages were modified for motor-train operation in October 1919.

ENGINE SUMMARY

No.	Date	Order No.	Carriage No.	Withdrawn
3	10/1905	H13	4314	7/1919
4	11/1905	H13	4315	7/1919
5	12/1905	H13	4306	11/1916
6	12/1905	H13	4307	11/1916
7	1/1906	H13	4308	11/1916
8	1/1906	H13	4309	11/1916
9	2/1906	H13	4310	11/1916
10	3/1906	H13	4260	7/1919
11	3/1906	H13	4316	11/1916
12	5/1906	A12	4311	11/1916
13	5/1906	A12	4312	11/1916
14	6/1906	B14	4313	11/1916
15	6/1906	B14	4317	11/1916

The engine units were built by Nine Elms Works and the coachwork by Eastleigh Carriage Works.

'C14' class No. 736, fully lined out in shops grey and with the numerals on the tank sides, outside Nine Elms Works on 28th September 1906. Note the roof-top organ pipe whistle and motor train cable pulleys and the lack of front footsteps.

J. B. Ashford

THE MOTOR TANKS
'C14' Class

In time experience with the railcars alleviated all the early operational problems except overcrowding and maintenance. To a degree and at a cost, the former could be overcome by substituting conventional trains at peak travel periods, but maintenance proved insolvable while the engine and carriage remained indivisible, for a defect in one inevitably halted the other, a failing which also affected cleanliness as the carriage had to trail the engine to the ash pit, coaling stage and running shed. Separation offered the only solution and this was taken on 21st March 1906, when Drummond ordered ten small 2—2—0 motor-train tanks from Nine Elms Works at a cost of £910 each. At the same time fifteen trailer cars were ordered from Eastleigh Carriage Works, although only six were commenced immediately, the remainder being spread over eight years.

Numbered 736-45 and classified 'C14', they entered traffic between September 1906 and February 1909. The design was based on the engine unit of the 'H13' series railcars, the cylinders, motion and wheel size being similar, but the boiler was larger. The dimensions were as follows:

Cylinders (outside)	10" x 14" (Nos. 739/41 later 11" x 14")	
Leading & driving wheels	3' 0"	
Wheelbase	8' 0"	
Boiler diameter	4' 0"	
Boiler length	4' 2" (Tubeplates 4' 5 1/8")	
Firebox length	4' 4"	
Heating surfaces:	Original	From Rebuilding
Tubes (216 x 1½")	379 sq. ft.	379 sq. ft.
Firebox	68½ sq. ft.	73 sq. ft.
Cross water tubes	119 sq. ft.	—
Total	566½ sq. ft.	452 sq. ft.
Working pressure	150 lb.	
Grate area	9½ sq. ft.	
Water capacity	500 gallons	
Coal capacity	1 ton	
Weights in working order:		
Leading wheels	12T 4C	
Trailing wheels	11T 16C	
Total	24T 0C	

The boiler was highly pitched in relation to the diameter and, with the engines being short, this gave the class the

'C14' class 2—2—0 motor tank in Nine Elms Works on 22nd September 1906, painted shops grey with alternative positions for the numerals chalked on the tank and bunker sides.

Author's collection

'C14' class No. 742 at Whitchurch with the 10.55 a.m. to Fullerton in October 1909; the carriages are not motor-train equipped.

appearance of being as long as they were tall and gave rise to the nickname of *Humpty-dumpties*. The side tanks, cab and bunker were of conventional pattern, while both sets of wheels were provided with separate splashers. Despite the earlier problems with organ pipe whistles, they were fitted on the cab roof, presumably because of their greater availability when travelling trailer car foremost. Standard whistles were substituted on rebuilding. Motor-train control was by means of a complicated array of wire cables, rods and pulleys, which gave drivers the means of operating from both the cab and a compartment at the outward end of the trailer cars. They were painted passenger green with the numerals carried on the side tanks beneath the company's initials, this position being chosen because of the narrow bunker panels, although the decision was not taken without the paint shop first chalking numerals for Drummond's inspection on both the tank and bunker panels of No. 736.

After running-in on local passenger duties around Eastleigh and Bournemouth, the following services were taken over:

Nos. 736/40	Exeter-Topsham and occasionally Exeter-Honiton.
Nos. 737/44	Bournemouth West-Christchurch/New Milton and Bournemouth Central-Hurn-Ringwood.
Nos. 739/42	Whitchurch-Hurstbourne-Fullerton (not apparently motor-train operated).
Nos. 741/3	Plymouth Friary-St. Budeaux and occasionally to Turnchapel also.
Nos. 738/45	Cosham-Havant (not motor-train operated).

The drawings of the six 1906 trailer cars (48 ft by 8½ ft) are lettered 'for the Plymouth District', three of which provided passenger accommodation, and the others also luggage and auxiliary driving compartments. They were intended to operate in pairs with both types having gangways at the inner ends. Despite this intention, only four cars were allotted to Plymouth, the remaining pair being stationed at Bournemouth. Until more trailer cars were constructed, most services were operated with a motley collection of elderly bogie carriages and six-wheeled 3rd class brakes. Of necessity engines having to run round their trains at the end of a journey or where a reversal was necessary was a method of working unlikely to please the unfortunate crews.

The ability to separate the units for servicing and repair removed another of the railcar failings, but overcrowding remained at peak periods for in his quest for economy Drummond had again provided power units incapable, except in favourable circumstances, of recuperating lost time or even on occasions maintaining schedule with two fully laden trailer cars. The lack of adhesion also proved troublesome in bad weather when restarting on adverse gradients, while slipping at speed occasionally damaged the motion. Difficulty was also met with the firebox cross water tubes for access was only possible by removing the side tanks.

Fast running between stops was not demanded by the schedules, which was probably as well for without the damping influence of attached carriage units, engines bucked and cork-screwed along the tracks at speeds in excess of 30 mph, a failing which, together with the lack of adhesion, led to the class losing favour for passenger service. By August 1911 only Nos. 737/8/40/2/4 remained in use, Nos. 737/40 working the Cosham-Havant shuttle trains, Nos. 738/44 the Bournemouth West-New Milton motor-services and No. 742 the Whitchurch-Fullerton trains (in partnership with 'O2' No. 224). Of the others, Nos.

739/43/5 were in or awaiting shops and Nos. 736/41 were shunting Southampton Town quay. If the mileages recorded by the August 1911 Coal Returns were standard for the whole year, then much time must have been spent in store. Details are:-

| No. | Mileage | | Coal Burnt per Mile | | Oil Consumed per 100 Miles | Duties |
	Passenger	Goods	Allowance	Actual		
751	480	78	17.0 lb	18.1 lb	4.5 lb	Cosham-Havant
740	133	17	17.0 lb	26.1 lb	7.3 lb	
738	684	—	20.0 lb	22.2 lb	4.7 lb	Bournemouth West-
744	1,098	—	20.0 lb	21.9 lb	5.1 lb	New Milton
742	424	64	20.0 lb	23.1 lb	5.3 lb	Whitchurch-Fullerton

No. 740 was ex-works in March 1911, so the excessive coal consumption could only be blamed on a heavy-handed fireman.

Just prior to his death Drummond accepted reality and agreed that more powerful motive power was necessary for the motor-train services and had 'M7' No. 481 and 'Terrier' No. 735 fitted experimentally with a system of rods, steel cables and pulleys so that the regulator, whistle and braking could be controlled from an auxiliary driving compartment at the end of two, three or four trailer cars. No report has survived of the trials, but the *South Western Gazette* mentions the use of both engines on the Clapham Junction-Kingston, Guildford-Effingham Junction-Leatherhead and Bournemouth West-New Milton services. Obviously the trials proved successful for over the next few years a number of 'M7s', 'T1s', 'O2s' and '0415s' were similarly equipped and took over all the motor-train and railcar services, except those at Wadebridge.

As a result, Urie decided to rebuild five 'C14s', probably Nos. 736/41/3-5, as four-coupled shunters at an estimated cost of £280 each in January 1913. On their return to traffic the remainder of the class were to be repaired and offered for sale at £700 each. The first conversion, No. 745, left Eastleigh Works on 26th April 1913 fitted with new 14 in. by 14 in. outside cylinders positioned conventionally

A hitherto rare view of 'C14' class No. 738 entering Mutley on a Plymouth Friary - St. Budeaux motor train service.   *Lt. Holberton RN*

below the smokebox, a conventional firebox, coupling rods, front footsteps and large running plate toolboxes. The weights in working order were:-

Leading wheels	13T 4C
Trailing wheels	12T 11C
Total	25T 15C

No. 743 was similarly rebuilt in June 1913 and with No. 745 was stationed at Eastleigh for shunting Southampton Town Quay or carriage piloting at the Town and West stations. No. 743 was transferred to Guildford in late 1914 and No. 745 hired by Dixon & Cardus Ltd. of Northam from February to June 1915. Other hirings at this period included No. 738 to Tongham Gasworks, Aldershot and No. 744 to W. Alban Richards Ltd; location unknown, but probably on the LSWR or GWR near Basingstoke for it was serviced by that shed on Sundays. In November 1916 the Inspector of Iron Structures on behalf of the Ministry of Munitions approached Urie regarding the purchase of any surplus tank engines weighing less than 32 tons. He was immediately offered 'S14s' Nos. 101/47 and Nos. 736-40/2/3, all of which were accepted subject to inspection, except No. 739 laid aside unserviceable following a pitch-in. Details of the sales are:-

December 1916: No. 740 sold for £900 to the Inland Waterways & Docks for service at Richborough, Kent. It was repaired at Ashford Works between October 1917 and January 1918 before being transferred to the Royal Engineers Garrison Railway, Shoeburyness.

March 1917: Nos. 736/8 sold for £1,050 each to the Ministry of Munitions, the former for service at Royds Green, Leeds and the latter at Dunball, Bridgwater.

November 1917: No. 742 sold for £1,050 to the War Department for service on the Royal Engineers Garrison Railway, Shoeburyness. It was offered for scrap at the New Ranges in April 1921 and later purchased by James Brown Ltd. of Sittingbourne.

December 1917: Nos. 737/43 sold for £1,100 to the Admiralty, the former for service at Grangemouth and No. 743 (on hire from March 1917) at Portsmouth Dockyard.

Nos. 741/4 also worked for the Admiralty, No. 741 from July 1917 to November 1919 at Portsmouth Dockyard and No. 744 from January 1917 to February 1920 at the Royal Naval Armaments Depot, Bedenham. No. 739 was purchased for £900 by the Bute Works Supply Company on 8th January 1917 and after repairs at Eastleigh

'C14' class No. 741 towards the end of its first general repair and repaint at Eastleigh Works in April 1911.   *W. Beckerlegge*

'C14' class No. 741 at Southampton on 14th April 1922 after rebuilding to 0—4—0 tank and being fitted with conventionally sited cylinders, front footsteps, toolboxes and a standard whistle.

H. C. Casserley

Works lasting until 24th February 1917, it was resold for £1,230 to the Ministry of Munitions for service at H.M. Ordnance Factory, Bramley. It was offered for sale in April 1921.

Of the other wartime disposals, Nos. 737/8/40/1/3 were advertised for sale by the Government Disposals Board in September 1921 under the caption of 'A new type of tank locomotive for railmotor trains'. Nos. 737/41 were purchased for scrap by James Brown Ltd. of Sittingbourne, Kent, about March 1922, while Nos. 738/43 would appear to have ended their days working for the Mazagon Dock Company, Bombay, for both were seen at Plantation Quay, Glasgow, in February 1923 labelled S.S. Clan MacAlpine, Mackinnon Mackenzie & Co. Bombay. No. 740 was transferred to Woolwich Arsenal for steam testing the boilers supplied under contract for the SE & CR 'N' class 2—6—0s. When most of these partially assembled engines were purchased by the Southern Railway, it was delivered in error to Ashford Works, where it was recorded as WA740 and broken up in July 1925.

Of those not sold, No. 745 (0745 from 12/1918) spent the early war years shunting at Southampton Town Quay, but in August 1917 it was noted working the Lee-on-Solent branch and in March 1919 was sub-shedded at Winchester. On returning from hire to Portsmouth Dockyard on 26th November 1919, No. 0741 was stationed at Strawberry Hill for tipping soil and ballasting at the new Feltham

sidings complex. It was joined there by No. 0744 in February 1920 on its return from hire to the Royal Navy Depot at Bedenham. Both engines still retained their cab roof top organ pipe whistles. No. 0741 was rebuilt to four-coupled in March 1922 and No. 0744 in October 1923.

All three survivors entered Southern Railway stock to be painted lined black and given the E-prefix, details being:-

No.	S.R. Livery	E-prefix Removed	
0741	2/1925	E0741	6/1932 3741
0744	7/1925	E0744	8/1931 3744
0745	7/1925	E0745	12/1937 77S (E77S 10/1927)

No. 0745 was transferred to Service Stock as E77S in October 1927 and henceforth was employed at the Redbridge Permanent Way Depot, Southampton. Nos. 0741/4 remained stationed at Eastleigh for shunting Southampton Town Quay.

This was the duty pattern throughout the 1930s and World War 2 until Nationalisation, when all three entered British Railways stock to be painted lined black and the two in general stock renumbered into the 30,000 series. Details are:-

No.	BR No.	Lined Black Livery
3741	12/1950 30588	12/1952
3744	8/1948 30589	5/1951
77S	6/1949	6/1949

'C14' class No. 3741 and Urie 'G16' class No. 494 provide an interesting contrast at Eastleigh in the 1930s.   *A. B. Macleod*

'C14' class No. 3744 at Eastleigh on 18th June 1933 in Southern Railway lined black livery with small numerals, boiler barrel clackboxes and leading end shunters handrailing.
H. C. Casserley

'C14' class No. 30589 (ex-No. 3744) at Eastleigh on 8th September 1956 in British Railways lined black with a B4 chimney, OP power classification above the numerals and the toolboxes removed. *E. W. Fry*

No. 30589 received a 'B4' class chimney in March 1951, but the other two retained the 'C14' pattern until withdrawal. It was this engine which headed the RCTS Bishops Waltham railtour of 14th June 1952 and amazed the participants by attaining a maximum speed of 35 mph, no mean feat for an engine having only 3 ft wheels, although the vibration and swaying led many to believe that the maximum was considerably higher.

The Southampton Town Quay shunting duties were shared by Nos. 30588/9 until June 1957, when the latter was condemned, leaving the 30588 in charge until it too succumbed in December 1957 and was replaced by Drewry shunter No. 11223. Unfortunately, some of the clearances were too tight and as Eastleigh had no suitable substitute, No. 77S had to be borrowed from Redbridge. Further trials were made with No. 11223 in March 1958 and when these also proved unsuccessful, No. 77S remained on loan until No. 11224, with cut back footsteps, became available on 12th January 1959. It then returned to Redbridge, but had barely recommenced work when a manning dispute with No. 11224 necessitated a hasty recall. This difficulty was overcome on 10th February 1959, with No. 77S being withdrawn on 21st March 1959 and broken up at Eastleigh Works on 2nd May 1959. Officially the final mileage was 321,643, although how this was calculated is difficult to imagine.

ENGINE SUMMARY

No.	Date	Order No.	Duplicated	Rebuilt	Withdrawn
736	9/1906	C14	–	–	3/1917
737	10/1906	C14	–	–	12/1917
738	10/1906	C14	–	–	3/1917
739	10/1906	C14	–	–	2/1917
740	11/1906	C14	–	–	12/1916
741	12/1906	D14	12/1918	3/1922	12/1957
742	12/1906	D14	–	–	12/1917
743	1/1907	D14	–	6/1913	11/1917
744	1/1907	D14	12/1918	10/1923	6/1957
745	2/1907	D14	12/1918	4/1913	3/1959

All built by Nine Elms Works. Disposal: Nos. 741/4/5 broken up at Eastleigh Works, the remainder sold. No. 745 was transferred to the Engineer's Department and became Service Stock 77S in October 1927.

Engineer's Department 'C14' No. 77S in British Railways lined black livery circa 1957. *R. C. Riley*

'S14' Class

The 'C14' motor tanks gave considerably better service than the railcars, although the diminutive boiler and poor adhesion forbade the use of two trailer cars except in the most favourable circumstances. As a result, Drummond prepared two larger four-coupled designs in 1909, a South Western variation of the Stroudley 'D1' class 0—4—2 tanks with 12 in. by 18 in. outside cylinders and a weight of 36 tons, priced at £1,480, and an 0—4—0 tank of 28 tons costing £1,055. On considering the designs the Locomotive Committee found the former too large and expensive, so five 0—4—0 tanks, Nos. 746-50, were ordered from the new locomotive works at Eastleigh.

The drawings were finalised on 3rd March 1910 but, because of the inevitable delays in gaining full production, it was mid-August before assembly commenced, by which date small motor-tanks had fallen into disrepute, so only the two most advanced were completed for the Bournemouth-New Milton and Lymington branch services. Before leaving the Paint Shop, they were renumbered 101/47. The three surplus boilers were converted for stationary duty, two providing power for the electric generators at Waterloo and the third for the well pump at Micheldever.

Classified 'S14', the dimensions were as follows:

Cylinders (outside)	12″ x 18″
Coupled wheels	3′ 8″
Wheelbase	6′ 8″
Boiler diameter	4′ 2″
Boiler length	4′ 8″
Firebox length	4′ 6″
Heating surfaces:	
Tubes	521 sq. ft.
Firebox	82 sq. ft.
Total	603 sq. ft.
Working pressure	150 lb.
Grate area	10½ sq. ft.
Tank capacity	600 gallons
Bunker capacity	1 ton
Weights in working order:	
Leading wheels	14T 18C
Trailing wheels	13T 4C
Total	28T 2C

Unlike the 'C14s', the firebox was without cross water tubes and the cylinders were sited conventionally below the smokebox and drove the rear pair of wheels. Again Walschaerts valve gear and organ pipe whistles were fitted.

In service Nos. 101/47 proved capable of hauling two fully laden trailer cars on the Lymington branch and Bournemouth West-New Milton services, but failed at Portland and Seaton, while the riding was rougher than the 'C14s' and the coal consumption little better than the 'O2s'. As a result, the Lymington branch returned to conventional operation in early 1911, but the New Milton services remained in their charge until mid-1914, when No. 101 was sent to Eastleigh for general repair and No. 147 transferred on loan to the Engineer's Department

for service at Salisbury where Tunnel Junction was being relaid and the drainage improved. Later both were stationed at Eastleigh for piloting at the locomotive or carriage works until March 1917, when they were sold to the Ministry of Munitions for £1,250 each. Having been repaired in September 1915, No. 147 only needed minor attention before being despatched in steam to No. 5 National Filling Factory, Quedgeley on 17th April 1917, but No. 101 required heavy repairs and it was 19th May 1917 before it could be sent to Stratton Filling Factory, Swindon. No. 147 was offered for sale in 1920 and in the following year was purchased by Joseph Pugsley & Sons Ltd., who sent it to the Avonside Engine Company in 1927 for repair and conversion to oil-firing. It was invoiced to Swansea docks on 20th July 1927 for shipment overseas.

No. 101 was offered for sale in April 1921 and towards the end of the year was purchased by the Branstone Blue Lias, Lime & Cement Company Ltd. (later Branstone Cement Company Ltd.), who obtained spares from Eastleigh Works in March 1925. It was next reported derelict in George Cohen's Stunningley Yard, Leeds, on 7th August 1939 just prior to being transported by road to Derby Works for repair. Later service was entered at the Royal Ordnance Factory, Chorley, where it was noted awaiting scrap in July 1951.

ENGINE SUMMARY

No.	Maker	Order No.	Date	Sold
101	Eastleigh Works	S14	9/1910	3/1917
147	Eastleigh Works	S14	9/1910	3/1917

'S14' class 0—4—0 motor-tank No. 101 outside Eastleigh Works in September 1910, painted grey with roof-top organ pipe whistle and motor-train cable pulleys.   *Author's collection*

THE 'TERRIERS'

LB & SCR 'Terrier' No. 668 *Clapham* upon arrival at Nine Elms on 12th March 1903 to be prepared with No. 646 *Newington* for service on the Axminster-Lyme Regis branch.   *W. Beckerlegge*

Nos. 734 and 735

Throughout the 1850s Lyme Regis was changing from a sleepy fishing village on the Channel coast to a bustling holiday resort, therefore it was only to be expected that the railway mania would inspire proposals for a swifter and more congenial means of access than provided by the roads of the period. Indeed, no less than three schemes were promoted offering rail communication with Bristol, Exeter and Salisbury. All failed to attract support, although a later proposal did obtain Parliamentary sanction in August 1871, only to suffer a similar fate after cutting the first sod. Over the next decade several other schemes were mooted, all equally unsuccessful until June 1899, when the Axminster & Lyme Regis Light Railway gained authority to construct a 6¾ mile branch from the South Western's Salisbury-Exeter line at Axminster. Construction commenced using the Cobb, Lyme's man-made harbour, to land the equipment, ballast, sleepers, rails and building materials, but, despite this advantage, progress was so severely disrupted by westerly gales, heavy rain, flooding and earth slips that it was 24th August 1903 before the Board of Trade sanctioned the opening. The services were operated by the

South Western under contract until the line was absorbed on 1st January 1907.

As construction was not to main line standards, the works were light, the curvature sharp and the gradients severe, which made the service both costly and difficult to operate for of necessity only small tank engines could be employed. No suitable motive power was available on the South Western, so Drummond, after considering the construction of two small 0—4—4 tanks with 4 ft. 6 in. wheels and 15 in. cylinders, decided to approach Robert Billinton at Brighton Works to ascertain whether the LB & SCR had a pair of Stroudley 'Terriers' for disposal. Several were available, therefore on 24th January 1903 two South Western inspectors travelled on the seven-carriage 7.10 a.m. Victoria-Stoats Nest headed by No. 668 *Clapham*, one of the engines on offer. The running on both outward and inward journeys was excellent, so after receiving his inspectors' report, Drummond recommended its purchase and No. 646 *Newington* at £600 each. This was authorised by the Locomotive Committee on 4th March 1903 and ten days later both were delivered to Nine Elms in LB & SCR livery. The actual price was £500 each, so obviously some 'horse-trading' occurred before agreement was reached. Both engines were photographed and then transferred to the Works to have the Westinghouse air brake replaced by vacuum ejectors and South Western livery applied.

They were not identical for *Newington* (LSWR No. 734) had 14 in. cylinders and cold boiler feed, whereas *Clapham* (LSWR No. 735) retained 13 in. cylinders and had exhaust steam heated feed. The dimensions were as follows:-

Cylinders	13″ or 14″ x 20″
Coupled wheels	4′ 0″
Wheelbase	6′ 0″ + 6′ 0″ = 12′ 0″
Boiler diameter	3′ 6″
Boiler length	7′ 10″
Firebox length	4′ 1″
Heating surfaces:	
Tubes (121 x 1¾″)	453 sq. ft.
Firebox	53 sq. ft.
Total	506 sq. ft.
Grate area	11¼ sq. ft.
Working pressure	150 lb.
Weights in working order:	
Leading wheels	8T 7C
Centre wheels	8T 3C
Trailing wheels	8T 2C
Total	24T 12C

Mileage: No. 734 – 574,266; No. 735 – 611,070

South Western service was entered on 4th April 1903 when No. 734 was sent to Guildford as shed pilot for several weeks before being despatched to Exmouth Junction for carriage piloting at Exeter station and working the Exmouth, Salterton and Sidmouth goods. It was derailed in the sidings at Topsham on 12th June 1903. No. 735 was employed around the shed yard at Nine Elms for several months before being transferred to Yeovil for working the Town-Junction shuttle services. Both were standing on Exmouth Junction shed on 17th July 1903, while no. 734 was working the Sidmouth Junction-Sidmouth services on August Bank Holiday Monday. In early August 1903, No. 735 ran a series of trials over the Lyme Regis branch, while for the official opening on 24th August both engines, suitably decorated and coupled together, spent the day working the well patronised services.

During the winter months one engine could operate the passenger and goods traffic, it being sub-shedded at Lyme in a small building near the station, with engines being exchanged weekly before services commenced on Monday mornings. The spare engine was usually employed carriage piloting at Exeter or working goods to Topsham, Exmouth and Sidmouth. In the summer many of the Lyme Regis services required piloting, which was not only uneconomical, but created problems if one of the branch engines failed or was stopped for repair because the engineer prohibited a

'Terrier' No. 734 (ex-No. 646 *Newington*) in LSWR livery with the Brighton works plates removed from the leading sandboxes and vacuum injectors substituted for the Westinghouse brake.

J. B. Ashford

'Terrier' No. 735 at Eastleigh on 19th August 1912 with a Drummond boiler, the feedwater heater pipes removed, and fitted with pulley and cable motor-train equipment.
Author's collection

'Terrier'-'O2' combination. As a result, 'O2' No. 228 was prepared for trials on the branch in May 1906 by giving the bogie greater play and restricting the coal and water carried to 1 ton and 500 gallons. It proved more capable than the 'Terriers', but nevertheless was unable to work unaided those services including through carriages to Waterloo, so Nos. 734/5 were left in control of the branch.

When the line was taken over by the South Western, the Engineer's Department lost little time easing the sharpest curves, improving the drainage, providing a short connecting line to the down platform at Axminster and relaying much of the track with second-hand but heavier rails. These very necessary improvements were completed by Easter 1908, when the services were taken over by specially modified 'O2s' Nos. 177/91, 202/28. For a time all piloting had to be performed by one of the 'Terriers', but by mid-1909 this was no longer demanded by the Engineer and most summer Saturdays found two 'O2s' working the services.

After being sub-shedded at Sidmouth for several months, No. 734 was transferred to Yeovil for the Town-Junction shuttle services, while No. 735 carriage piloted at Exeter and worked the Sidmouth Junction-Sidmouth-Exmouth trains. Later No. 734 was transferred to Fratton and appeared on the Gosport, Cosham-Havant and Lee-on-the-Solent services. Neither was essential for these duties, therefore when the Stroudley boilers required renewal in 1911-12, Drummond recommended withdrawal, but was

overruled by the Locomotive Committee, who ordered reboilering for use on the motor-train services. No. 735 was returned to traffic in June 1912 and No. 734 in the following September. The changed dimensions were:-

Boiler diameter	3' 3½"
Boiler length	7' 10" (Tubeplates 8' 1½")
Firebox	4' 0"
Heating surfaces:	
Tubes (113 x 1¾")	420 sq. ft.
Firebox	57 sq. ft.
Total	477 sq. ft.
Working pressure	150 lb.
Grate area	11¼ sq. ft.
Weights in working order:	
Leading wheels	7T 6C
Centre wheels	9T 17C
Trailing wheels	9T 0C
Total	26T 3C

The boilers were of Drummond pattern with dome top direct loaded safety valves, continuous hand railing and injectors. At the same time new 13 in. cylinders, steam carriage heating and reconditioned crank axles (from Brighton Works at £11 6s. 4d. each) were fitted, while the feed water heating equipment was removed from No. 735.

After being run-in, No. 735 was fitted with mechanical motor-train gear and, with 'M7' No. 481, used for a series of trials in the London area and at Bournemouth before being set to work on the Lee-on-the-Solent branch. No. 734

was stationed at Eastleigh and employed carriage piloting at Southampton Town or shunting the Town Quay until hired by the Freshwater, Yarmouth & Newport Railway in mid-1913.

No. 735 remained working the Lee-on-the-Solent branch until laid aside pending withdrawal in October 1919, but, when no suitable substitute could be found, it was reinstated, repaired and returned to traffic in January 1920 with an Adams stove pipe chimney welded to the Stroudley base, boiler barrel clackboxes and cast-iron brake shoes attached to the original hangers.

Southern Railway stock was entered at Grouping and in May 1925 it was painted Maunsell green and received the E-prefix. For a time regular appearances were made on the Lee-on-the-Solent branch, but when ex-LB & SCR Marsh boilered 'Terriers' Nos. B655/61 were fitted with Drummond pattern motor-train gear and transferred to Fratton in September 1925, they were preferred by the men and tended to monopolise the services, leaving No. 735 to carriage pilot at Cosham or work the Gosport goods. Light repairs were received at Eastleigh Works in January 1927, but these only proved a temporary expedient for the firebox was practically worn out and little serious work was performed before a further visit to shops in February 1930 to have the Drummond boiler replaced by the LB & SCR A1X pattern from No. B658. No other modifications occurred, therefore when returned to traffic in May 1930, the Adams stove pipe and motor-train brackets were retained. After some

weeks carriage and coal-stage piloting at Eastleigh, it was transferred to Ashford for piloting at the Wagon Works, a duty retained, apart from several brief periods of loan to Chislet Colliery, until condemned in December 1936.

No. 734 was shipped to the Isle of Wight on 25th June 1913 and, in partnership with a six-coupled Manning Wardle saddle tank, commenced working the Newport-Freshwater passenger and goods services of the small Freshwater, Yarmouth & Newport Railway on 1st July 1913, the day on which that company accepted responsibility for operating its own services. Hitherto they had been worked under contract by the Isle of Wight Central Railway. The Manning Wardle tank was painted emerald green and numbered 1 shortly after reaching the island, but being on hire, the 'Terrier' retained LSWR livery until purchased for £900 in February 1915, when it was painted light green with dark green and yellow lining. For some reason it ran without identification until repairs at Ryde Works (IWR) during early 1919, when the tanks were lettered FYN and No. 2 added to the bunker sides.

After Grouping it was painted Maunsell green and renumbered W2 in March 1924, when the vacuum ejectors were removed, the Westinghouse air brake fitted and the bunker extended in the same manner as the ex-IWCR 'Terriers'. Employment remained on the Newport-Freshwater services, usually in partnership with No. W10.

At the January 1927 general repair, carriage heating and compressed air motor-train equipment was fitted, while the

'Terrier' No. E735 at Fratton on 14th July 1928 in Southern Railway green livery with Drummond motor-train equipment, an Adams stove-pipe chimney, boiler barrel clackboxes and cast iron blocks attached to the original brake hangers.   *O. J. Morris*

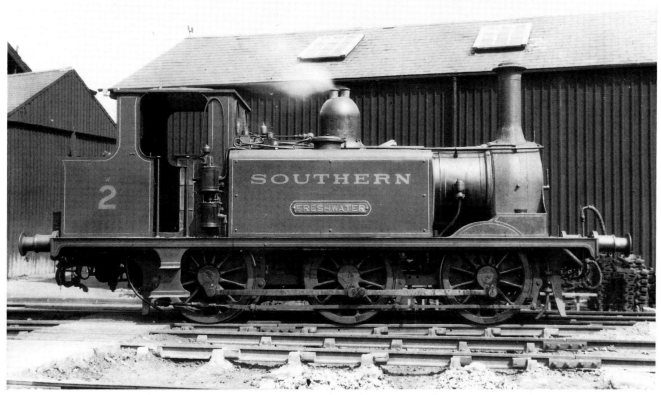

'Terrier' No. W2 *Freshwater* (ex-LSWR No. 734 and FY & NR No. 2) in Southern Railway (Isle of Wight Section) Maunsell green livery and refitted with the Westinghouse brake. *O. J. Morris*

name *Freshwater* was added in October 1928. The standard Southern pattern nameplates were mounted on the side tanks between the W-prefix and the numerals, but in November 1929 they were repositioned lower down the side tanks with the prefix and numerals transferred to the bunker to accord with standard Isle of Wight practice.

The Drummond boiler remained *in situ* until January 1932, when the firebox was condemned and a spare 'A1X' class boiler was sent across from the mainland. On returning to traffic in April 1932, *Freshwater*, after a twenty year break, again carried an LB & SCR boiler. At the same time it was renumbered W8, fitted with an organ pipe whistle and a Drummond chimney. Usually employment was on the Merstone-Ventnor West motor-trains, but occasional appearances were still made on the Newport-Freshwater services. After the outbreak of war in September 1939, it was stored for some months at Newport, but thereafter was found spasmodic employment until the Island services returned to normal in September 1945, by which date the Maunsell green livery had given way to plain black.

At Nationalisation only two 'Terriers', Nos. W8 *Freshwater* and W13 *Carisbrooke* remained working on the island, one piloting at Newport and the other in charge of the Ventnor West services. However, the long presence on the island was rapidly drawing to a close and in May 1949 both were returned to the mainland, where Eastleigh Works gave superficial repairs and renumbered them 32646/77 before transfer to Fratton for the Hayling Island branch.

Later No. 32646 worked from Brighton and Newhaven before being withdrawn from Fratton on 4th November 1963, the day the Hayling Island services ceased. Latterly, it ran painted BR lined black and carrying a copper-capped chimney. After a period in store, it was purchased by the Sadler Rail Car Company for £600, while following a final run in steam over the Meon Valley line on 13th May 1966, it was resold to Brickwoods Brewery for display outside the Hayling Billy public house. There it proved an excellent attraction and undoubtedly added to the custom, but by 1979 the ravages of time had caused serious deterioration and thought had to be given to the future. Fortunately, *Freshwater's* historic value was appreciated by Whitbread Wessex Ltd., successors to Brickwoods, and on 18th June 1979, following renewal of the paintwork, it was transferred to the custody of the Wight Locomotive Society and shipped to the island, where it was returned to steam.

ENGINE SUMMARY

LSWR No.	LB & SCR No. & Name	Built	Purchased	Remarks
734	646 *Newington*	1/1877	3/1903	On hire to FY & NR 6/1913, purchased 2/1915, to W2 3/1924, named *Freshwater* 10/1928, to W8 4/1932, to 32646 8/1949, withdrawn 11/1963.
735	668 *Clapham*	8/1874	3/1903	To E735 5/1925, withdrawn 12/1936.

Built at Brighton Works, No. 734 preserved and No. 735 broken up at Ashford Works 2/1937.

'K14' class No. 82 shunting at Plymouth Friary on 14th June 1926.

H. C. Casserley

'K14' CLASS SHUNTERS

The five 0—4—0 tanks forming this class were ordered at a cost of £1,210 each from Nine Elms Works in May 1907 and delivered as Nos. 82-4, 746 *Dinan* and 747 *Dinard* in April-June 1908. They had the following dimensions:

Cylinders (outside)	16" x 22"
Coupled wheels	3' 10"
Wheelbase	7' 0"
Boiler diameter	3' 7"
Boiler length	10' 8" (Tubeplates 10' 11½")
Firebox length	3' 9"
Heating surfaces:	
Tubes (142 x 1¾")	709 sq. ft.
Firebox	55 sq. ft.
Total	764 sq. ft.
Working pressure	140 lb.
Grate area	10.8 sq. ft.
Water capacity	600 gallons
Coal capacity	½ ton
Weights in working order:	
Leading wheels	14T 13C
Trailing wheels	18T 5C
Total	32T 18C

Nos. 82-4 were stationed at Eastleigh and Nos. 746/7, as their names suggest, at Southampton Docks. Since these five engines were based on the Adams 'B4s', worked similar duties and were absorbed into that class in 1913, their later history is to be found in pages 103-11 of the Adams volume of this series.

ENGINE SUMMARY

No.	Date	Order No.	Name	Withdrawn
82	6/1908	K14	—	6/1957
83	6/1908	K14	—	11/1959
84	6/1908	K14	—	8/1959
746	4/1908	K14	Dinan	11/1948
747	4/1904	K14	Dinard	2/1949

All were built at Nine Elms Works, No. 84 being the last engine constructed there. Nos. 746/7 were renumbered 101/47 in February 1922. Disposal: Nos. 82/3 were broken up at Eastleigh Works, No. 84 at Ashford Works and Nos. 746/7 (101/47) sold.

'K14' class No. 747 *Dinard* with a full cab, dome lock-up safety valves and vacuum ejectors at Southampton Docks circa 1909.

L & GRP, courtesy David & Charles

SUMMARY OF DRUMMOND CLASSES

4—6—0s

F13 class (1905)	Nos. 330-4	5	
E14 class (1907)	No. 335	1	
G14 class (1908)	Nos. 453-7	5	
P14 class (1910)	Nos. 448-52	5	
T14 class (1911-2)	Nos. 443-7/58-62	10	
			26

4—4—0s

C8 class (1898)	Nos. 290-9	10	
T9 class (1899-1901)	Nos. 113-22, 280-9, 300-5/7/10-4/ 36-8, 702-19/21-32/73	66	
K10 class (1901-3)	Nos. 135-46/9/50-3, 329/40-5/7/80-94	40	
S11 class (1903)	Nos. 394-404	10	
L11 class (1903-7)	Nos. 134/48/54-9/61/3-75, 405-14/35-42	40	
L12 class (1904-5)	Nos. 415-34	20	
D15 class (1912-3)	Nos. 463-72	10	
			196

DOUBLE SINGLES

T7 class (1897)	No. 720	1	
E10 class (1901)	Nos. 369-73	5	
			6

0—6—0s

700 class (1897)	Nos. 687-716 (Nos. 702-16 were renumbered 306/8/9/15/7/25-7/ 39/46/50/2/5/68, 459 in 1898)	30	
			30

0—4—4 TANKS

M7 class (1897-1911)	Nos. 21-60, 104-12/23-33, 241-56, 318-24/8/56/7/74-9, 479-81, 667-76	105	
			105

0—4—0 TANKS

K14 class (1908)	Nos. 82-4, 746/7	5	
S14 class (1910)	Nos. 101/47	2	
			7

2—2—0 TANKS

C14 class (1906-7)	Nos. 736-45	10	
			10

INSPECTION SALOON

F9 class (1849)	No. 733	1	
			1

RAIL CARS

K11 class (1903)	Joint LB & SCR Nos. 1, 2	2	
H12 class (1904)	Nos. 1, 2	2	
H13 class (1905-6)	Nos. 3-15	13	
			17
TOTAL			398

LOCOMOTIVES PURCHASED

0—6—0 TANKS

Terriers (1903)	Nos. 734/5 (from LB & SCR)	2	
Total			2

ADAMS LOCOMOTIVES COMPLETED BY DRUMMOND

4—4—0s

T6 class (1895-6)	Nos. 677-86	10	
X6 class (1895-6)	Nos. 657-66	10	
			20

0—4—4 TANKS

T1 class (1896)	Nos. 358-67	10	
			10

0—6—0 TANKS

G6 class (1896-1900)	Nos. 160/2, 237-40/67-79, 348/9/51/3/4	24	
			24
Total			54

'T7' CLASS DOUBLE-SINGLE

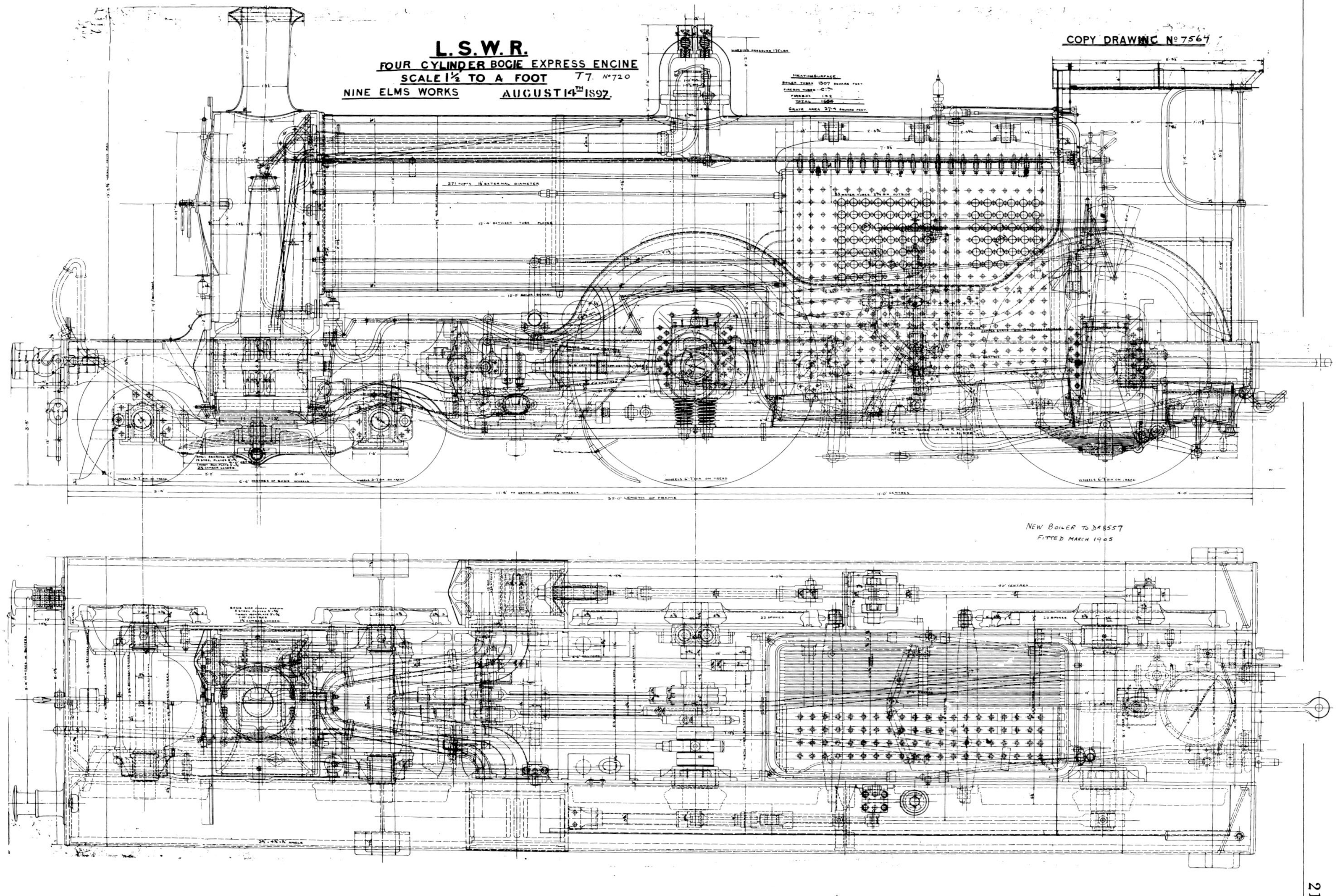

COPY DRAWING Nº 7567

NEW BOILER TO Nº 4557
FITTED MARCH 1905

L.S.W.R.
FOUR CYLINDER BOGIE EXPRESS ENGINE   77. Nº 720
SCALE 1½ TO A FOOT   AUGUST 14TH 1892.
NINE ELMS WORKS

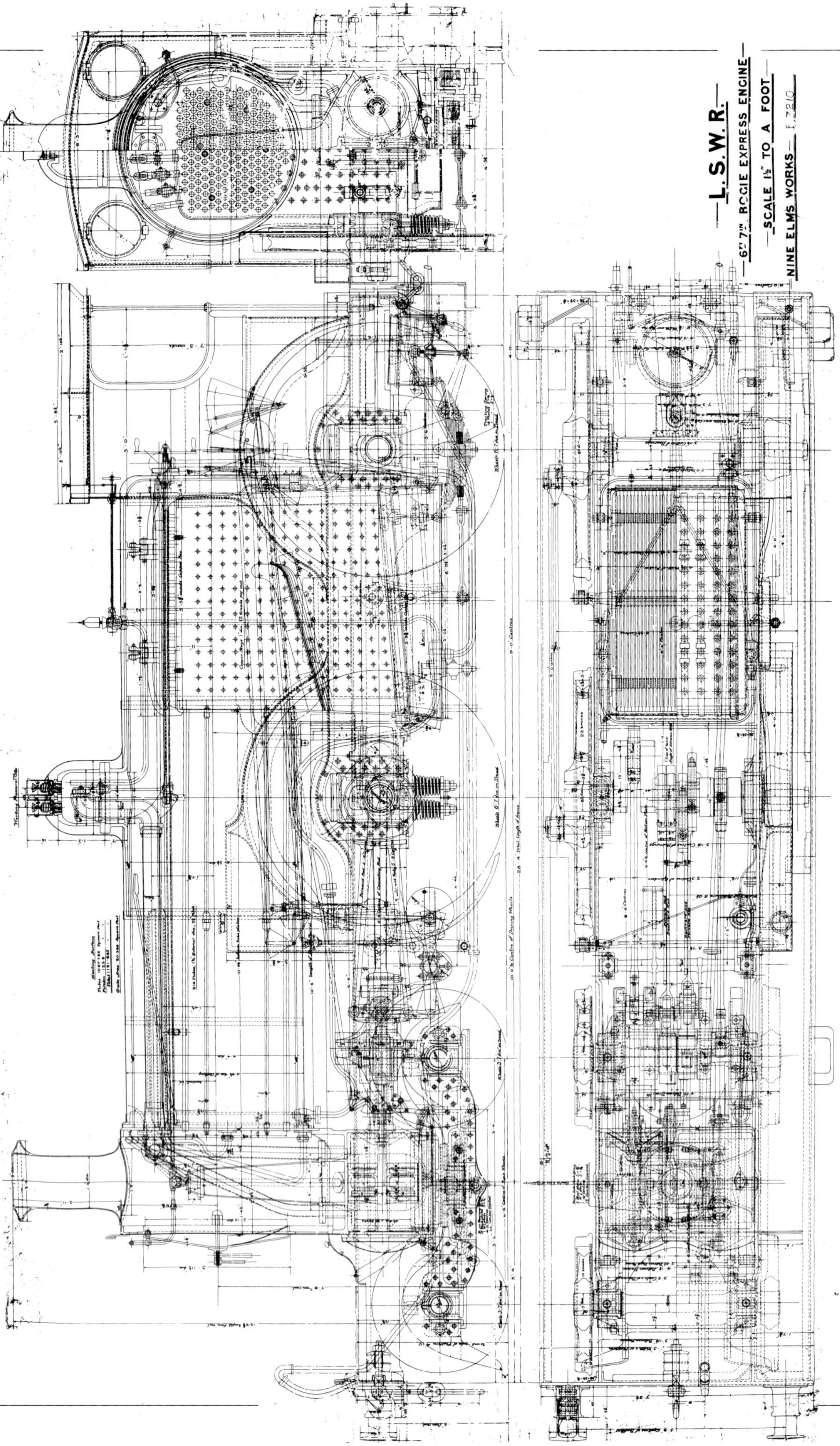

'C8' CLASS EXPRESS 4—4—0

L.S.W.R.

6" 7IN BOGIE EXPRESS ENGINE

SCALE 1½" TO A FOOT

NINE ELMS WORKS — F.7210

'T9' CLASS EXPRESS 4–4–0

214

URIE MODIFIED 'T9' CLASS

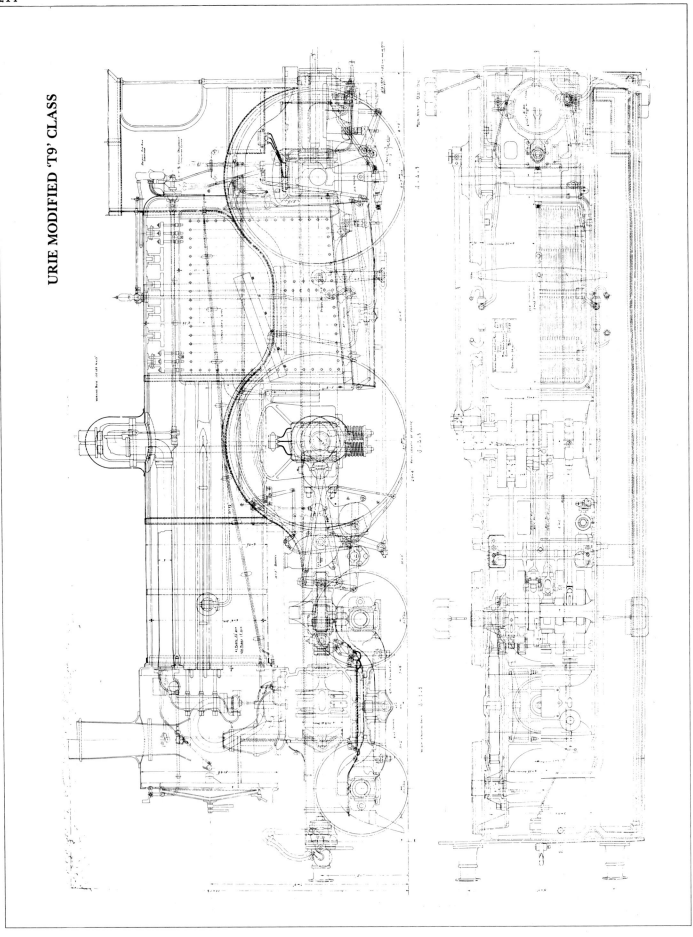

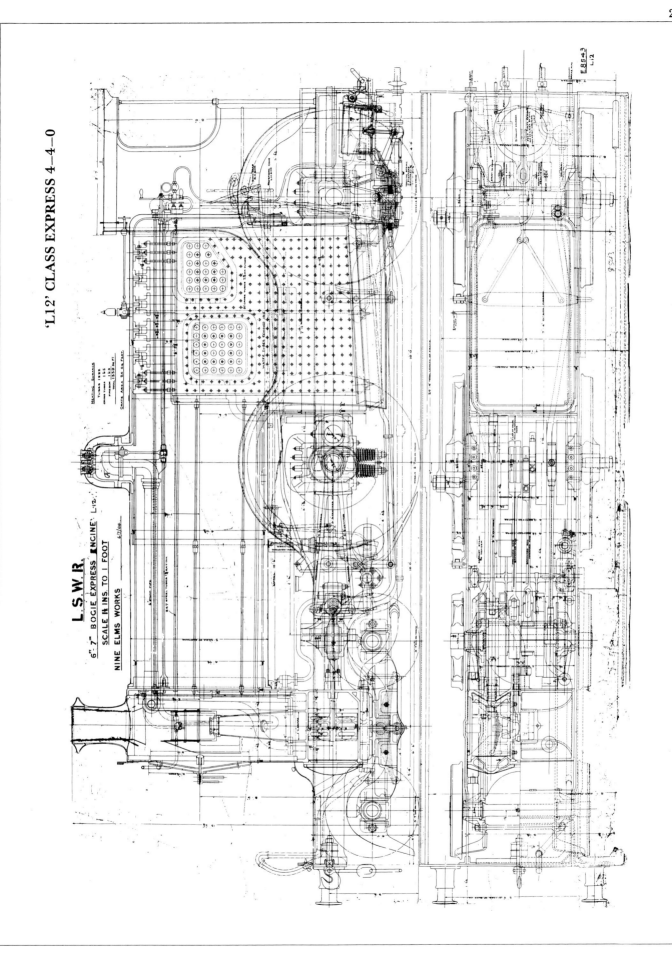

'L12' CLASS EXPRESS 4–4–0

L.S.W.R.
6"–7" BOGIE EXPRESS ENGINE 'L.12.'
SCALE 1½ INS. TO 1 FOOT
NINE ELMS WORKS

E.8543
L.12

'D15' CLASS EXPRESS 4–4–0

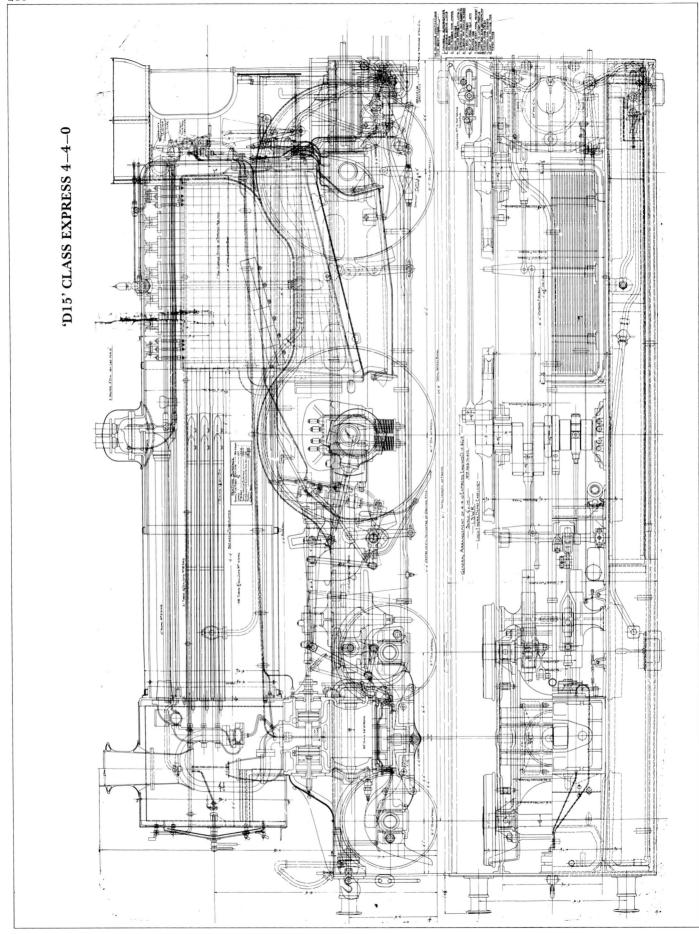

GENERAL ARRANGEMENT OF 4–4–0 EXPRESS ENGINE 'D15' CLASS

'S11' CLASS MIXED TRAFFIC 4–4–0

218

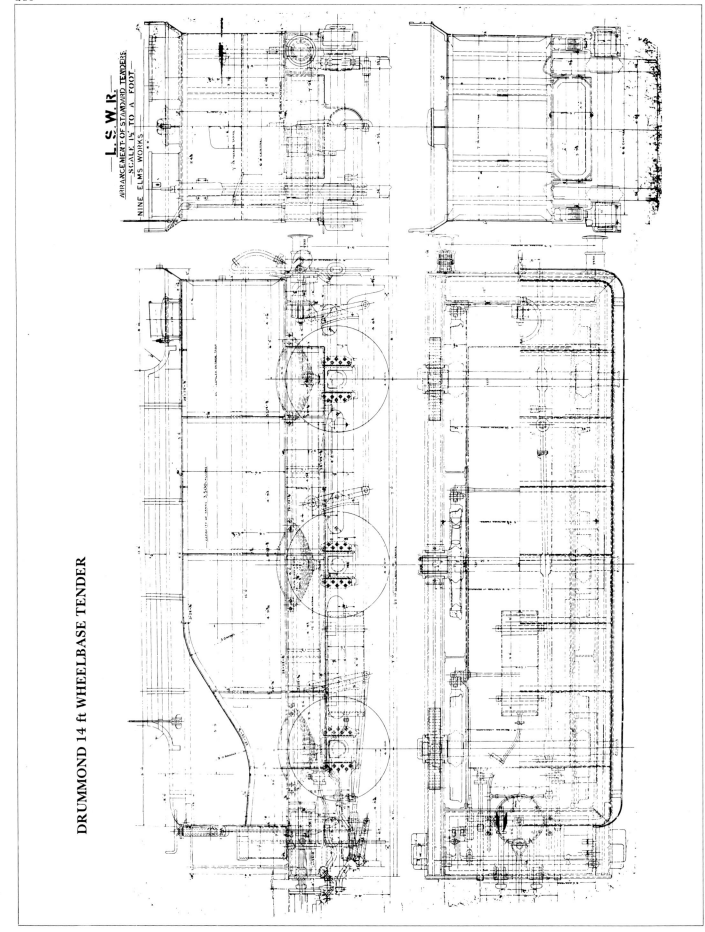

DRUMMOND 14 ft WHEELBASE TENDER

L.S.W.R.
ARRANGEMENT OF STANDARD TENDERS.
SCALE 1½ TO A FOOT.
NINE ELMS WORKS.

DRUMMOND BOGIE TENDER

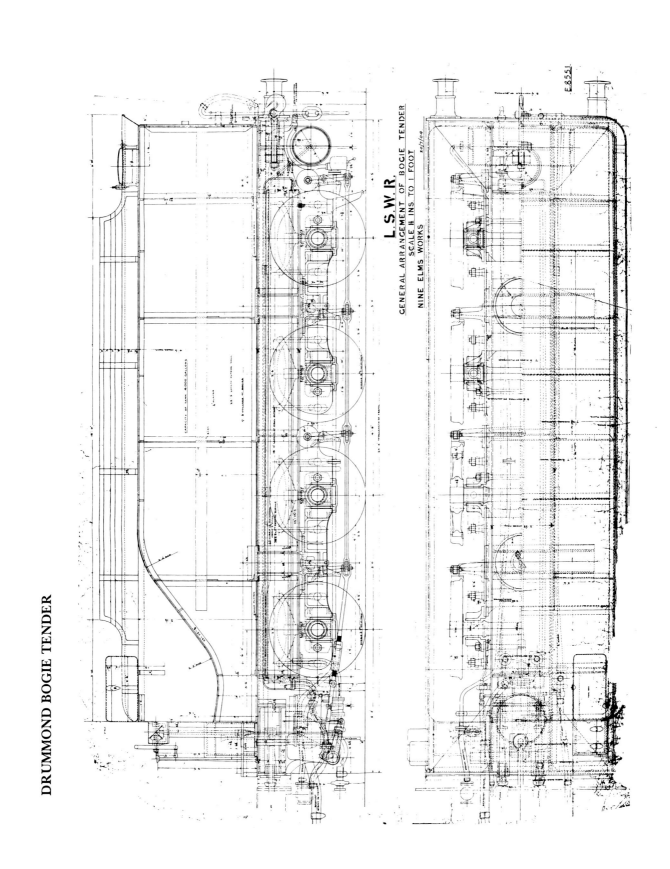

L.S.W.R.

GENERAL ARRANGEMENT OF BOGIE TENDER

SCALE 1½ INS TO 1 FOOT

NINE ELMS WORKS

E.8551

'T14' CLASS 4-6-0

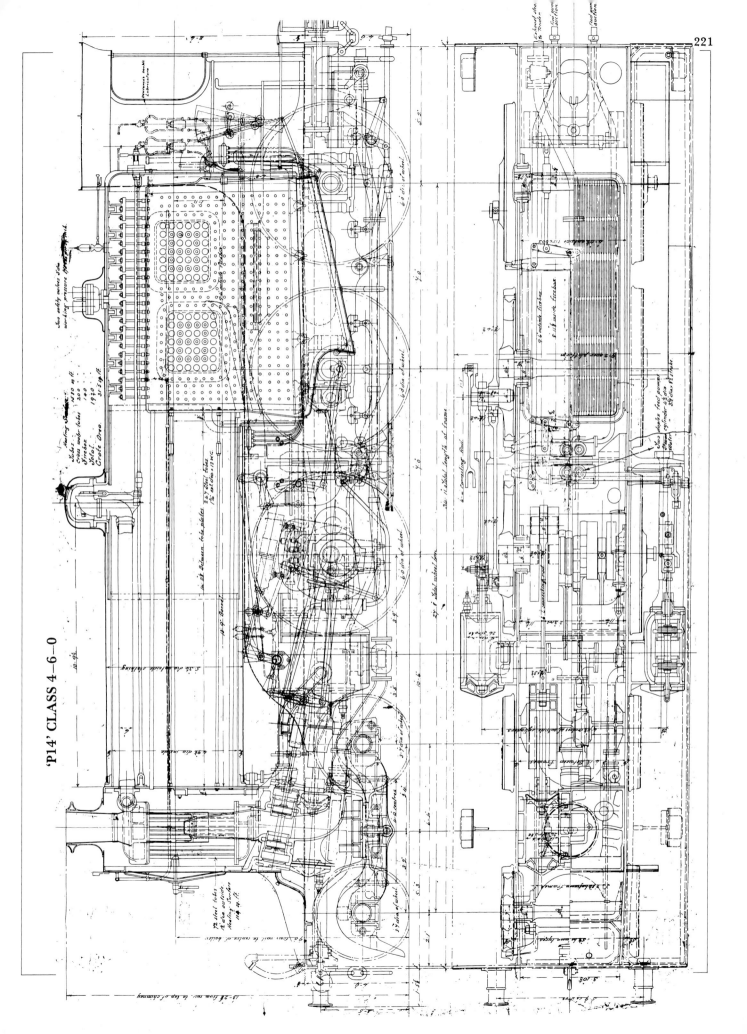

'P14' CLASS 4-6-0

'G14' CLASS 4–6–0 .

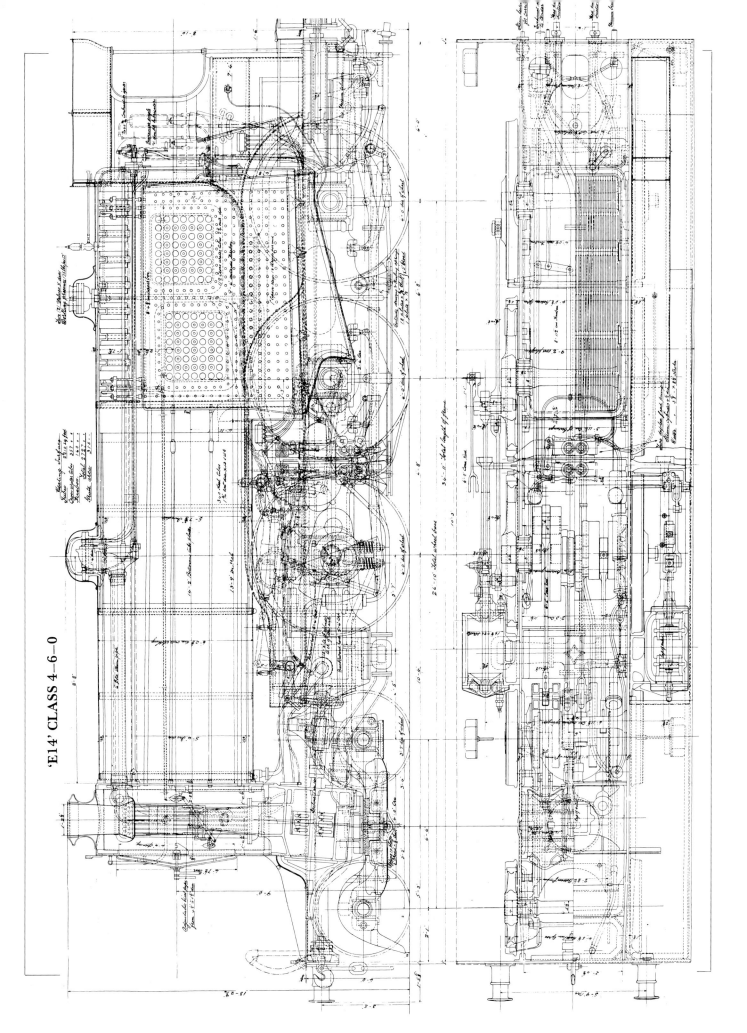

'E14' CLASS 4–6–0

'T14' CLASS

'P14' CLASS

E10142

'G14' CLASS 'E14' CLASS

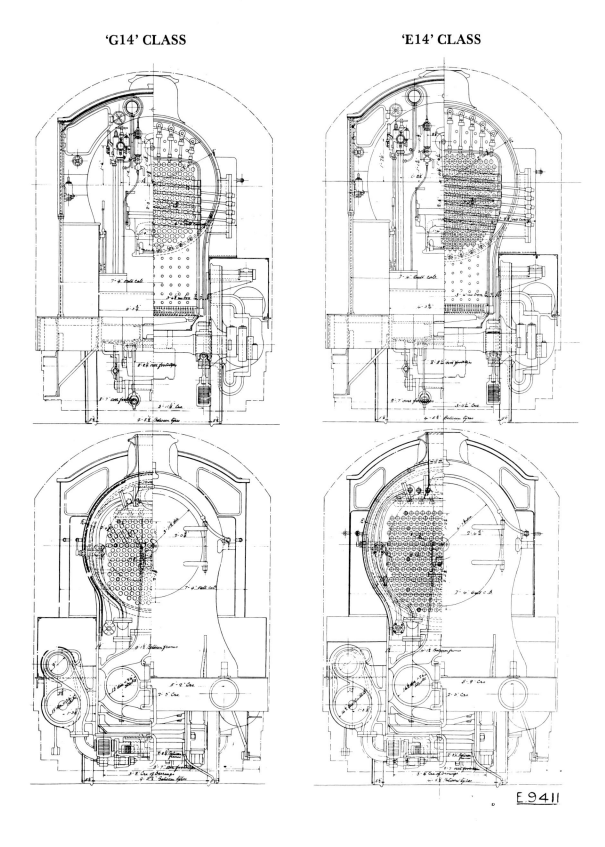

E.9411

'F13' CLASS 4–6–0

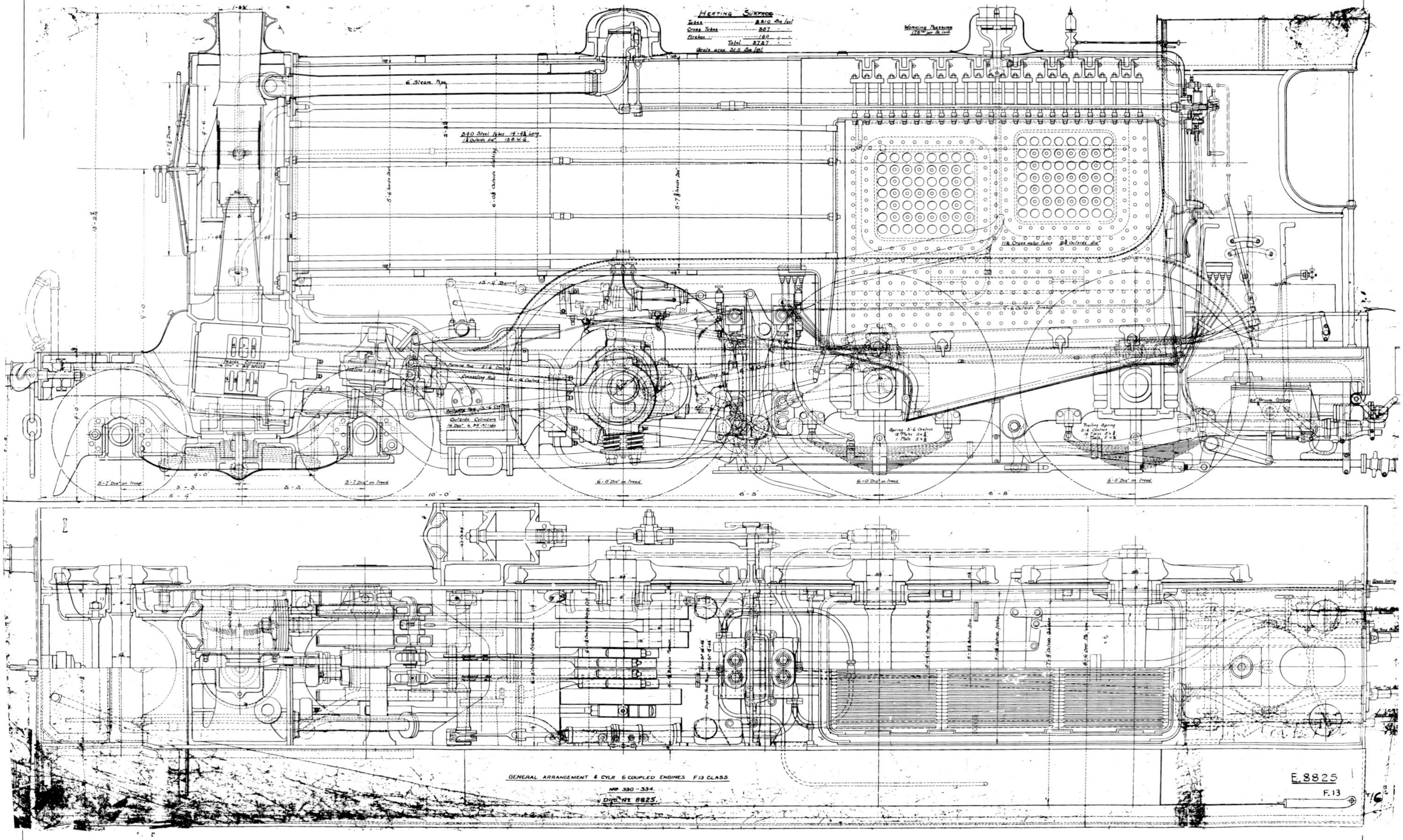
HEATING SURFACE
WORKING PRESSURE
GENERAL ARRANGEMENT 4 CYLR 6 COUPLED ENGINES F13 CLASS
E.8825
F.13

'700' CLASS 0–6–0

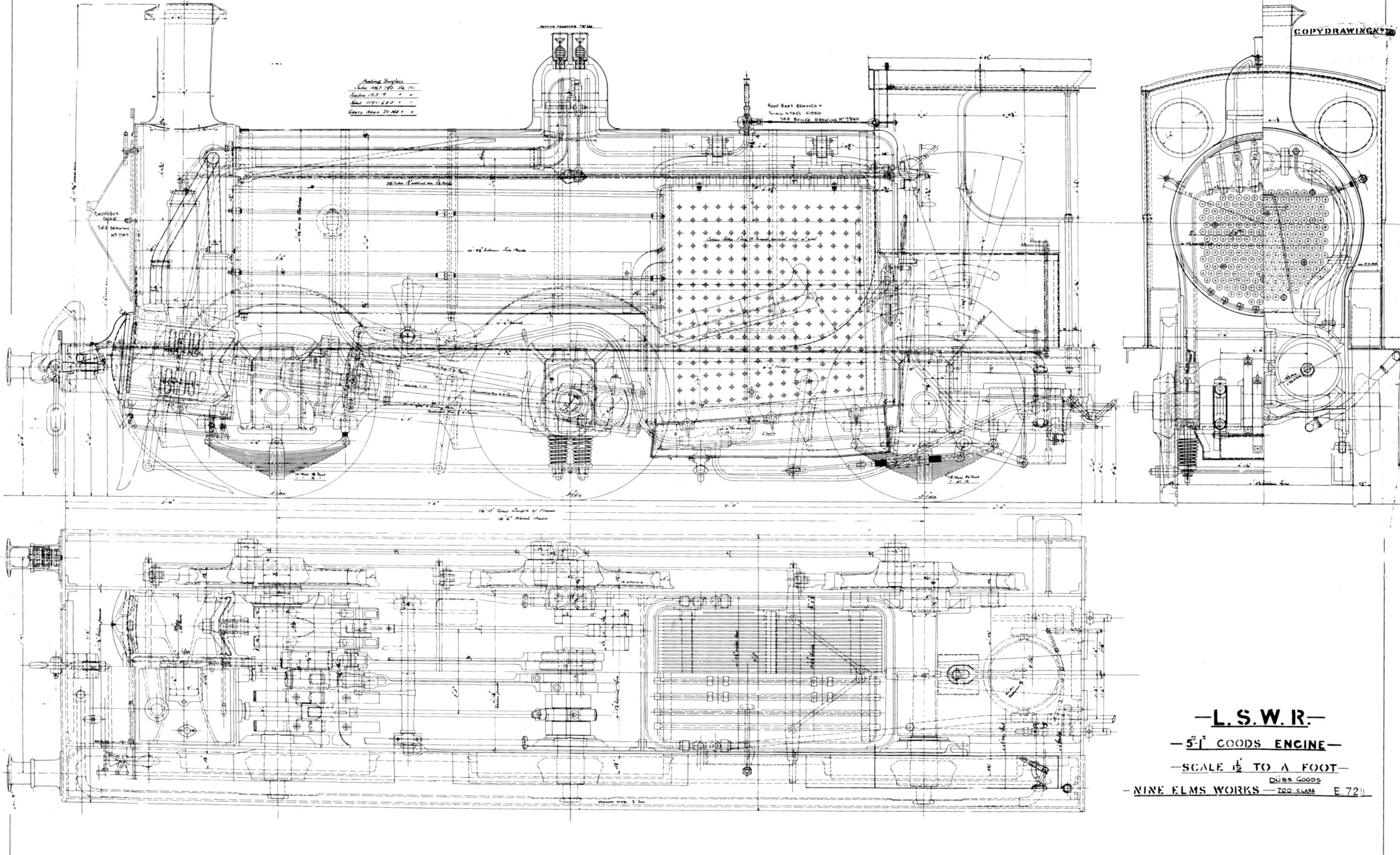

—L.S.W.R.—

5'1" GOODS ENGINE

—SCALE 1½" TO A FOOT—

—NINE ELMS WORKS— DUBS GOODS 700 CLASS E 72"

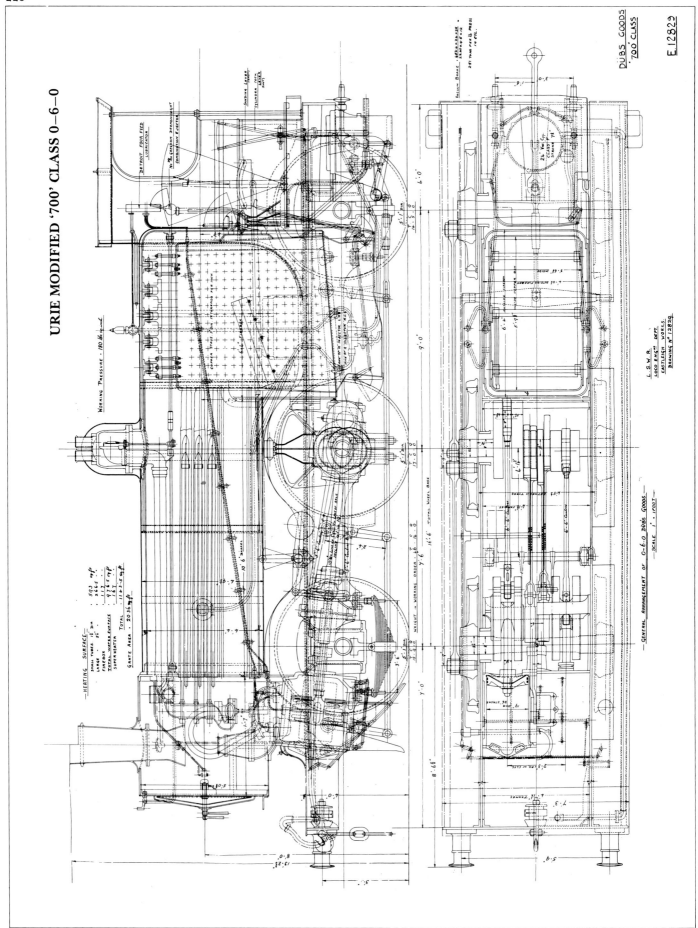

URIE MODIFIED '700' CLASS 0—6—0

WORKING PRESSURE 180 lbs. per sq. inch.

— HEATING SURFACE —

SMALL TUBES . 1⅝ DIA . . 503 sq.ft.
LARGE . . 5⅛ . . . 2466 .
FIREBOX . . . . 117 .
TOTAL WATER SURFACE . 9765 sq.ft.
SUPERHEATER . . . 1167 sq.ft.
                Total . 2036 sq.ft.

GRATE AREA . . . 2036 sq.ft.

DÜBS GOODS
'700' CLASS

E.12829

L.S.W.R.
LOCO. ENG'G DEPT.
EASTLEIGH WORKS.
DRAWING N.º 12829.

— GENERAL ARRANGEMENT OF O—6—0 DÜBS GOODS —
— SCALE 1" = 1 FOOT —

SHORT FRAME 'M7' CLASS 0-4-4T

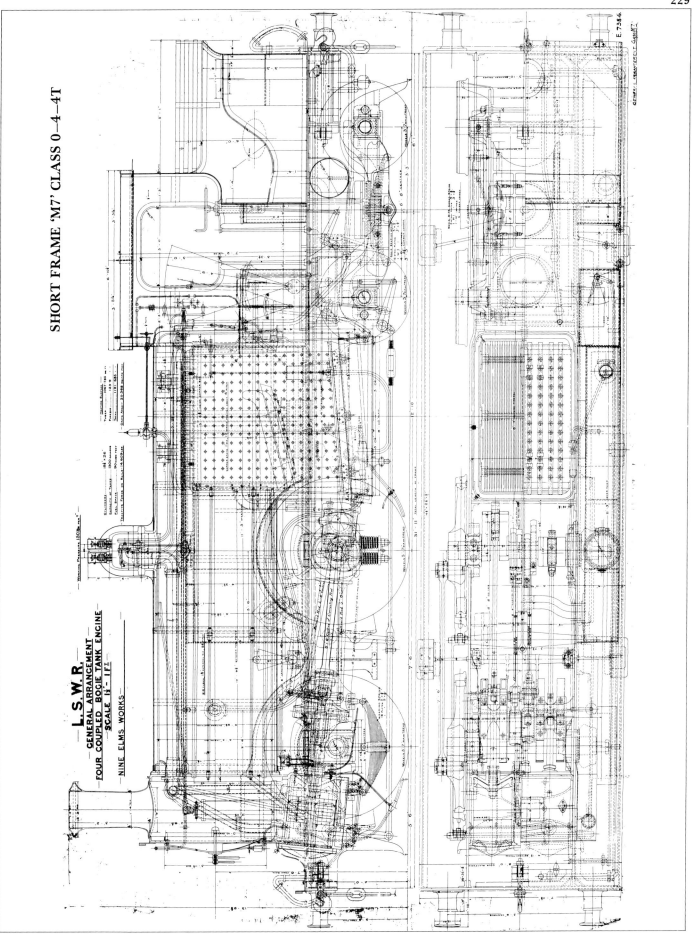

L.S.W.R.

— GENERAL ARRANGEMENT —

— FOUR COUPLED BOGIE TANK ENGINE —

— SCALE 1½"–1 F.T. —

— NINE ELMS WORKS —

LONG FRAME 'M7' CLASS 0–4–4T

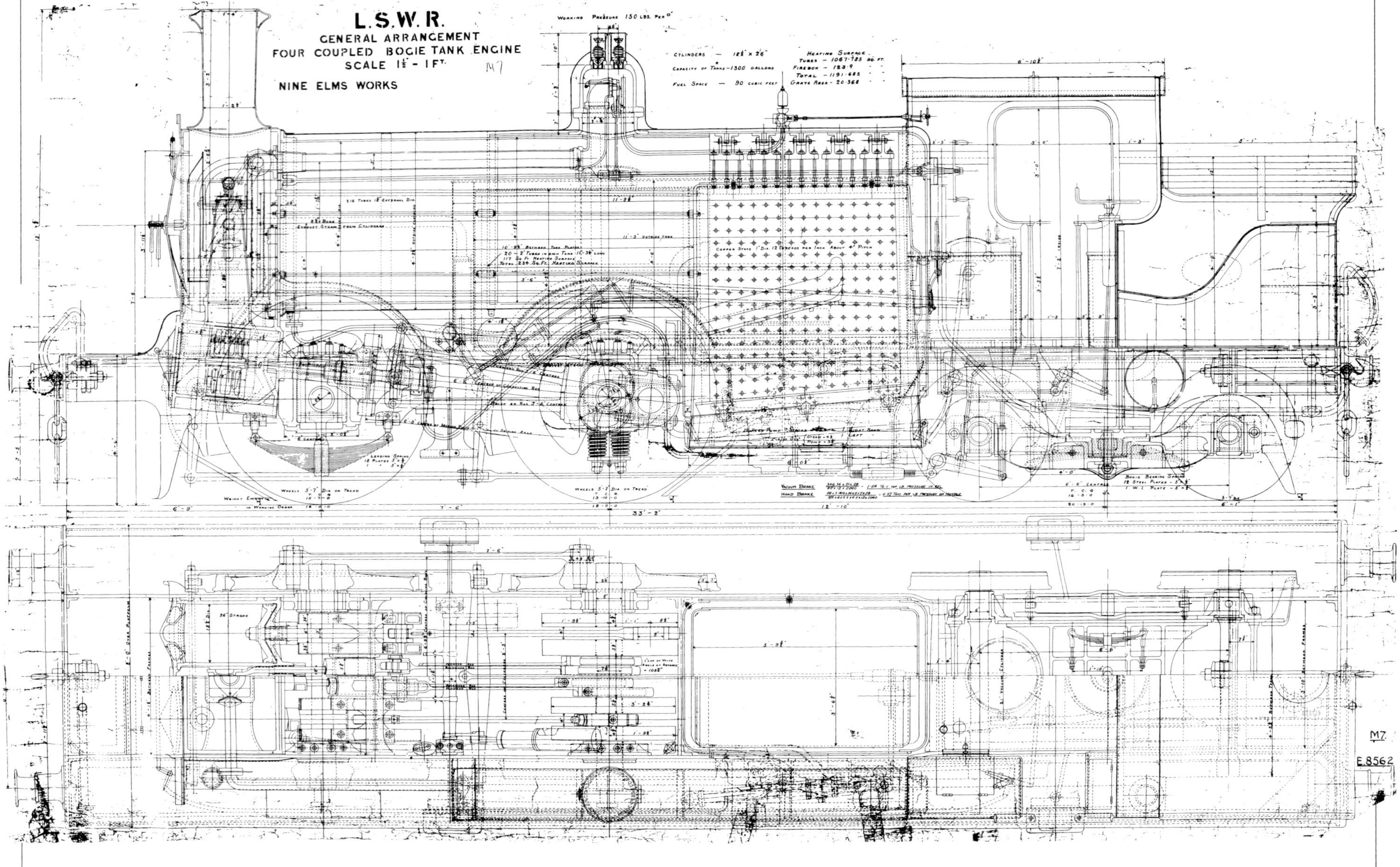

M7
E.8562

L.S.W.R.
GENERAL ARRANGEMENT
FOUR COUPLED BOGIE TANK ENGINE
SCALE 1½ = 1 FT.

NINE ELMS WORKS

Working Pressure 150 lbs. per □"

CYLINDERS — 18½" × 26"

Capacity of Tanks — 1300 Gallons

Fuel Space — 50 cubic feet.

Heating Surface
Tubes — 1067·785 sq. ft.
Firebox — 102·8 □
Total — 1170·585
Grate Area — 20·368

'H12' CLASS RAILCAR

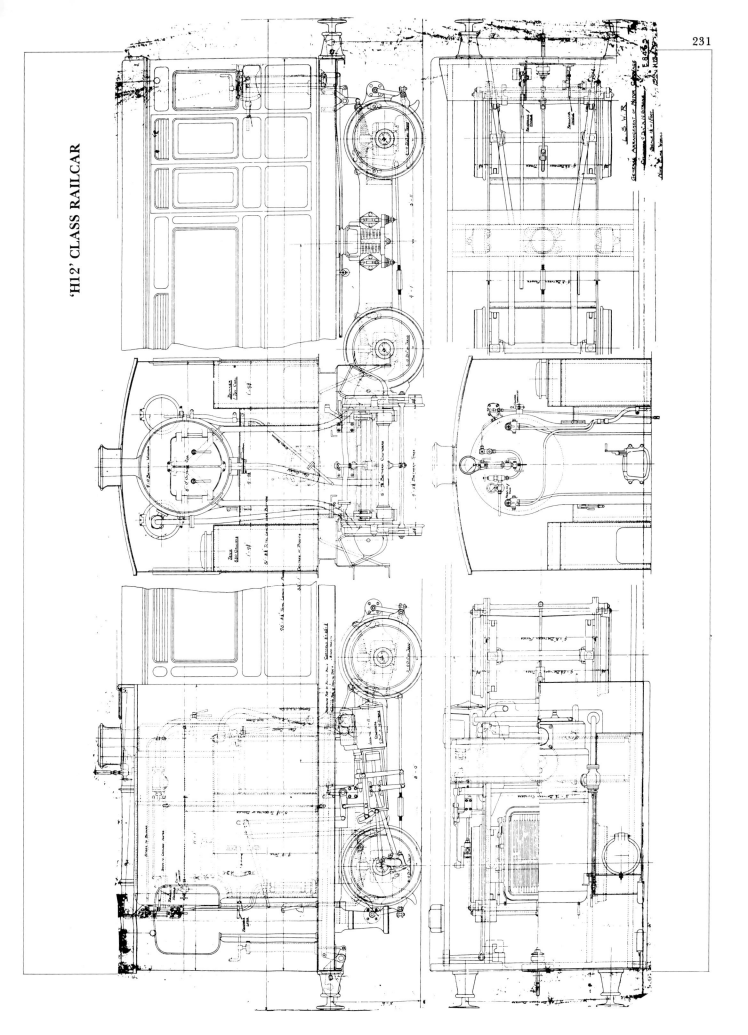

'C14' CLASS MOTOR TANK

ROD & PIPE ARRANGE^{MT}
4 WHEEL PASS^R TANK
CYL 10 × 14
WHEELS 3'·O· DIA
GROUP C14
SCALE

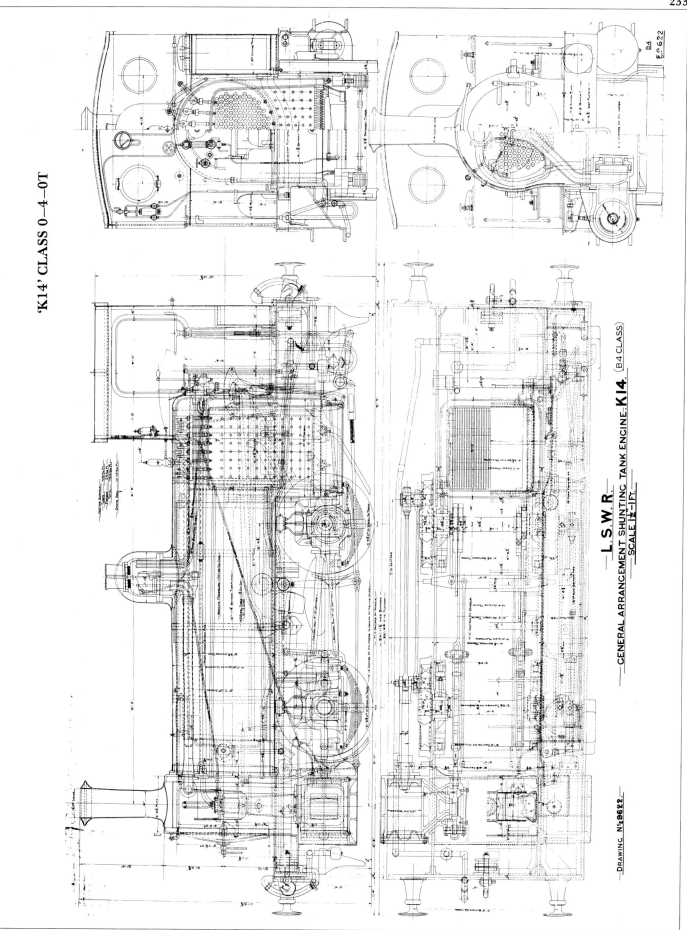

'K14' CLASS 0-4-0T

B4
E<u>o</u> 622

L.S.W.R.
— GENERAL ARRANGEMENT SHUNTING TANK ENGINE. **K14**. (B4 CLASS) —
— SCALE 1¼ =1FT. —

— DRAWING N<u>o</u> **8622**. —

DRUMMOND CHIMNEYS

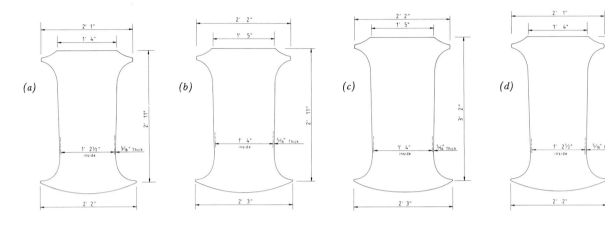

(a) 'T7' and 'T9' class chimney. (b) 'C8' class chimney. (c) 'M7' class (short) and '700' class chimney. (d) 'M7' class long chimney.

Numberplate of Drummond design which was used on both NBR and CR prior to its use on the LSWR. This is of the 'flat' or, more correctly, 'intaglio' pattern. The characters are said to have been filled with black wax. Its use was first noted on 'X6' class No. 658, new in December 1895. Plates of this design were then fitted to classes 'T1', '700', 'M7', 'T7', 'C8', 'T9', 'E10', 'K10' and 'G6'. Possibly the last new locomotive to be fitted was 'M7' class No. 123 of February 1903. There is no sign of its use on rebuilds or duplicate locomotives. Works photographs, by Neilson and Dübs suggest that the plates were the same size as those on CR No. 123, i.e. 17½ in. x 11 in., and these are the dimensions quoted in the HMRS *LSWR Livery Register*. No original plates seem to have survived. Numerals appear to be 3½ in. and lettering 1 5/8 in.